Microsoft

# Microsoft
# Office for iPad
# Step by Step

Joan Lambert

PUBLISHED BY
Microsoft Press
A division of Microsoft Corporation
One Microsoft Way
Redmond, Washington 98052-6399

Library of Congress Control Number: 2014951858
ISBN: 978-0-7356-9695-2

Printed and bound in the United States of America.

First Printing

Microsoft Press books are available through booksellers and distributors worldwide. If you need support related to this book, email Microsoft Press Support at mspinput@microsoft.com. Please tell us what you think of this book at http://aka.ms/tellpress.

This book is provided "as-is" and expresses the author's views and opinions. The views, opinions, and information expressed in this book, including URLs and other Internet website references, may change without notice.

Some examples depicted herein are provided for illustration only and are fictitious. No real association or connection is intended or should be inferred.

Microsoft and the trademarks listed at http://www.microsoft.com on the "Trademarks" webpage are trademarks of the Microsoft group of companies. All other marks are property of their respective owners.

**Acquisitions Editor:** Rosemary Caperton
**Developmental Editor:** Carol Dillingham
**Project Editor:** Carol Dillingham
**Editorial Production:** Online Training Solutions, Inc. (OTSI)
**Technical Reviewers:** Barb Levy and Linda Larkan (OTSI)
**Copyeditor:** Kathy Krause (OTSI)
**Indexer:** Susie Carr (OTSI)
**Cover:** Twist Creative • Seattle

# Contents

# Part 1: Get started with Microsoft Office for iPad

**Give us feedback**
Tell us what you think of this book and help Microsoft improve our products for you. Thank you!
*http://aka.ms/tellpress*

## 2 Get connected . . . . . . . . . . . . . . . . . . . . . . . . . . . . . . . . . . . . . . . . . . . . 27

## 3 Create and manage files . . . . . . . . . . . . . . . . . . . . . . . . . . . . . . . . . . . 49

# Part 2: Microsoft Word for iPad

# Part 3: Microsoft Excel for iPad

# Part 4: Microsoft PowerPoint for iPad

# Part 5: Microsoft OneNote for iPad

**Give us feedback**
Tell us what you think of this book and help Microsoft
improve our products for you. Thank you!
*http://aka.ms/tellpress*

# Introduction

Welcome! This *Step by Step* book has been designed so you can read it from the beginning to learn about the infrastructure that supports the Microsoft Office for iPad apps, the common user interface elements, and the skills you can use when working in any of them; and then build your skills as you learn to perform increasingly specialized procedures. Or, if you prefer, you can jump in wherever you need ready guidance for supporting the apps or performing tasks in Microsoft Word for iPad, Excel for iPad, PowerPoint for iPad, and OneNote for iPad. The how-to steps are delivered crisply and concisely—just the facts. You'll also find informative, full-color graphics that support the instructional content.

## Who this book is for

*Microsoft Office for iPad Step by Step* is designed for use as a learning and reference resource by home and business users of Office programs who want to use Word, Excel, PowerPoint, and OneNote to create and edit documents, workbooks, presentations, and notebooks on iPads. The content of the book is designed to be useful for people who have previously used Word, Excel, PowerPoint, and OneNote on other platforms and for people who are discovering Office apps for the first time.

## The *Step by Step* approach

The book's coverage is divided into parts representing general Office app skills or specific apps. Each part is divided into chapters representing skill set areas, and each chapter is divided into topics that group related skills. Each topic includes expository information followed by specific procedures. At the end of the chapter, you'll find a series of practice tasks you can complete on your own. You can use the practice files that are available from this book's website to work through the practice tasks, or you can use your own files.

# Download the practice files

Before you can complete the practice tasks in this book, you need to download the book's practice files to your Microsoft OneDrive or OneDrive for Business storage drive from *http://aka.ms/iPadOfficeSBS/files*. Follow the instructions on the webpage.

 **IMPORTANT** The Office for iPad apps are not available from this website. You should install those apps before using this book.

You can open the files that are stored on your OneDrive from within the Office for iPad apps and save a duplicate copy of each file on your iPad. The apps automatically save changes to the practice files. If you later want to repeat practice tasks, you can download the original practice files again.

 **SEE ALSO** For information about opening and saving files, see "Create, open, and save files" in Chapter 3, "Create and manage files."

The following table lists the practice files for this book.

| Chapter | Folder | File |
| --- | --- | --- |
| 1: Office for iPad basics | iPadOfficeSBS\Ch01 | None |
| 2: Get connected | iPadOfficeSBS\Ch02 | None |
| 3: Create and manage files | iPadOfficeSBS\Ch03 | NavigateOffice.docx |
| | | OpenFiles.xlsx |
| | | PrintSheets.xlsx |
| | | PrintSlides.pptx |
| | | SearchReplace.docx |
| | | SearchScope.xlsx |
| | | SendCopy.pptx |
| | | SendLink.xlsx |
| | | SendReview.docx |
| 4: Create professional documents | iPadOfficeSBS\Ch04 | ArrangeText.docx |
| | | FormatParagraphs.docx |
| | | FormatText.docx |
| | | PastePractice.docx |
| | | StructureContent.docx |

| Chapter | Folder | File |
| --- | --- | --- |
| 5: Add visual elements to documents | iPadOfficeSBS\Ch05 | ArrangeImages.docx<br>CreateLists.docx<br>CreateTables.docx<br>FormatPictures.docx<br>FormatShapes.docx |
| 6: Enhance document content | iPadOfficeSBS\Ch06 | ConfigurePages.docx<br>CreateColumns.docx<br>CreateTextBoxes.docx<br>InsertReferences.docx<br>ReviewContent.docx |
| 7: Store and retrieve data | iPadOfficeSBS\Ch07 | DisplayData.xlsx<br>EnterData.xlsx<br>ManageCells.xlsx<br>ManageStructure.xlsx<br>ManageWorksheets.xlsx |
| 8: Process and present numeric data | iPadOfficeSBS\Ch08 | CreateCharts.xlsx<br>CreateTables.xlsx<br>PivotData.xlsx<br>ProcessData.xlsx<br>ReviewComments.xlsx |
| 9: Create compelling presentations | iPadOfficeSBS\Ch09 | AddGraphics1.pptx<br>AddGraphics2.docx<br>AddText1.pptx<br>AddText2.docx<br>AddText3.xlsx<br>ChangeSize.pptx<br>ManageSlides.pptx |
| 10: Prepare and deliver slide shows | iPadOfficeSBS\Ch10 | AnimateTransitions.pptx<br>EnterNotes.pptx<br>ManageRecordings.pptx<br>PresentShow.pptx |
| 11: Store information in digital notebooks | iPadOfficeSBS\Ch11 | MoveNotes.one<br>StoreNotes.one |
| 12: Locate and share notebook content | iPadOfficeSBS\Ch12 | ShareNotes.one |

## Adapt exercise steps

This book contains many procedures for performing tasks in Word, Excel, PowerPoint, and OneNote on your iPad. The procedural instructions use this format:

1. To select the paragraph that you want to format in columns, triple-tap the paragraph.

2. On the **Layout** tab, tap **Columns** to display the scrollable menu of column layout options.

3. On the **Columns** menu, tap **Three**.

On subsequent instances of instructions that require you to follow the same process, the instructions might be simplified in this format because the working location has already been established:

1. Select the paragraph that you want to format in columns.

2. On the **Columns** menu, tap **Three**.

The instructions in this book assume that you're interacting with on-screen elements on your iPad by tapping the screen (with your finger or a stylus) and interacting with on-screen elements on desktop computers by clicking (with a mouse, touchpad, or other hardware device). If you're using a different method—for example, if you have an external keyboard connected to your iPad or if you use a touchscreen computer—substitute the applicable tapping or clicking action when you interact with a user interface element.

Instructions in this book refer to iPad user interface elements that you tap on the iPad screen as *icons*, to Office app user interface elements that you tap on the iPad screen as *buttons*, and to physical buttons that you press on the iPad device as *buttons*, to conform to the standard terminology used in documentation for these products.

When the instructions tell you to enter information, you can do so by typing on a connected external keyboard, tapping an on-screen keyboard, or even speaking aloud, depending on your iPad or computer setup and your personal preferences.

Images in this book depict the iPad interface as it appears when the iPad is oriented horizontally. This maximizes the ribbon width in the Office for iPad apps so the buttons aren't crowded. (And, as a bonus, the horizontally oriented images require less vertical space on the page than vertical images, leaving more space available for words.) You can orient your iPad vertically or horizontally depending on your preference. For example, when the ribbon and on-screen keyboard are both open, you might want to work with your iPad oriented vertically to have more space available between those elements. When the iPad is oriented vertically, some elements of the Office app user interface might appear slightly different from those depicted in the book. For example, some buttons on the ribbon might be represented by icons instead of words.

# Ebook edition

If you're reading the ebook edition of this book, you can do the following:

- Search the full text
- Print
- Copy and paste

You can purchase and download the ebook edition from the Microsoft Press Store at *http://aka.ms/iPadOfficeSBS/details*.

# Get support and give feedback

This topic provides information about getting help with this book and contacting us to provide feedback or report errors.

## Errata and support

We've made every effort to ensure the accuracy of this book and its companion content. If you discover an error, please submit it to us at *http://aka.ms/iPadOfficeSBS/errata*.

If you need to contact the Microsoft Press Support team, please send an email message to *mspinput@microsoft.com*.

For help with Microsoft software and hardware, go to *http://support.microsoft.com*.

## We want to hear from you

At Microsoft Press, your satisfaction is our top priority, and your feedback our most valuable asset. Please tell us what you think of this book at *http://aka.ms/tellpress*.

The survey is short, and we read every one of your comments and ideas. Thanks in advance for your input!

## Stay in touch

Let's keep the conversation going! We're on Twitter at *http://twitter.com/MicrosoftPress*.

# Part 1

# Get started with Microsoft Office for iPad

# Office for iPad basics

1

*Microsoft Office for iPad* is the collective name for a group of individual apps you can use on your iPad to display, create, and work with different kinds of information. The Office for iPad family includes three core apps:

- Word for iPad
- Excel for iPad
- PowerPoint for iPad

Another useful Office app that is available for the iPad is Microsoft OneNote for iPad. This book includes coverage of all four of these Office apps, which are widely used in home, business, and school environments.

Other Microsoft products that are available for the iPad include the Microsoft SharePoint Newsfeed and Yammer networking tools, the Skype and Skype for Business (formerly Microsoft Lync) online communication apps, the Microsoft Outlook Web App enterprise communication app, and apps that help you access and manage content in Microsoft OneDrive and OneDrive for Business online storage locations.

This chapter provides information about the environment necessary to support the Office apps on an iPad. It then guides you through procedures related to installing, configuring, updating, removing, and reinstalling Office apps and configuring iPad settings for features and functions that can be used in the Office apps.

## In this chapter

- Install Office for iPad apps
- Configure iPad and Office app settings
- Update Office apps
- Remove and reinstall Office apps

## Practice files

No practice files are necessary to complete the practice tasks in this chapter.

# Install Office for iPad apps

The Office for iPad apps are free, as are the features necessary to display, create, and edit Word documents, Excel workbooks, PowerPoint presentations, and OneNote notebooks. All you need is a free Microsoft account (which you probably already have). You can use Word for iPad, Excel for iPad, PowerPoint for iPad, and OneNote for iPad to open and explore Office files regardless of whether the files were originally created on a computer running Windows, a Mac computer, or an iPad.

You install the individual Office apps from the App Store. After you sign in to an app by using your Microsoft account credentials, you can get right to work.

> ⚠ **IMPORTANT** You have the option of unlocking premium app features by associating the apps with an Office 365 account. Premium features include advanced change-tracking features, unlimited use of paragraph styles, and advanced chart, table, and picture formatting tools.

>  **SEE ALSO** For information about Microsoft accounts and Office 365 accounts, see "Microsoft account options" and "Office 365 subscription options" later in this topic.

## Hardware requirements

The Office apps can be installed on any iPad running iOS 7 or iOS 8 (the current version at the time of this writing). Each app requires about 450 megabytes (MB) of local storage space (on the iPad) to install. The documents, workbooks, presentations, and other files you create or work with require additional storage space, but you can store those either locally on the iPad or in a remote storage location such as a OneDrive, SharePoint, or Dropbox site.

>  **SEE ALSO** For information about remote storage locations, see "Connect to additional storage locations" in Chapter 2, "Get connected."

> ✓ **TIP** If your iPad doesn't have enough free space to install the Office apps you want, you can regain space by deleting other apps, or by moving photos, music, and other files to remote storage locations. If you want to make an entirely clean start, you can restore the iPad to its original state and then install the most recent version of iOS. Always synchronize iPad content with your computer before you restore an iPad to its original state.

# iTunes support for the iPad

You can manage the content, software, and data on iPads and other Apple devices by installing iTunes on your computer. When your iPad is connected to the computer, clicking or tapping the iPad icon on the toolbar displays information that includes the total storage capacity and the iOS version.

*iTunes provides information about your connected device*

From the Summary page, you can also configure backup settings and other options. Two notable options for the iPad-to-computer connection are:

- **Open iTunes when this iPad is connected**  This option is selected by default. Clear it if you want to start iTunes manually.

- **Sync with this iPad over Wi-Fi**  Select this option to save yourself the trouble of connecting the iPad to the computer by using a USB cable.

From the File Sharing area at the bottom of the Apps page, you can add files from your computer to the iPad and save files from the iPad to your computer.

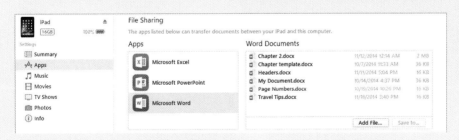

*Connected devices are available from the toolbar*

**SEE ALSO**  You can learn about and install iTunes from *itunes.apple.com*.

There are several ways to find out about your iPad's operating system version and available storage space. You can check directly on the iPad or, if the iPad is connected to a computer, from iTunes or the file explorer system on the computer.

**To display information about your iPad operating system and storage space**

1. On the Home Screen, tap the **Settings** icon to start the Settings app.

2. In the **Settings** list, tap **General**.

3. At the top of the **General** page, tap **About**.

   The Available entry displays the available storage space. The Version entry displays the installed iOS version.

4. Return to the **General** page.

5. About halfway down the **General** page, tap **Usage** to display the total used and available storage space on the device.

6. On the **Usage** page, tap **Manage Storage** to display the totals and the storage space consumed by each app and its related documents and data.

7. Tap any app to display a breakdown of the content stored for that app.

*Or*

1. Connect the iPad to a computer that iTunes is installed on.

2. Start iTunes if it doesn't start automatically.

3. On the iTunes toolbar, tap or click the **iPad** button.

>  **IMPORTANT** The iPad button isn't labeled, other than by an icon that looks like an iPad device.

The first section of the Summary page displays the total storage capacity on the left side, and the iOS version on the right side. The bar at the bottom of the window displays used and available storage space.

| Apps | Other | 7.58 GB Free |

*Colored blocks indicate the portion of storage used by photos, apps, and other content*

>  **SEE ALSO** For information about deleting apps to free up storage space, see "Remove and reinstall Office apps" later in this chapter.

## Installation options

You always install the Office apps from the App Store. To install an app directly from the App Store, you must first locate it by searching for the app and then identifying it among the related results. This approach seems straightforward, but many apps have been released that support or resemble the Office apps, so you might have to scroll through a lot of search results to identify the actual app you want to install.

A more direct path to the Office apps is through the Office website. You can learn about and link to the App Store listings for all the Office apps that are available for a specific mobile device (in this case, the iPad) from the Office website for mobile devices at *office.microsoft.com/mobile.*

*The Office for Mobile Devices website provides information for iPad, iPhone, Windows Phone, and Android phone users*

When you start an app installation, the app icon is automatically added to the iPad Home Screen. Until the app is ready to use, the icon is screened (dark) and labeled with the installation status rather than the app name.

*The Installing status appears during the initial app installation and subsequent updates*

When the app is ready for use, the icon is unshaded and labeled with the app name.

**To locate Office for iPad apps in the App Store**

1. Display any view of the App Store (Featured, Top Charts, Near Me, Purchased, or Updates).

2. In the **Search** box in the upper-right corner, enter Office 365 or the name of the specific app you want to locate.

3. Tap a corresponding search term in the **Results** list.

4. Scroll the page if necessary to locate the official apps.

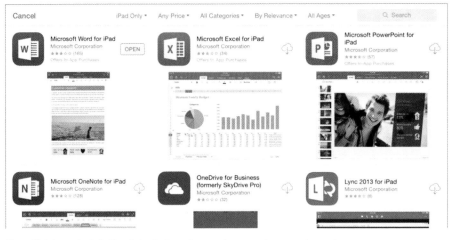

*The official app installation links feature the app icons and names shown here*

> **TIP** If you're accustomed to working with Office programs on other platforms, you might notice that the names of the iPad app versions of Word, Excel, PowerPoint, and OneNote don't include version numbers (such as *2013*) like the desktop programs. The Office for iPad apps automatically update when new versions become available. The current version is shown on the app page in the App Store and on the splash screen that appears after the installation of an update.

## To install Office for iPad apps from the App Store

1.  In the App Store, locate the app you want to install.

2.  To begin the installation, do one of the following:

    *   In the upper-right corner of the app listing, tap the **Install** icon.

    *   Tap the app listing, and then on the app information page, tap the **Install** icon to begin the installation.

> **TIP** The Install icon depicts a downward-pointing arrow on a cloud. If an app is already installed on the iPad, the app information page displays an Open button instead of an Install icon.

Install icon          Installation progress indicator

*The Install icon changes to indicate the progress of the installation*

## To install Office for iPad apps from the Office website

1.  On the iPad, using Safari or another web browser, go to *office.microsoft.com /mobile*.

2.  With **iPad** selected at the top of the page, scroll to the **Introducing Office for iPad** section, and then tap **Get Word**, **Get Excel**, or **Get PowerPoint** to open the information page for the selected app in the App Store.

3.  On the app's information page, tap the **Install** icon.

## Microsoft account options

If you use Skype, OneDrive, Xbox Live, Outlook.com, or a Windows Phone, you already have a Microsoft account. (Microsoft account credentials are also used by many non-Microsoft products and websites.) If you don't already have a Microsoft account, you can register any existing account as a Microsoft account, sign up for a free Outlook.com or Hotmail.com account and register that as a Microsoft account, or create an alias for an Outlook.com account and register the alias.

> **TIP** Many software programs and websites authenticate transactions by using Microsoft account credentials. For that reason, it's a good idea to register a personal account that you control, rather than a business account that your employer controls, as your Microsoft account. That way, you won't risk losing access if you leave the company.

You can start the process of creating a Microsoft account while signing in to an Office app, or you can create the account independently of the sign-in process.

> **SEE ALSO** For information about creating a Microsoft account while signing in to an Office app, see "Start and activate apps" in Chapter 2, "Get connected." You can learn about Microsoft accounts, register an existing email address, or sign up for a new Microsoft account at *www.microsoft.com/account*.

### To create a Microsoft account from any computer

1.  If necessary, sign out of the current computer user's Microsoft account.

    > **IMPORTANT** If the current user is signed in to a Microsoft account on the computer or iPad, the management page for that account appears instead of the Create An Account page. To create a new account, first sign out of the existing account.

2.  Go to *https://signup.live.com* to display the **Create an account** page.

    >  **TIP** You can use a different password for the Microsoft account than the one you use to access your email.

**1**

3. If you want to register an existing email account as a Microsoft account, enter your identifying information, the email address you want to register, and the password you want to assign to the Microsoft account.

*Or*

If you want to obtain a new email account for use as a Microsoft account, tap or click **Or get a new email address**. Then enter your identifying information, the email address you want to create (choose Outlook.com or Hotmail.com in the list), and the password you want to assign to the account.

> **TIP** The site immediately checks whether the email address you enter is available. If the requested address is already taken, the site recommends other email addresses based on your name and the address you requested.

4. Enter the code shown at the bottom of the page to verify that a person is creating the account (rather than a computer program), and then tap or click the **Create account** button.

## Office 365 subscription options

Office 365, which was originally available only to businesses, now has many subscription options designed for individual home and business users, students, households, small businesses, midsize businesses, enterprises, government agencies, academic institutions, and nonprofits; in other words, whatever your needs may be, there is an Office 365 subscription option that will be a close fit. Subscription prices range from about $2 to $22 per user per month (and some versions are free).

Many of the Office 365 subscription options include licensing for the desktop Office programs and unlock the premium features of the Office for iPad apps. Most subscriptions that include licensing permit each user to run Office on up to five devices, including computers running Windows, Mac computers, tablets, and iPads.

>  **SEE ALSO** For information about associating Office for iPad apps with an Office 365 subscription, see "Start and activate apps" in Chapter 2, "Get connected."

If you have an Office 365 subscription, you can find out whether you have the licensing necessary to activate the premium app features on the Software page of the Office 365 portal, which you can access at *portal.microsoftonline.com*.

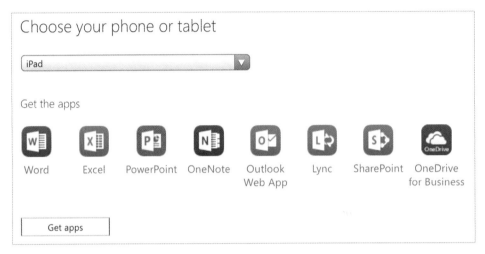

*You can access your licensed software from the Office 365 Settings page of the Office 365 portal*

If you intend to run Office apps only on your iPad and don't need a higher-level subscription, you can subscribe to Office 365 Personal for about $6 per month. An Office 365 Personal subscription allows you to install and use full versions of the following software:

- The current versions of Microsoft Access, Excel, OneNote, Outlook, PowerPoint, Publisher, and Word on one computer running Windows

    *Or*

    The current versions of Excel, OneNote, Outlook, PowerPoint, and Word for Mac on one Mac computer

- Office apps on one iPad or Windows tablet

- Office apps on Android phones, iPhones, and Windows Phones

An Office 365 Personal subscription also provides 1 terabyte (TB) of online storage and 60 minutes of international Skype calling per month.

> ⚠️ **IMPORTANT** You can purchase desktop versions of Office programs for use on a computer running Windows or a Mac computer. These stand-alone versions don't include the licensing necessary to activate the premium features of the Office apps on an iPad.

If you don't already have an Office 365 subscription for business or personal use and want to try out the premium features on your iPad, you can sign up to try Office 365 Home for free for a month. (Specific versions are also available to educational institutions and government organizations for 30-day trials.)

An Office 365 subscription must be associated with either your Microsoft account credentials or the credentials provided to you by your organization.

**To check your Office for iPad app licensing in the Office 365 portal**

1. On the iPad or a computer, using Safari or another web browser, go to *portal.microsoftonline.com*.

   If you're already signed in to Office 365 on the iPad or computer, your name or account picture appears near the right end of the Office 365 toolbar and you can skip to step 3.

2. If you aren't signed in to Office 365, enter your organizational account credentials, and then tap or click **Sign in**.

3. In the Office 365 portal, tap or click the **Settings** button to the right of your name or account picture.

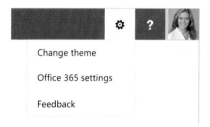

*The Settings button is shaped like a gear*

4. On the **Settings** menu, tap **Office 365 settings**.

5. On the **Office 365 settings** page, tap **Software**.

6. In the left pane of the **Software** page, tap **Phone & tablet**, and then in the **Tablet** list, tap **iPad** to display the iPad apps that you're licensed to use.

### To sign up for a free 30-day trial of Office 365 Home

1. On your iPad or any computer, go to *office.microsoft.com/try*.

2. On the **Try Office 365** page, tap or click **Start your free month**.

3. On the Microsoft account sign-in page, provide your Microsoft account credentials, and then tap or click **Sign in**.

   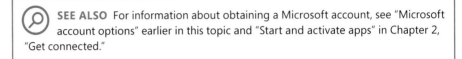 **SEE ALSO** For information about obtaining a Microsoft account, see "Microsoft account options" earlier in this topic and "Start and activate apps" in Chapter 2, "Get connected."

4. Select an existing payment method or add a new payment method, and then tap or click **Next**.

   You will not be charged for the 30-day free trial period, but payment information is necessary in the event that you extend the subscription.

5. On the **Review and confirm** page, note the trial period end date and the monthly Office 365 Home subscription price thereafter. Then tap or click **Purchase** to start your subscription.

   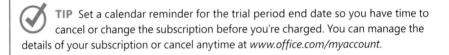 **TIP** Set a calendar reminder for the trial period end date so you have time to cancel or change the subscription before you're charged. You can manage the details of your subscription or cancel anytime at *www.office.com/myaccount*.

 **SEE ALSO** Current information about Office 365 subscription options is available from the Office website at *office.microsoft.com*.

# Configure iPad and Office app settings

As a rule, settings for iPad apps are configured centrally from the iPad Settings app rather than from each individual app. Some of the settings that affect your Office app experience are specific to the iPad, including the following:

- **Wi-Fi** An active Internet connection is necessary to install the app and updates, to validate your Microsoft account and Office 365 subscription, to view online content (such as Help file content) from within the apps, and to connect to online storage resources.

- **General** You can configure many user experience settings, such as those that do the following:

  - Make features and commands easier to access for people with limited vision, hearing, or dexterity.

  - Specify the length of time before the iPad screen automatically locks.

  - Require a passcode to install or delete apps; purchase content, upgrades, or subscriptions from within apps; or use the AirDrop functionality to transfer files to nearby devices.

  - Permit or restrict access to app content and website content based on content ratings.

  - Control whether apps can access the microphone (for use when dictating content in Word).

  - Provide access to alternative on-screen keyboards so you can easily enter characters from other alphabets or add emoticons to your content.

  Make sure that you're familiar with the available options so that you recognize areas within the apps that would benefit from changes.

- **iCloud** Manage your iCloud Drive storage options and app sharing settings.

- **iTunes & App Store** Turn on or off the option to automatically install purchased apps on all the devices registered to your iTunes account.

- **Photos & Camera** Configure storage locations for pictures that you can insert in Word documents, PowerPoint presentations, and other Office files.

Each configurable app you install on your iPad has a page in the Settings app. The iPad versions of the Office apps have far fewer configurable settings than the desktop versions that you might be familiar with. Each app has a Reset option that you can use to delete the credentials associated with the app and any locally stored files.

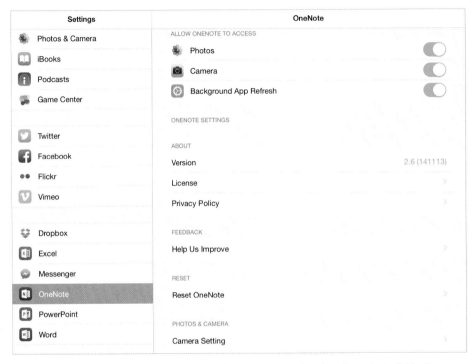

*Office app settings are configured from the iPad Settings app rather than from the individual apps*

### To display the configurable settings for an Office app

1. Start the Settings app.

2. Scroll to the bottom of the **Settings** list, and locate the app name in the list.

3. Tap the app name to display the related settings in the right pane.

 **SEE ALSO** For information about app updates, see "Update Office apps" later in this chapter.

**To install an alternative on-screen keyboard**

1. Start the Settings app and display the **General** page.

2. On the **General** page, tap **Keyboard**, and then tap **Keyboards**.

   The Keyboards page displays the currently installed keyboards.

3. On the **Keyboards** page, tap **Add New Keyboard**.

   More than 60 keyboards are available, representing different languages and character styles.

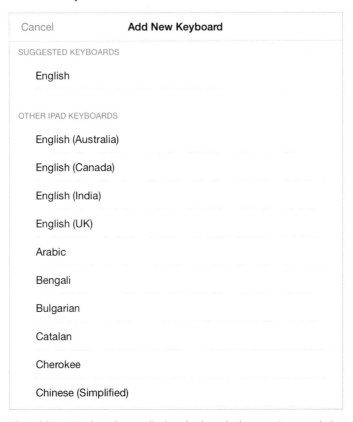

| Cancel | **Add New Keyboard** |
| --- | --- |

SUGGESTED KEYBOARDS

English

OTHER IPAD KEYBOARDS

English (Australia)

English (Canada)

English (India)

English (UK)

Arabic

Bengali

Bulgarian

Catalan

Cherokee

Chinese (Simplified)

*The Add New Keyboard page displays keyboards that aren't currently installed on your iPad*

4. Tap the keyboard you want to install.

> **TIP** From the *Emoji* keyboard, you can enter emoticons rather than letters and numbers. You can switch between installed keyboards by tapping the globe icon in the lower-left corner of the on-screen keyboard. As you switch keyboards, the name of the new keyboard appears briefly on the spacebar.

# Update Office apps

From time to time, Microsoft releases updates to the Office apps, usually for the purpose of adding functionality but sometimes to fix or avoid problems.

When you install an Office app such as Word, Excel, or PowerPoint on your iPad from the App Store, you're installing the most recent version that is available. When the iPad is online, the App Store periodically checks for any available app updates and downloads them to the iPad.

After updates are downloaded, the number of currently available updates appears in a red circle on top of the App Store icon. Updates that have been downloaded but not installed are shown in the Pending Updates section of the Updates page of the App Store.

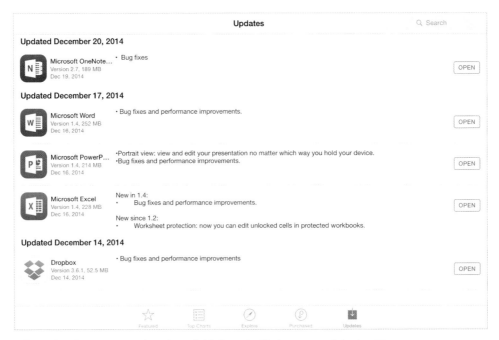

*Information about recent updates is available from the Updates page of the App Store*

**1**

You can install updates from this page, or you can configure the iPad to automatically install downloaded updates. The automatic installation option is useful if you want to be certain that you have the most current version of all apps on your iPad for optimal functionality and security.

> **TIP** Information about available and recently installed updates is available from the Updates page of the App Store. A history of all the updates installed for an individual app is available from the app's information page.

When you start an Office app after installing an update, a splash screen describes the changes implemented by the update.

*The splash screen provides the version number and the name and description of each new product feature*

**To display a list of downloaded updates**

1. Open the App Store.

2. At the bottom of the App Store window, tap the **Updates** icon.

**To manually install an update**

1. On the **Updates** page of the App Store, locate the pending update you want to install.

2. Tap the **Update** button to the right of the update description.

**To configure your iPad to automatically install updates**

1. Start the Settings app.

2. In the **Settings** list, tap **iTunes & App Store**.

3. In the **Automatic Downloads** list, tap the slider to the right of **Updates**.

*A green background on the Updates slider indicates that automatic updates are turned on*

> ✓ **TIP** If you have multiple iPads connected to your App Store account, turning on the Automatic Download feature for apps instructs the App Store to automatically propagate any app that you install on one device to the other devices.

**To display the version history of a specific app**

1. Open the App Store.

2. At the bottom of the App Store window, tap the **Purchased** icon.

1

3. On the **Purchased** page of the App Store, locate the app you want to display version history for. Tap the app name to display the app information page.

 **IMPORTANT** The app information page opens only when you tap the app name, not when you tap the Open or Install button to the right of the name.

4. In the **Details** view of the page, scroll to the **Version History** heading, and then tap **Show Version History**.

Installed app versions are listed in order from most recent to least recent.

*The version number, update date, and description of changes is provided for each update*

✓ **TIP** You can display information about the app only from the app information page in the App Store, not from within the app itself. Program design decisions like this help to minimize the local storage space requirements of the app so it runs efficiently on the iPad and other mobile devices.

# Remove and reinstall Office apps

If at some point you want or need to remove an Office app from your iPad, you can do so in the same way that you do any other app. The process of removing an app from an iPad is referred to as *deleting* the app. You can delete apps from the Home Screen or from the Settings app.

Deleting an app from one device doesn't affect the state of the app on any other devices. If you've installed the app on multiple iPads, either manually or through the Automatic Downloads feature, the app will remain active on the other iPads. Deleted apps remain in the list of purchased apps and can be easily reinstalled from the Purchased page of the App Store, or from iTunes when the iPad is connected to a computer.

**To remove an app from your iPad**

1. On the Home Screen, locate the page or folder containing the app icon.

2. Tap and hold any app icon to activate all the app icons on the screen for editing.

3. In the upper-left corner of the icon that represents the app you want to delete, tap the ×.

*When an icon is active, you can reposition it or delete the related app*

4. In the **Delete "*App*"** message box, tap **Delete**.

5. Press the Home button to deactivate the remaining icons.

*Or*

1. Start the Settings app and display the **General** page.

2. On the **General** page, tap **Usage**.

3. In the **Storage** list, tap the app you want to remove.

4. In the **Delete App** message box, tap **Delete App**.

> ⚠️ **IMPORTANT** Deleting an app removes the app from the iPad and also deletes any locally stored files associated with that app. If you want to keep files, move or send them to an alternative storage location before deleting the app.

**To reinstall a deleted app**

1. Display the **Purchased** page of the App Store.

2. At the top of the **Purchased** page, tap **Not on This iPad**.

3. Locate the app you want to reinstall, and tap the **Install** icon for the app.

4. Accept any required installation terms.

# Skills review

In this chapter, you learned how to:

- Install Office for iPad apps

- Configure iPad and Office app settings

- Update Office apps

- Remove and reinstall Office apps

# Practice tasks

No practice files are necessary to complete the practice tasks in this chapter.

## Install Office for iPad apps

Perform the following tasks:

1. Display the Office for Mobile Devices website on your iPad and review the Office apps that are available for iPad devices.

2. Locate all the available Office apps in the App Store.

3. Install Word, Excel, PowerPoint, and OneNote on your iPad, if you haven't already done so.

## Configure iPad and Office app settings

Perform the following tasks:

1. Display the configurable settings for Word. Tap each setting that displays an arrow to display information about the setting options.

2. Display and explore the configurable settings for Excel.

3. Display and explore the configurable settings for PowerPoint.

4. Display and explore the configurable settings for OneNote.

## Update Office apps

Perform the following tasks:

1. Display the list of all pending and installed updates.

2. On the **Updates** page of the App Store, review all pending and recently installed updates.

3. From the **Updates** page, install any pending updates for Office apps.

4. Display the version history of the Word for iPad app.

5. If you want to, configure the iPad to automatically install downloaded updates.

## Remove and reinstall Office apps

Perform the following tasks:

1. Begin the process of deleting an Office app.

2. When prompted to delete the app or cancel the process, cancel the process.

   *Or*

   If you want to, delete the app and then reinstall it.

   >  **IMPORTANT** Deleting the app will also delete your locally stored files that are associated with that app.

3. Display the list of purchased apps.

4. On the **Purchased** page of the App Store, locate the Excel for iPad app.

5. From the **Purchased** page, display the Excel information page and review the app version history.

# Get connected

As mentioned in Chapter 1, "Office for iPad basics," the only credentials necessary for displaying, creating, and editing files by using Word for iPad, Excel for iPad, PowerPoint for iPad, and OneNote for iPad is a registered Microsoft account. You can activate premium features of the Word, Excel, and PowerPoint iPad apps by associating a Office 365 subscription with the apps.

Microsoft accounts and Office 365 accounts provide access to specific online storage locations associated with the account: either a OneDrive or OneDrive for Business site, and possibly a SharePoint site.

You can access content on your OneDrive and SharePoint sites, and also on a Dropbox site if you have one, from within the Office for iPad apps or from individual iPad apps created specifically for those resources.

This chapter guides you through procedures related to starting and activating Office apps, connecting to user accounts, storing files locally and online, locating helpful resources, and exiting files and apps.

## In this chapter

- Start and activate apps
- Connect to additional storage locations
- Get help with Office apps
- Exit files and apps

## Practice files

No practice files are necessary to complete the practice tasks in this chapter.

# Start and activate apps

Before you can start using an Office app, you need to activate the app. Depending on the method you choose, you can end up with any one of three versions of the apps: display only, standard, or premium.

## Connect to an account

When you first start Word for iPad, Excel for iPad, or PowerPoint for iPad, the app displays a series of informational screens. The final screen prompts you to sign in to the app. You have three options for continuing from this screen to the app:

- **Sign In** You can sign in to the app by using any Microsoft account or Office 365 account. If the account you sign in with is associated with an Office 365 subscription that supports the premium Office for iPad features, the app starts with  full functionality. If the user account is not associated with a qualified subscription, the app presents you with two options after you enter your credentials:

  - **Create and Edit for Free** This option activates the basic feature set of the app, which enables you to display, edit, and create documents, workbooks, presentations, and notebooks.

  - **Go Premium** This option displays a selection of current personal Office 365 subscription plans. You can follow the subscription process to activate the premium features of Word for iPad, Excel for iPad, and PowerPoint for iPad. (OneNote for iPad doesn't have a premium version.)

- **Create an Account** This option starts the process of creating a Microsoft account, and then returns you to the Sign In screen. You can sign in with your new Microsoft account to activate the standard version of the app, or subscribe to Office 365 to activate the premium version of the app.

- **Sign In Later** This option starts the app in a limited functionality mode in which you can display (but not edit) documents, workbooks, and presentations. If you choose this option, you can connect to an account (and activate the standard or premium feature set) at a later time.

 **TIP** At any time, you can continue to the app by clicking an option, or cancel the sign-in process by closing the window.

2

One activation option that isn't obvious is that of connecting to an Office 365 subscription that is associated with your Apple ID but that is not yet connected to the iPad you're working on. You can access the process necessary to reconnect to a disconnected account by following the Go Premium path and selecting any of the subscription options.

Activating any one Office product on your computer, iPad, or other device automatically activates all the Office apps on the device.

Sidebars in the first chapter of each app-specific part of this book provide information about the features that are available in the iPad, online, and desktop versions of Word, Excel, PowerPoint, and OneNote. Outside of the procedures in *this* topic that are specific to connecting to Microsoft accounts and Office 365 accounts, the procedures in this book assume that you have access to the full feature sets of each app.

 **SEE ALSO** For information about the functionality available in Word for iPad, see Chapter 4, "Create professional documents"; in Excel for iPad, see Chapter 7, "Store and retrieve data"; in PowerPoint for iPad, see Chapter 9, "Create compelling presentations"; and in OneNote for iPad, see Chapter 11, "Store information in digital notebooks."

**To start an Office app**

1. On the Home Screen, locate the icon for the app you want to start, and then tap the icon.

   > **TIP** It might be necessary to swipe left or right to a different Home Screen to find the app icon or the folder that contains the app.

   *Or*

   Locate the app on any page of the App Store, and tap the **Open** button next to the app name.

   *Or*

   Display the app information page, and then tap the **Open** button.

# Organize apps in folders

To simplify the process of finding the Office apps (or any set of related apps) that you've installed on your iPad, you can put them all into one folder. Grouping apps in folders also cuts down on the amount of swiping you have to do to locate apps on the Home Screen. This is especially useful if you have a lot of apps installed.

To create a folder, follow these steps:

1. On the Home Screen, tap and hold any app icon to activate all the app icons.

2. Locate the icons for two of the apps you want to group. Drag one app icon on top of the other app icon and hold it there briefly until a box appears around the icons.

   When you release the icon, the new folder opens. Depending on the apps you grouped, the folder might already have a meaningful name.

To add apps to an existing folder, simply drag the app icons onto the folder to drop them inside it. You can access all your folders from the Home Screen. (You can't create subfolders within these top-level folders.)

To change a folder name, follow these steps:

1. Open the folder and activate the app icons.

2. Tap the existing folder name to activate it for editing. Then edit or replace the name.

3. Press the Home button to leave the editing mode.

To remove an app from a folder, follow these steps:

1. Open the folder and activate the app icons.

2. Drag the app icon from the box that denotes the folder to the space outside the box.

When only one app remains in the folder, the folder is automatically deleted.

**To connect to an Office app for the first time**

1. Tap or flick through the Office 365 sign-in screen series.

2. On the **Sign in now** screen, do one of the following:

   - To sign in with an existing account, tap **Sign In**, enter your credentials on the **Sign in** screen that appears, and then follow the process to activate the standard or premium versions of the Office for iPad apps.

   - To create a Microsoft account that you can use to activate the standard versions of the Office for iPad apps, tap **Create an Account**, and then follow the process for creating a Microsoft account.

   >  **SEE ALSO** For information about creating Microsoft accounts, see "Install Office for iPad apps" in Chapter 1, "Office for iPad basics."

   - To start the app in read-only mode, tap **Sign In Later**.

## Manage account connections

When you start Word, Excel, or PowerPoint on your iPad for the first time, or if you weren't working in a specific file the last time you exited the app, the app displays the Open page of the Backstage view. (This is different from the experience on the desktop version of the program, which displays a blank file.)

If the app isn't connected to a user account, the words *Sign In* appear below the Account button and only the local iPad storage is available.

*OneDrive, SharePoint, and Dropbox storage locations aren't shown until you connect to an account*

>  **TIP** In this book, information that applies both to Microsoft accounts and to organizational accounts refers generically to the account you use to sign in to Office apps as a *user account*. The process of connecting an app to a user account is accomplished by signing in using the account credentials.

If you signed in to the app with a user account, the Account button displays your name, and the Account menu that appears when you tap the Account button provides access to your connected storage resources, and to account-specific settings.

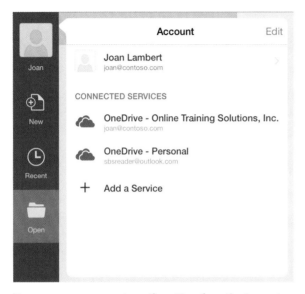

*You can manage account-specific settings from the Account menu*

 **SEE ALSO** For information about cloud storage options, see "Connect to additional storage locations" later in this chapter.

Until you activate the premium features of an app, the Go Premium button (which is represented by a shopping cart icon) appears at the bottom of the File bar. Although the button displays a shopping cart, if you have an existing Office 365 subscription, no purchase is required.

**2**

**To connect to an account from within an Office app**

1. If necessary, tap the **Back** button (located at the left end of the ribbon) to display the Backstage view of the app.

   The Account button at the top of the File bar is labeled *Sign in*.

2. On the **File** bar, tap the **Account** button.

3. On the **Sign In** screen, enter the email address associated with your Microsoft account or Office 365 account, and then tap **Next**.

4. On the secondary **Sign In** screen, re-enter the email address, enter the associated account password, and then tap **Sign In**.

   The Account button displays your account name to indicate that you're signed in.

**To activate premium features from within an app**

1. Connect (sign in) to Office by using an account that has an associated Office 365 license.

*Or*

1. Display the Backstage view of the app.

2. At the bottom of the **File** bar, tap the **Go Premium** button, and then do one of the following:

   - Tap **Activate by Signing In**, and then provide the credentials of an account that has an Office 365 subscription.

   - Tap one of the available subscription options, review the details and price, tap **Buy Now**, and provide the necessary account information.

   - Tap one of the available subscription options, tap **Restore Previous Purchase**, tap **Buy**, and enter the password for your Apple ID to sign in to the iTunes Store and restore a previously connected subscription.

# Alternative file access methods

If you're accustomed to working with Word, Excel, or PowerPoint on other platforms, one experience that you might find different when working with the iPad apps is that the most usual method of working in a file is to first start the app, and then open the file you want to work with from within the app. Because the iPad doesn't have a native browsable file storage system like those provided by the Windows and Mac operating systems, you can't navigate to and open the files stored on your iPad from outside of the app.

**SEE ALSO** For information about managing files from iTunes, see the side-bar "iTunes support for the iPad" in Chapter 1, "Office for iPad basics."

Methods for opening files on your iPad from outside of the apps include the following:

■ You can browse through the contents of your OneDrive or OneDrive for Business site by using the related iPad app, and open files directly in Word, Excel, PowerPoint, or OneNote from within those apps.

■ You can browse through the contents of your Dropbox site and open files directly in Word, Excel, or PowerPoint from within the Dropbox app.

■ You can open a OneDrive, OneDrive for Business, SharePoint, or Drop-box site in Safari or another web browser and open files from that site.

■ If you receive a document, workbook, or presentation as an attach-ment to an email message, you can display the file content or open the file for editing.

■ If you receive a link to a OneNote notebook in an email message, you can open the notebook from the message in OneNote Online, and from there you can open the notebook in OneNote.

# Connect to additional storage locations

Signing in to a user account connects the Office apps to the online storage location associated with that account. Microsoft accounts have associated OneDrive storage sites, personal Office 365 accounts have OneDrive storage sites, and business Office 365 accounts have OneDrive for Business storage sites.

 **SEE ALSO** For more information about Microsoft accounts and Office 365 accounts, see "Install Office for iPad apps" in Chapter 1, "Office for iPad basics."

The default storage location for Office files you save to your iPad is your iPad. You can connect to multiple online storage locations, including OneDrive, OneDrive for Business, SharePoint, and Dropbox sites.

**IMPORTANT** Apple offers the iCloud online storage solution. iCloud is not available as a storage location for files you create and edit in Word, Excel, or other Office apps. You can configure iCloud as a backup location for the contents of your iPad.

Each storage location is referred to as a Place. You can add Places by connecting to services or specifying locations. You can open files that are stored in any of the Places you connect to, and save files to those same Places.

*Individual SharePoint sites are organized within the SharePoint Place*

 **TIP** You can connect to multiple OneDrive sites or SharePoint sites. Each OneDrive site appears as a place and each SharePoint site as a subset of the SharePoint place.

# Use OneDrive to work anywhere

If you're new to the world of OneDrive, here's a quick tutorial to help you get started.

OneDrive is a cloud-based storage solution. The purpose of OneDrive is to provide a single place for you to store and access all your files. Although this might seem like a simple concept, it provides major value for people who use Word or other Office products on multiple devices, including computers running Windows, Mac computers, iPads and other tablets, and Windows, iPhone, and Android smartphones.

For example, you can create a file on your desktop computer at work, edit it on your iPad at home, and review it on your smartphone while you're waiting for your lunch to be served at a restaurant. If you use the full suite of Office products within your organization, you can even present the file in a Skype for Business (formerly Lync) meeting from your tablet PC, all while the file is stored in the same central location.

There are currently two types of OneDrive—one for personal use and one for business use:

- **OneDrive**  A *personal* OneDrive storage site, formerly known as a SkyDrive, is provided free with every Microsoft account. Each OneDrive is linked to a specific account.

- **OneDrive for Business**  An *organizational* OneDrive storage site, formerly part of SharePoint MySites, is provided with every business-level Office 365 subscription license. These storage locations are part of an organization's Office 365 online infrastructure.

You might have both types of OneDrive available to you; if you do, you can connect to both from the Office for iPad apps.

In this book, the personal and organizational versions are referred to generically as OneDrive sites except in instructions that are specific to one version or the other.

**2**

To make OneDrive a realistic one-stop storage solution, Microsoft has chosen to support the storage of very large files (up to 10 gigabytes [GB] each) and to provide a significant amount of free storage—from a minimum of 15 GB for every Microsoft account, to unlimited storage for Office 365 subscribers!

By default, files that you store on your OneDrive site are password-protected and available only to you. You can share specific files or folders with other people by sending a personalized invitation or a generic link that allows recipients to view or edit files. You can also create a collaboration space called a OneDrive Group, in which multiple people can freely create and manage files.

You can access files stored on your OneDrive from your iPad in several ways:

- From within the Word, Excel, PowerPoint, or OneNote apps when opening or saving a file.

- Through the OneDrive or OneDrive for Business apps.

- Through a web browser such as Safari. Personal OneDrive sites are available at *https://onedrive.live.com*; organizational OneDrive sites have addresses linked to your Office 365 account, such as *https://contoso-my.sharepoint.com/personal/joan_contoso_com/*.

When you're working on a computer, you have even more access to the files that are stored on your OneDrive site:

- On a computer running Windows, you can synchronize your OneDrive site contents with the computer to make the OneDrive contents available in File Explorer.

- On a Mac computer, you can install a OneDrive app and synchronize your OneDrive with the app.

Because OneDrive and OneDrive for Business file storage locations are easily configurable in all versions of Word, Excel, PowerPoint, and OneNote, OneDrive is a simple and useful cloud storage option. And best of all, it's completely free!

## Connect to a remote storage location

Creating a Microsoft account simultaneously creates a OneDrive online storage account on which you can store files that you create in Office apps or other apps. Since the inception of OneDrive, the amount of free storage granted to OneDrive users has continually increased.

OneDrive for Business is the online storage provided to each user who has a business subscription to Office 365. You access this storage from your organization's SharePoint site by using your Office 365 credentials. You can also add it to the list of Places that is available in an Office app.

**To add a storage location from within an Office app**

1. At the left end of the ribbon, tap the **Back** button to display the Backstage view.

2. On the **File** bar, tap **Open** to display the storage locations you're connected to.

3. On the **Open** page, tap **Add a Place**.

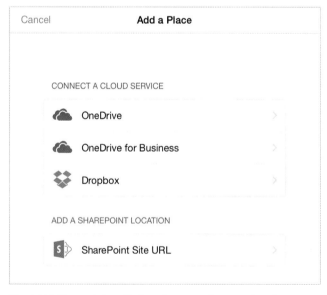

*The Add A Place window displays the types of storage locations you can connect to*

2

4.  In the **Add a Place** window, do one of the following:

    *   Tap **OneDrive**, enter your Microsoft account credentials, and then tap the **Sign In** button.

    *   Tap **OneDrive for Business**, enter your organizational credentials, and then tap the **Sign In** button.

    *   Tap **Dropbox**, enter the email address and password associated with your Dropbox account, and then tap the **Sign in** button.

    *   Tap **SharePoint Site URL**, enter the SharePoint site address (including *https://* if it's a secure site), and then tap the **Next** button. Enter your SharePoint site credentials if prompted to do so.

*Or*

1.  On the **File** bar, tap the **Account** button, and then tap **Add a Service**.

2.  In the **Add a Service** window, do one of the following:

    *   Tap **OneDrive**, enter your Microsoft account credentials, and then tap **Sign In**.

    *   Tap **OneDrive for Business**, enter your organizational credentials, and then tap **Sign In**.

>  **TIP** SharePoint sites you're connected to appear in the Connected Services list for the account, but you can't add a SharePoint site from that location.

# Synchronize OneDrive with desktop computers

Your OneDrive is easy to access from within the Office apps on the iPad, but to fully take advantage of it as a central file storage location, you can synchronize it with your desktop computer and browse its contents as you would those of any storage folder.

To synchronize your OneDrive contents with a computer running Windows 7 or Windows 8, follow these steps:

1. In Internet Explorer or another web browser, display the OneDrive download site at *https://onedrive.live.com/about/en-us/download.*

2. With **Windows** selected in the operating system list, tap or click the **Download now** button for the OneDrive software you want to install.

3. Run the **OneDriveSetup** installation file and configure your preferences.

To synchronize your OneDrive contents with a Mac, follow these steps:

1. Install the OneDrive app from the App Store (not from iTunes—the full app is available only from the App Store).

2. Start the OneDrive app, and then configure your preferences, which include:

   - Whether to start OneDrive automatically.

   - Which folders to synchronize with OneDrive.

   - Whether to display the OneDrive icon in the Dock.

3. To simplify the process of saving files to OneDrive, add the OneDrive folder to your **Favorites** list by dragging the folder to the Finder.

The OneDrive app for the Mac requires Mac OS X Lion (10.7) or later. For more information, go to *windows.microsoft.com/en-us/onedrive /mac-app-faq.*

# Get help with Office apps

While you're working in Word, Excel, PowerPoint, or another Office app on your
iPad, you can access general information and helpful tips from the Help module.

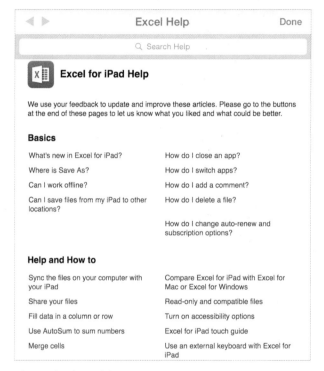

*The Excel Help module*

 **IMPORTANT**  The content of the Help module is stored online, so you can access it
only when your iPad is connected to the Internet.

If you don't find the information you're looking for in the Help file, you can consult online resources including these:

- **Microsoft Office Mobile website**  Visit *office.microsoft.com/mobile* and tap the links on the top link bar to display information about apps, subscriptions, support options, and your account.

- **Microsoft Community forum**  Product experts and users participate in moderated online discussions about specific product features and issues. You can search the forum discussions to find out whether other people have had the same problem and what they've done to resolve it.

- **Microsoft Answer Desk**  Product advisors provide technical support, account information, and product recommendations through a live chat interface.

**To open the Help module for the current app**

1. Open any file in the app to display the ribbon.

2. Near the left end of the ribbon, tap the **File** button.

3. On the **File** menu, tap **Help and Support**.

**To access community discussions relevant to the current app**

1. Visit *answers.microsoft.com/en-us/office/forum/office_mobile* from any computer.

*Or*

1. Open the Help module.

2. Scroll to the **Still have questions?** section at the end of the main page.

3. In the paragraph that follows the heading, tap the **Microsoft Community** link.

**To chat with a support person**

1. Visit *support.microsoft.com/contactus* from any computer.

*Or*

1. Open the Help module.

2. In the **Still have questions?** section at the end of the main page, tap the **Answer Desk** link.

# Exit files and apps

In any Office for iPad app, you can have only one file open in the app window at a time. Opening a second file doesn't start a second instance of the app, as you might be accustomed to when working with Office files on other platforms—the second file simply replaces the first file in the same app window.

When working in the primary Office for iPad apps, you can't simply close an open file. You have the following options for leaving a Word, Excel, or PowerPoint file:

- Delete the file, if you haven't yet saved it for the first time.

>  **SEE ALSO** For information about deleting unsaved files, see "Create, open, and save files" in Chapter 3, "Create and manage files."

- Open a different file in the current app window (thereby closing the current file).
- Exit the app.

You can't exit an Office for iPad app from within the app window; you must first display the list of running apps and then exit the app by dismissing it from the list.

*App icons and app preview screens help you quickly identify apps*

**To exit an Office app**

1.  Use one of the following methods to display the currently open apps:

    *   From within the app window, flick up with four or five fingers.

    *   Press the Home button twice.

2.  Flick left or right if necessary to locate the app you want to exit.

 **SEE ALSO** For information about multitasking gestures, see the sidebar "Switch among running apps" on the next page.

3.  Flick the app preview screen up past the top of the window.

# Skills review

In this chapter, you learned how to:

*   Start and activate apps

*   Connect to additional storage locations

*   Get help with Office apps

*   Exit files and apps

2

# Switch among running apps

It's likely that you'll run more than one app at a time on your iPad (for example, you might concurrently run the Word, Excel, Mail, and FaceTime apps), but you can interact with only one app at a time. The process of navigating among apps is different from that of navigating among program windows on a desktop computer. If you're not already familiar with iPad app-switching techniques, here is a quick tutorial.

You can switch among apps in two ways:

- From within an app, use four or five fingers to flick left or right between the open apps.

- Use one of the following techniques to display the open apps:

  - Use four or five fingers to flick up from within the app window.

  - Press the Home button twice.

  Then flick left or right to locate the app you want to make active, and tap the app preview screen or icon.

The four-finger and five-finger techniques work only when multitasking gestures are turned on (as they are by default). You can turn multitasking gestures on and off from the General page of the Settings app.

**SEE ALSO** For related information, see the sidebar "Switch among files" in Chapter 3, "Create and manage files."

# Practice tasks

No practice files are necessary to complete the practice tasks in this chapter.

## Start and activate apps

Perform the following tasks:

1. Start the Excel for iPad app.

2. If the app is not already connected to a user account, provide your Microsoft account or Office 365 account credentials.

3. Connect to a user account.

4. If the app is not already activated, link to an existing Office 365 subscription or subscribe to Office 365.

5. Activate Office.

## Connect to additional storage locations

Start Word for iPad, and then perform the following tasks:

1. Add your OneDrive or OneDrive for Business storage site to your Places list, and browse its contents from within Word.

2. Install the appropriate OneDrive management app or apps on your iPad:

   - If you have only personal OneDrive storage sites, install the OneDrive app.

   - If you have only organizational OneDrive storage sites, install the OneDrive for Business app.

   - If you have personal *and* organizational OneDrives, install both apps.

3. Connect the app or apps you installed in step 2 to your OneDrive storage sites.

4. If you work with files that are stored on a SharePoint site, add the site to your Places list, and browse its contents from within Word.

## Get help with Office apps

Start PowerPoint for iPad, and then perform the following tasks:

1. Display the PowerPoint Help module.

2. Locate information in the Help module about new features in PowerPoint for iPad.

3. Locate information about accessibility options for PowerPoint.

4. Visit the Microsoft Community forum for PowerPoint, and read at least two discussions.

## Exit files and apps

With the Word for iPad, Excel for iPad, and PowerPoint for iPad apps running, perform the following tasks:

1. Display the list of running apps.

2. Exit each of the apps.

# Create and manage files

3

The elements that control the appearance of an iPad app or computer program and the way we interact with it are collectively referred to as the user interface. Some user interface elements, such as the color scheme, are cosmetic. Others, such as toolbars, menus, and buttons, are functional. Many apps and programs allow users to modify cosmetic and functional user interface elements (the "look and feel" of the app) to accommodate individual preferences.

The Office for iPad apps—Word, Excel, and PowerPoint—share many common user interface features and functions. The ways in which you interact with each app to perform standard tasks such as opening, saving, sharing, searching, and printing files are standardized across the apps so that you can concentrate your learning efforts on the skills and features that are specific to the app or to the document, workbook, or presentation you're creating.

This chapter guides you through procedures that are common to Word for iPad, Excel for iPad, and PowerPoint for iPad. It includes procedures related to opening and creating files, saving files, sharing files, searching file content, and printing documents, workbooks, worksheets, or specific portions thereof.

## In this chapter

- Create, open, and save files
- Use common Office interface features
- Search file content
- Print file content
- Distribute files

## Practice files

For this chapter, use the practice files from the iPadOfficeSBS\Ch03 folder. For practice file download instructions, see the Introduction.

# Create, open, and save files

When you start an Office app from the Home Screen, it displays the Backstage view. From the File bar on the left side of the window, you can create new files, open files that you worked with previously, or browse through your connected storage locations to find and open a file.

## Create files

When creating a file in an Office app, you can create a blank file of the default file type or create a file based on one of the templates provided with each app. Each template incorporates specific design elements such as fonts and colors. Many templates also include typical information that you can modify or build on to create a useful document, workbook, or presentation.

*Some of the available Excel workbook templates*

> **TIP** You can't open online or custom templates from the New page of an iPad app. To use a template other than those that are available by default from the New page, save the template to one of your connected storage locations and open it from that location.

If you create a file that contains content (either from a template or content that you enter) and display the Backstage view before naming and saving the file, the app prompts you to save or delete the file.

> **SEE ALSO** For information about creating files in Word for iPad, see Chapter 4, "Create professional documents"; in Excel for iPad, see Chapter 7, "Store and retrieve data"; and in PowerPoint for iPad, see Chapter 9, "Create compelling presentations."

**3**

You can open an existing file from within the corresponding Office app, from its storage location, or from an email message. If the file is stored remotely, the app downloads a copy of the file before opening it.

If you no longer need a file that you've stored on your iPad or a connected storage location, you can delete files from the Open page of the Backstage view.

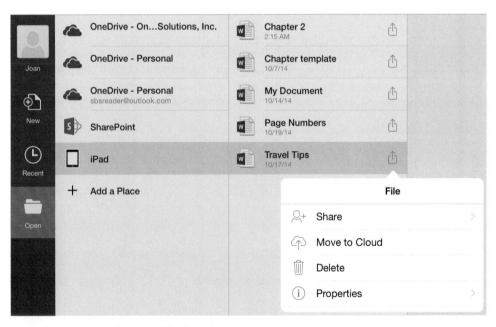

*You can perform several tasks on files from the Open page*

> **TIP** It can take a short time for files that you post to a SharePoint or OneDrive site to appear in a folder structure that you've previously opened. If you don't want to wait, you can manually refresh the display of the folder contents by swiping the folder structure down the Open page.

**To create a new document, workbook, or presentation**

1. Start the app or, if you're already working in a document, tap the **Back** button to display the Backstage view.

2. On the **File** bar, tap **New**.

3. On the **New** page of the Backstage view, tap the type of file you want to create.

**To delete a new file instead of saving it for the first time**

1. At the left end of the ribbon, tap the **Back** button.

    If you haven't yet named the file and selected a file storage location, the Save As window opens.

2. In the upper-left corner of the **Save As** window, tap **Delete** to delete the current file and display the **New** page of the Backstage view.

 **IMPORTANT** The Delete command is available only in the Save As dialog box that appears when you tap the Back button in an unsaved file. It is not available when you are using the Name or Duplicate function.

**To delete a file that has already been saved**

1. Display the Backstage view.

2. On the **File** bar, tap **Open**.

3. On the **Open** page of the Backstage view, navigate to the folder that contains the file you want to delete.

4. Tap the **File Actions** button to the right of the file name, and then tap **Delete**.

5. In the confirmation message box, tap **Delete**.

## Open files

From the Open page of the Backstage view, you can navigate to files stored locally on your iPad or on a remote storage resource such as a OneDrive site or a SharePoint site. Each app displays only the files that can be opened by that app.

*The Open page displays only the app-specific files in the selected location*

The Open page displays up to three levels of the storage structure in columns. Initially, the Place is in the leftmost column and subsequent sites or folders are in adjacent columns. Each column represents one level of the storage structure and displays the folders and files at that level in alphabetical order. When you navigate through a deep folder structure, the columns move to the left. You can scroll the page left and right to display the entire storage path.

If you want to access files that are stored on a OneDrive site directly from your iPad (rather than through the apps), you can install the OneDrive or OneDrive for Business app on your iPad. These apps allow you to browse through the folders on your storage site and manage the files that are stored there.

> **TIP** When you open a file that is stored in a remote storage location, the words *read-only* appear in parentheses to the right of the file name on the title bar, and a yellow banner at the top of the content pane provides an Edit button that you must tap before you can make changes to the file. If you don't intend to modify the file content, you can hide the banner by tapping the × at its right end.

Office keeps track of the files that you work with on any device and makes the list available from any other device. (The data is linked to your user account.) This is one of the tremendous benefits of the Office 365 subscription model and the cloud storage that comes with it—you can be up and running on a new computer in minutes, without having to move files or configure settings and preferences.

# Switch among files

When you're working in an Office program on a desktop computer, you can have multiple files open at the same time and easily switch among them. When you're working in an Office app on your iPad, however, you can have only one file open at a time in each app. To switch to another file, you must open the file from the Backstage view.

After you create a new, blank file and add content to it, you can't open a different file in the same app until you name and save the new file or delete it. The Open page of the Backstage view displays the files and folders stored in connected storage locations, but the files are dimmed so you can't open them. This safeguard is built into the Office for iPad apps to protect you from losing unsaved information, due to the limitation of having only one file open at a time in an iPad app.

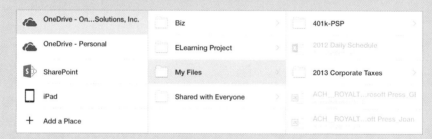

*Dimmed files are visible but not available to open*

**SEE ALSO** For related information, see the sidebar "Switch among running apps" in Chapter 2, "Get connected."

The Recent page of the Backstage view provides quick access to the files you've worked with recently on your iPad, desktop computer, or other device. The Recent page displays only files that are related to the app you're working in: documents in the Word app, workbooks in the Excel app, and presentations in the PowerPoint app.

> **TIP** Each app recognizes the file types commonly associated with the desktop version of the program. For example, Word for iPad recognizes the current and previous default Word Document file types (.docx and .doc), and templates created for those standards.

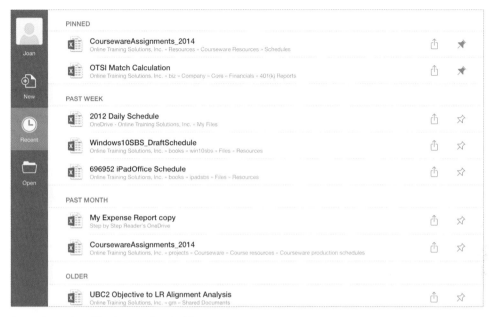

*Recently used workbooks associated with a user account*

To ensure that you can find a specific file quickly regardless of whether you've worked with it recently, you can pin it to the Recent page. Pinned files appear in the Pinned section at the top of the list and are indicated by a colored thumbtack.

**To open a recent file from within the relevant app**

1. Display the **Recent** page of the Backstage view.

2. If necessary, scroll through the list to locate the file you want to open. Then tap the file.

3. If the app prompts you to do so, enter the credentials necessary to gain access to the file or storage location.

**To pin a file to the Recent file list**

1. Display the **Recent** page of the Backstage view.

2. If necessary, scroll through the list to locate the file you want to pin.

3. Tap the **Pin** button located to the right of the file name to add the file to the **Pinned** area at the top of the **Recent** page.

# Font substitution

The desktop versions of the Office programs support more fonts than the Office for iPad apps. The Office for iPad apps have been programmed to handle this situation gracefully by substituting an available font for any unsupported font. Because of this, the file content is fully visible and available for editing.

When you open a file on your iPad that uses fonts that aren't installed on the iPad, a black warning banner appears briefly below the ribbon to inform you that text in the file might look different than in the original file.

Only the appearance of the text is changed; the original font is still assigned to the text, and any edits you make to the text will be in the assigned font. When the file is displayed on a computer that supports the assigned font, it will appear correctly.

The Font list displays the original font name. You can apply that font to other text within the document by copying the text and then pasting the format onto other text.

If you apply other fonts to the document content while working with it on your iPad, the new fonts will be visible in the document to people who display or edit the document in a desktop version of the program.

**SEE ALSO** For information about copying and pasting formats, see "Change the appearance of text" in Chapter 4, "Create professional documents."

**To open a file directly from a OneDrive storage site**

1. From the App Store, install the OneDrive app.
2. Start the OneDrive app.
3. In the OneDrive app window, browse to and tap the file you want to open.
4. If prompted to do so, enter the Microsoft account credentials associated with the OneDrive, and then tap **Sign in**.

**To open a file directly from a OneDrive for Business storage site**

1. From the App Store, install the OneDrive for Business app.

2. Start the OneDrive for Business app.

3. If prompted to do so, enter your organizational account credentials, and then tap **Sign in**.

4. In the OneDrive for Business app, browse to and tap the file you want to open.

**To open an Office file attachment from the Mail app**

1. Open or preview the email message that has the attached file.

2. Tap the attachment to display a read-only version of the file content. Then in the upper-right corner of the screen, tap the arrow icon to display a list of apps you can open the file in.

   *Or*

   Tap and hold the attachment to display a list of apps you can open the file in.

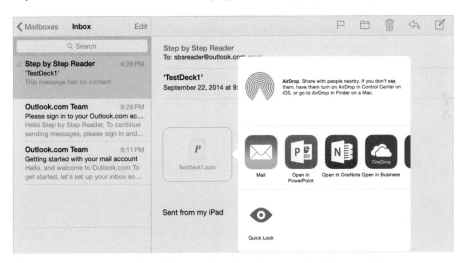

*The options that appear in the window vary based on the apps installed on your iPad*

3. Tap the icon of the Office app in which you want to open the attachment.

## Save files

By default, the Office apps automatically save the file you're working on and track saved file versions online so that you can revert to earlier versions when necessary.

When the AutoSave function is turned on:

- If you're working in a new, unnamed file, the app saves a temporary copy of the file to your default storage location.

- If you're working in a previously saved file, the app saves a copy of the file to the location in which you opened or last saved it.

You can turn off the automatic file-saving function if you prefer to save changes manually.

> **TIP** When using the Office for iPad apps, you can save files only in the default file format for the app you're working in. To save a file as a template, macro-enabled file, or one of the many other available formats, use the desktop or online version of the program.

**To save and name a file for the first time**

1. Tap the **File** button.

2. On the **File** menu, tap **Name** or **Save**.

> **TIP** The File menu includes the Name command when AutoSave is turned on, and the Save command when AutoSave is turned off. The command is active until a name is assigned to the file; then it becomes dimmed to indicate that it is unavailable.

3. On the **Save As** screen, enter a file name in the **Name** box.

4. In the **Choose Name and Location** pane, tap the place where you want to store the file.

5. If a list of folders associated with the selected storage location appears in the center pane, tap the folder in which you want to store the file.

6. In the upper-right corner of the pane, tap **Save**.

**To save a copy of a file**

1. On the **File** menu, tap **Duplicate**.

2. In the **Choose Name and Location** pane, tap the place where you want to store the file copy. Then if necessary, flick the folder structure to the right to display the top-level folders.

3. In the **Name** box, enter a name for the new version of the file.

4. In the upper-right corner of the pane, tap **Save**.

## View and edit files online

Most Office 365 subscriptions that include licensing for premium features of Word for iPad, Excel for iPad, and PowerPoint for iPad also include licensing for Word Online, Excel Online, and PowerPoint Online. These Office Online apps—formerly known as the Office Web Apps—run entirely within your web browser and don't require the installation of an app or desktop software. In spite of this, you can sometimes do more in the Office Online apps than you can in the iPad apps—but only with files that are stored in cloud storage locations that support the Office Online apps, such as OneDrive and SharePoint sites.

If you find that you need more editing functionality than is provided by the iPad app version of a program—for example, if you want to insert footnotes in a Word document—you can start a web browser (such as Safari), browse to the storage location on *onedrive.live.com* or your SharePoint site, and then open and edit the file in the relevant Office Online app.

# Use common Office interface features

The Office apps designed for the iPad share common user interface features, so if you know how to find your way around one app, it's a less daunting task to learn to use another.

## Identify standard features

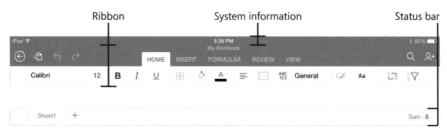

*The user interface of a typical Office for iPad app*

Word for iPad, Excel for iPad, and PowerPoint for iPad each have a colored pane at the top of the app window, containing these standard window elements:

■ The system information bar, which displays the time, battery charge, and information about the iPad's network connections. This system information is independent of the Office app.

■ The ribbon, which provides access to commands for working with the app, the current file, and the file content.

■ The name of the active file, which is displayed between the system information bar and the ribbon.

> ⊘ **TIP** The pane color is specific to the app you're using—blue for Word, green for Excel, orange for PowerPoint, and purple for OneNote—so you can quickly differentiate between apps when looking at file thumbnails or quick views of app windows.

Excel for iPad also has a status bar at the bottom of the window, which provides information about the currently selected file content.

> ⊘ **TIP** The user interface elements of the Office for iPad apps are designed to be easy to access and control by using touch (with fingers) rather than an external pointing device such as a mouse. You can use the iPad's on-screen keyboard or an external keyboard to input information. If you're using an external keyboard, the on-screen keyboard doesn't appear when you're working in the file content. For more information about the on-screen keyboard, see the sidebar "Reconfigure the on-screen keyboard" later in this chapter.

The Office apps, like other iPad apps, open in full-screen windows. You can't minimize, resize, or close the apps from within the window.

# Change the magnification level of file content

The Office for iPad apps don't have built-in zoom controls like those in the desktop Office programs—they aren't necessary, because the iPad is a touch-centric device, and the functionality is built in. You can use gestures to change the magnification level of a document:

- Stretch two fingers apart to zoom in, so that the file content appears larger.

- Pinch two fingers together to zoom out, to display more of the file content.

You can turn on additional magnification tools in the iPad settings, including these tools, which are useful for working in the Office for iPad apps:

- **Zoom** When this function is turned on, you can display a magnifying tool by double-tapping with three fingers. You can then drag the magnifier around the screen by its handle, or drag the screen with three fingers to change the area shown in the magnifier.

- **Zoom Controller** This round control is available on the screen when the Zoom tool is turned on, and dims when it is idle. Tapping the controller displays a menu of zoom-related commands. Dragging within the controller moves the magnifier around the screen.

To turn on the iPad zoom controls you want to use, follow these steps:

1. In the Settings app, display the **General** page.

2. Tap **Accessibility**, and then tap **Zoom**.

3. On the **Zoom** page, do any of the following:

    - Tap the **Zoom** slider to turn on the magnifying tool.

    - Tap the **Show Controller** slider to turn on the Zoom Controller.

    - Tap **Zoom Region** and then tap either **Full Screen Zoom** or **Window Zoom** to specify the area you want to magnify by using the controls.

# Work with the ribbon

The commands and procedures available for creating and modifying the content of a Word document, Excel workbook, or PowerPoint presentation are located on the tabs grouped in the center of the ribbon and vary among apps. Each Office app has Home, Insert, and Review tabs, and additional function-specific tabs that provide commands specific to working with content in that app.

*The Home tab for each app contains the most commonly used commands for that app*

Tool tabs appear to the right of the primary tabs when certain types of content such as pictures, tables, and shapes are active. A tool tab has a white shadow under the tab name when it isn't active, to differentiate it from the standard tabs.

*Tool tabs contain commands specific to working with the selected element*

Because the screen area of the iPad and iPad Mini devices is limited, active areas of the user interface change to make relevant features and commands available. For example, the standard ribbon tabs move to the left to make space for each active tool tab.

Commands that relate to managing, searching, and sharing files are grouped on the left and right ends of the ribbon.

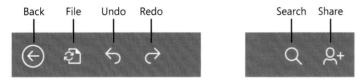

*Tapping the Back, File, Search, and Share buttons displays additional screens or menus*

The buttons at the left end of the ribbon provide access to the Backstage view and the File menu, and allow you to undo (and redo, if you change your mind) recent actions. The buttons at the right end of the ribbon display options for distributing the file to other people and for either searching the file content (in Word and Excel), or playing a slide show (in PowerPoint).

 **SEE ALSO** For information about searching and sharing, see "Search file content" and "Distribute files" later in this chapter.

Tapping the Back button displays the Backstage view of the app. The Backstage view of each Office for iPad app provides access to commands for connecting to your user account and file storage locations, and for creating and opening files. Some of the information in the Backstage view is shared among all the Office apps that are installed on your iPad. Other information is specific to the app you're working in.

 **SEE ALSO** For hands-on practice working in the Backstage view, see "Start and activate apps" and "Connect to additional storage locations" in Chapter 2, "Get connected."

### To undo, redo, and repeat recent changes

1. To undo individual changes sequentially, tap the **Undo** button.

2. To reinstate undone changes, or to repeat the last action, tap the **Redo** button.

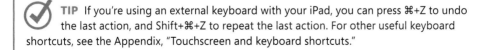 **TIP** If you're using an external keyboard with your iPad, you can press ⌘+Z to undo the last action, and Shift+⌘+Z to repeat the last action. For other useful keyboard shortcuts, see the Appendix, "Touchscreen and keyboard shortcuts."

## Manage files

Commands for managing the currently open file (not its content) are available from the File menu that expands when you tap the File button.

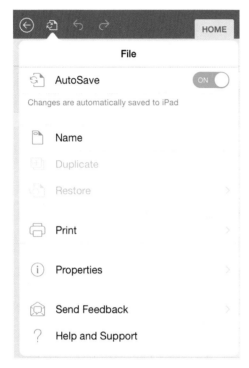

*The available commands vary based on the settings configured for saving the file*

> ⚠ **IMPORTANT** If the File menu doesn't display all the commands shown here, tap one of the commands that expands a submenu (such as Print) and then tap Cancel (in the upper-left corner of the submenu) to refresh the display of the File menu.

You control the following functions from the File menu:

- **AutoSave** This function, which is turned on by default, saves a temporary copy of the file at regular intervals.

- **Name** This function is available in a new file until the file is saved. Use this function to save a file for the first time in a specific storage location, with a specific name.

- **Duplicate** This function is available only in files that have previously been saved. Use this function to create a copy of the current file. You can set the file name and storage location of the copy.

>  **TIP** Duplicating a file is an easy way of moving a file to a different location—simply save the duplicate in the new location and then delete the original file.

- **Restore** Periodically you might want to experiment with structural or content modifications, or you might simply find that a change you've made didn't work as intended, and want to undo your changes. The Office for iPad apps provide three levels of change reversion:

  - You can undo one change at a time (and redo that change if you want to).

  - You can undo all the changes in the current app session.

  - You can roll back to a previous version of the document.

- **Print** Standard printing options include printer selection, print range, and number of copies to print.

>  **TIP** In Excel for iPad, the Print command also provides access to layout options such as page size, orientation, and scaling. More extensive layout options are available for Word documents, from the Layout tab of the ribbon.

In addition to these functions, you can display the properties of the current file, send feedback about an app feature that you like or don't like, and access online Help information about the app.

> **SEE ALSO** For information about the Name and Duplicate functions, see "Create, open, and save files" earlier in this chapter. For information about online Help, see "Get help with Office apps" in Chapter 2, "Get connected."

The Office for iPad apps display only a few of the available properties for each file, including information such as its location, size, author, and creation date.

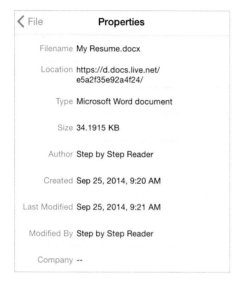

*Only basic file properties are displayed*

### To display file management commands

1. Near the left end of the ribbon, tap the **File** button.

### To stop Office from automatically saving open files

1. Tap the **File** button.

2. On the **File** menu, tap the **AutoSave** slider to change its background to white.

### To display file properties

1. Tap the **File** button, and then tap **Properties**.

2. Tap anywhere outside of the **Properties** menu to hide it.

### To restore previous file versions

1. To undo all changes made in the current app session, tap the **File** button, tap **Restore**, and then tap **Restore to Last Opened**.

*Or*

1. To undo changes made in a previous session, tap the **File** button, tap **Restore**, and then tap **View Version History Online** to display the history of changes to the document in your default web browser.

2. Tap the document version you want to restore, and then tap **Restore**.

| Delete All Versions | | | |
| --- | --- | --- | --- |
| No. ⬇ Modified | | Modified By | Size |
| 22.0 | 10/10/2014 6:29 PM | ■ Joan Lambert | 36.8 KB |
| 21.0 | 10/10/2014 6:21 PM | ■ Joan Lambert | 36.8 KB |
| 20.0 | View | ■ Jeanne Craver | 35.3 KB |
| 19.0 | Restore | ■ Kathy Krause | 36.8 KB |
| 18.0 | Delete | ■ Joan Lambert | 36.9 KB |
| 17.0 | 10/8/2014 12:03 AM | ■ Joan Lambert | 37.2 KB |

*A SharePoint library offers multiple options for working with file versions*

# Hide and show the on-screen keyboard

When you tap in a location that permits text entry, the on-screen keyboard appears at the bottom of the app window. Elements such as the File menu that expand into the keyboard space are cut off by the keyboard. To display the full menu content, you have to hide the keyboard.

To hide and display the on-screen keyboard:

1. To hide the keyboard, tap the **Keyboard** key that is located in its lower-right corner.

2. To display the keyboard, tap any text-entry area.

# Reconfigure the on-screen keyboard

By default, the on-screen keyboard extends across the bottom half of the screen and covers the content of the file you're working in. If you prefer to display more of the file content, you can split the keyboard into two halves.

*A document open in Word with the split on-screen keyboard*

With the active file between the keyboard halves, more of the file content is available while the keyboard is open. You can change the magnification of the file content, but the keyboard halves remain in the same position.

To change the keyboard configuration:

1. To split the keyboard, do one of the following:

   - Drag with two fingers from the center of the keyboard to the left and right sides of the screen.

   - Press and hold the **Keyboard** key, and then on the menu that appears, slide to the **Split** command.

2. To rejoin the keyboard halves, do one of the following:

   - Drag the halves with two fingers to the center of the screen.

   - Press and hold the **Keyboard** key, and then on the menu that appears, slide to the **Dock & Merge** command.

# Search file content

You can use the Search function to quickly locate specific information in a docu-ment, workbook, or worksheet. (No search functionality is available in PowerPoint for iPad.) After you display the search pane, entering a search term in the Find box immediately displays the number of instances of that term that are in the document or workbook, and selects the first instance. You can move to the next or previous instance by tapping the arrows at the right end of the search pane.

> **TIP** You can copy a search term from the document or elsewhere and paste it into the Find box to ensure that it is spelled correctly. Tap and hold in the Find box to display the shortcut bar, and then tap Paste.

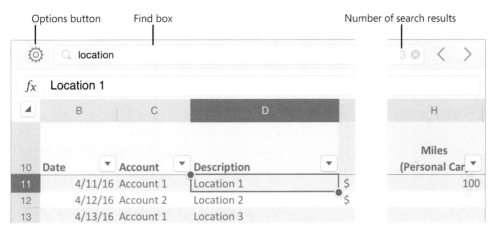

The Search function displays the number of instances of the found term

By default, the Search function locates every instance of the search term. You can restrict the results to only those that exactly match the capitalization of the term as you specify it in the Find box. When searching in an Excel workbook, you can also restrict the search results to cells that contain nothing other than the search term, and restrict the range of the search to the current worksheet.

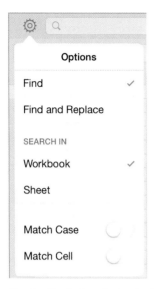

*Tapping the Options button in the search pane displays the search options for the current file type*

You can also use the Search feature to easily substitute a specific word or phrase for another. When replacing a search term that occurs multiple times in the current file, you can evaluate each search result independently and choose whether to replace it, or you can replace all instances of the search term at the same time.

Replace box

*The Replace box and replacement scope options appear in the search pane*

> **TIP** If you have an external keyboard connected to your iPad, you can move between the Find and Replace boxes by pressing the Tab key. The active box is indicated by the Delete button at the right end of the box.

### To search the current file

1. Near the right end of the ribbon, tap the **Search** button.

2. In the search pane, enter the search term in the **Find** box.

**3**

## To move among search results

1. At the right end of the search pane, tap the right arrow to move to the next result.

2. Near the right end of the search pane, tap the left arrow to move to the previous result.

## To restrict search results in Word for iPad

1. At the left end of the search pane, tap the **Options** button.

2. On the **Options** menu, specify any of the following restrictions:

   - Tap the **Match Case** slider to find only instances of the search term that are capitalized exactly as you enter it in the **Find** box.

   - Tap the **Whole Words** slider to find only freestanding instances of the search term (not partial words).

>  **TIP** Sliders change from white to green to indicate that the associated function is turned on.

## To restrict search results in Excel for iPad

1. At the left end of the search pane, tap the **Options** button.

2. On the **Options** menu, specify any of the following restrictions:

   - Tap **Sheet** to search only the current worksheet.

   - Tap the **Match Case** slider to find only instances of the search term that are capitalized exactly as you enter it in the **Find** box.

   - Tap the **Match Cell** slider to find worksheet cells that contain only the search term.

## To replace one or more instances of the search term

1. At the left end of the search pane, tap the **Options** button.

2. On the **Options** menu, tap **Find and Replace**.

3. In the search pane, enter the search term in the **Find** box and the replacement term in the **Replace** box.

4.  If one or more results are returned, do any of the following:

    - Tap **All** to replace all instances of the search term.

    - Tap **Replace** to replace the current instance of the search term and move to the next instance.

    - Tap the right arrow or left arrow to move to the next or previous result without replacing the current instance.

**To close the search pane**

1.  Tap anywhere in the document or workbook content.

# Print file content

You can print a document, worksheet, or presentation to a wireless printer on your network. It isn't necessary to "install" the printer (or drivers); the iPad uses a technology called AirPrint, which is also incorporated into most modern printers. Your iPad will automatically locate available AirPrint printers on your wireless network.

 **IMPORTANT** The printing function will locate only printers that support AirPrint technology. A list of these printers is available at *support.apple.com/kb/HT4356*.

You can configure various options for printing files. The options that are available depend on the file type:

- When printing any file, you can select the printer and the number of copies of the file you want to print.

- If the selected printer supports double-sided printing, you can turn that function on or off.

- When printing a document or presentation, you can specify the range of pages or slides you want to print.

- When printing a workbook, you can specify additional layout options, including the page size and orientation, the range of data to print, and whether to fit the entire worksheet, all rows, or all columns on the page.

 **TIP** The printing function doesn't currently offer the opportunity for you to preview the file content before printing it.

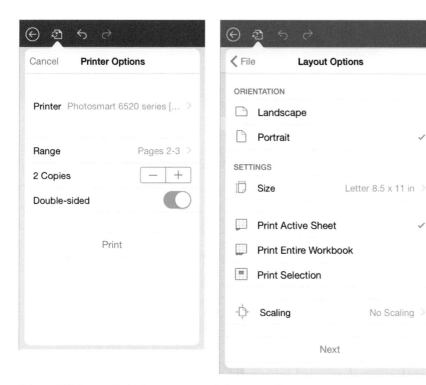

3

*Print to AirPrint-enabled printers on your wireless network*

### To print document or presentation content

1. On the **File** menu, tap **Print**.

2. On the **Printer Options** submenu, tap **Printer**, and then tap the printer you want to use.

    **IMPORTANT** The Print command is available only when a printer is available. If you recently printed from the iPad, the printer might already be selected.

3. If you want to print only part of the document or presentation, tap **Range**. On the **Page Range** submenu, scroll to the numbers of the first and last pages or slides in the range you want to print. Then tap **Back**.

4. If you want to print more than one copy of the document or presentation, tap the plus sign (or minus sign) to specify the number of copies to print.

5. Tap **Print** to print the document or presentation content according to your specifications.

**To print workbook content**

1. On the **File** menu, tap **Print**.

2. On the

3. **Layout Options** submenu, do any of the following:

   - To change the page orientation, tap **Landscape** or **Portrait**.

   - To change the paper size from the default, tap **Size**, tap the paper size you want, and then tap **Layout Options**.

   - To print the currently displayed worksheet, tap **Print Active Sheet**.

   - To print all worksheets in the workbook, tap **Print Entire Workbook**.

   - To print only the currently selected cells, tap **Print Selection**.

   - To shrink or expand the content to fit the paper, tap **Scaling**. On the **Scaling Options** submenu, tap **Fit Sheet on One Page**, **Fit All Rows on One Page**, or **Fit All Columns on One Page**. Then tap **Layout Options**.

4. On the **Layout Options** submenu, tap **Next** to display the printer options.

5. On the **Printer Options** menu, tap **Printer**, and then select the printer you want to use.

6. If you want to print more than one copy of the workbook, tap the plus sign (or minus sign) to specify the number of copies to print.

7. Tap **Print** to print the workbook content according to your specifications.

# Distribute files

When your file is complete or ready for review, there are several ways in which you can distribute it to other people:

- You can print the file or some portion of it.

- You can attach a copy of the original file or a PDF version of the file to an email message.

- You can send a link to the file in an email message, instant message, or other online communication if the file is stored in a shared location. You have the option of sending a link that permits read-only access or a link that permits read-write access.

**To attach a file to an email message**

1. At the right end of the ribbon, tap the **Share** button.

2. On the **Share** menu, tap **Email as attachment**, and then do one of the following:

   • To attach a copy of the current file to the message, tap **Send** *File Type*.

   • To create a PDF file and attach that file to the message, tap **Send PDF**.

   The Mail app creates an email message with the specified file attached. The message subject is automatically set to the name of the attached file.

3. In the message window, enter the recipient information, modify the subject if you want to, and enter any additional message content.

*The file attachment is represented by the app icon*

4. In the upper-right corner of the message window, tap **Send**.

**To send a file link in an email message**

1. Save the file in a shared location such as your OneDrive online storage site or a SharePoint site.

2. At the right end of the ribbon, tap the **Share** button.

3. On the **Share** menu, tap **Email as Link**, and then do one of the following:

    - To send a link that permits the recipient to display but not modify the file content, tap **View Only**.

    - To send a link that permits the recipient to display and modify the file content, tap **View and Edit**.

    The Mail app generates an email message that contains the specified link. The subject of the message states that a file has been shared with the recipient.

4. In the message window, enter the recipient information, modify the subject if you want to, and enter any additional message content.

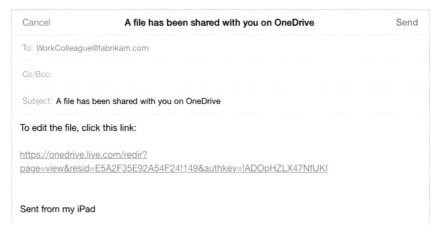

| Cancel | A file has been shared with you on OneDrive | Send |
| --- | --- | --- |

To: WorkColleague@fabrikam.com

Cc/Bcc:

Subject: A file has been shared with you on OneDrive

To edit the file, click this link:

https://onedrive.live.com/redir?
page=view&resid=E5A2F35E92A54F24!149&authkey=!ADOpHZLX47NfUKI

Sent from my iPad

*The file link includes the necessary credentials*

5. In the upper-right corner of the message window, tap **Send**.

**To create and share a file link**

1. Save the file in a shared location such as your OneDrive online storage site or a SharePoint site.

2. At the right end of the ribbon, tap the **Share** button.

3. On the **Share** menu, tap **Copy Link**, and then do one of the following:

   - To create a link that permits the recipient to display but not modify the file content, tap **View Only**.

   - To create a link that permits the recipient to display and modify the file content, tap **View and Edit**.

   The app generates a link with the selected permissions. You can paste the link into a message, file, or electronic communication.

# Skills review

In this chapter, you learned how to:

- Create, open, and save files

- Use common Office interface features

- Search file content

- Print file content

- Distribute files

# Practice tasks

The practice files for these tasks are located in the iPadOfficeSBS\Ch03 folder.

## Create, open, and save files

Start Excel for iPad, and then perform the following tasks:

1. Create a new workbook based on the **Household Budget** template.

2. Delete the new workbook instead of saving it for the first time.

3. Create a new workbook based on the **Simple To-Do List** template.

4. Name the workbook My To-Do List and save it on your iPad.

5. Pin the **My To-Do List** workbook to the **Recent** page.

6. From the **Open** page of the Backstage view, browse to the practice files folder and open the **OpenFiles** workbook.

7. Save a copy of the **OpenFiles** workbook on your iPad as My Expenses.

8. From the **Recent** page, open the **My To-Do List** workbook.

## Use common Office interface features

Open the NavigateOffice document in Word for iPad, and then perform the following tasks:

1. Display each tab of the ribbon and familiarize yourself with the available commands.

2. In the document, tap the image and then the table to activate the corresponding tool tabs.

3. Display the file management commands, and turn off the AutoSave function.

4. Display the file properties, and note the information displayed there.

5. Modify the design of the table, and then undo the change.

6. Add a row to the table, and then add another row by repeating the change.

7.  Save a copy of the document in the **Ch03** folder as My Travel List.

8.  Restore the previous version of the file.

9.  Turn on the **AutoSave** function so that Word automatically saves documents for you.

10. Close the file.

## Search file content

Open the SearchReplace document in Word for iPad, and then perform the following tasks:

1.  Search for the word *Agency* and replace all but the first instance with Agent.

2.  Search for the word *Name*, and replace only the second instance with name.

3.  Switch to Excel for iPad, and open the **SearchScope** workbook.

4.  Search for the word *Itinerary* in the following scopes and note the different results:

    a.  Search only the *Vacation Items Checklist* worksheet.

    b.  Search the entire workbook.

    c.  Search for cells that contain only the search term.

5.  Close the search pane.

## Print file content

Open the PrintSlides presentation in PowerPoint for iPad, and then perform the following tasks:

1.  Print only slide **1**.

2.  Print the entire presentation, double-sided if your printer has that capability.

3.  Switch to Excel for iPad, and open the **PrintSheets** workbook.

4.  On the **Vacation Items Checklist** worksheet, select cells **C4:D22**. Then print only the selection.

5.  Configure the printer settings to fit all columns on one page, and then print the worksheet.

## Distribute files

Open the SendCopy presentation in PowerPoint for iPad, and then perform the following tasks:

1. Send yourself an email message that has a copy of the presentation attached to it. Set the message subject to **SBS attachment**.

2. Switch to Excel for iPad and open the **SendLink** workbook.

3. Send yourself an email message that has a link to the workbook in the message body. Set the message subject to **SBS file link**.

4. Switch to Word for iPad and open the **SendReview** document.

5. Create a link to the document that permits recipients to display the document, but does not permit them to modify the document content.

6. Send the link to yourself or someone else in any message format other than email.

# Part 2

# Microsoft Word for iPad

# Create professional documents

The development and strong adoption of the Office for iPad apps signal the start of an important new era in which the iPad is evolving from a device that is primarily used for entertainment and other content consumption purposes to a device that supports content creation and can serve as a useful business tool.

Word is the undisputed frontrunner among the Office apps. Entering and editing text in a Word document can be more challenging on an iPad than on a computer, because the iPad doesn't have an external keyboard for fast text entry and a mouse to navigate within or rearrange content. However, you can easily connect an external Bluetooth keyboard to your iPad if you plan to generate a lot of text from scratch.

You can create a simple document with a couple of taps. Whether you create a blank document or start from a prepopulated template, the importance of the document is in the words and images it contains. You can enter text in a document by tapping, typing, or dictating. Then you can provide structure and meaning by formatting the text in various ways.

This chapter guides you through procedures related to creating Word documents, entering and manipulating text, formatting paragraphs, structuring content by using line breaks and tabs, and applying character formats, text effects, and predefined styles to text.

## In this chapter

- Create documents from templates
- Enter text in documents
- Move, copy, and delete text
- Align, space, and indent paragraphs
- Structure content manually
- Change the appearance of text

## Practice files

For this chapter, use the practice files from the iPadOfficeSBS\Ch04 folder. For practice file download instructions, see the Introduction.

# The Word feature set

As the platforms we work on have expanded from computers to tablets to smartphones, Microsoft has developed versions of Word and other programs in the Microsoft Office suite for each of these platforms. The experience of working in each version is similar, but the functionality in some versions is restricted by the limitations of the platform. The good news is that they all work with the same files.

Here is a brief comparison of the features you can use in each version. If you can't perform a specific task in a document on one platform, you can put the finishing touches on the document in a different version of Word.

## Word for iPad features

After you sign in by using a Microsoft account, you can do the following:

- Open and edit existing documents and document templates.
- Create new documents, modify document content, and manually or automatically save changes.
- Connect to storage locations, and open, edit, and save documents from SharePoint, OneDrive, and Dropbox sites.
- Apply a limited number of fonts and character formats to text, and lay out text horizontally or vertically.
- Apply a standard set of paragraph styles and character styles, or the styles that are saved in the active document.
- Create lists that use built-in bullet styles and numbering styles.
- Create and format tables, shapes, and text boxes.
- Insert and format locally stored photos.
- Provide reference information by using hyperlinks and footnotes.
- Configure page size and margins within a limited set of options.

- Insert page breaks.

- Insert and modify headers, footers, and page numbers.

- Track, review, and manage changes and comments.

- Check spelling as you type.

- Set and modify tab stops on the ruler.

- Display document statistics including page count, word count, and character count.

- Coauthor documents that are stored online, or work offline with local copies.

- Send a document, a link to a document, or a PDF of a document by email.

- Print documents (with limited print options).

The following premium features require that you sign in by using an account that is associated with a qualified Office 365 subscription:

- Insert section breaks, and configure text in up to three columns.

- Customize headers and footers for different pages.

- Change page orientation.

- Track and review changes.

- Add custom colors to shapes.

- Insert and edit WordArt.

- Add shadows and reflection styles to pictures.

- Add and modify chart elements.

If you find that you need to perform tasks within a Word document that aren't available in Word for iPad, you can save the document to a shared storage location and edit it by using Word Online or a desktop version of Word.

4

## Word Online features

Word Online has greater functionality than Word for iPad in some areas and lesser functionality in others. You can use Word Online to do the following:

- Create documents based on professionally designed templates that are available from the Office website.

- Display (but not edit) citations, bibliographies, tables of contents, and indexes.

- Translate document content.

- Apply theme fonts and theme colors.

- Provide reference information in endnotes.

- Insert pictures from local and online sources.

- Mark comments as done.

- Coauthor documents in real time (with presence indicators and real-time changes).

- Use the Tell Me search feature to quickly find a way to accomplish tasks.

For more information about Word Online, visit *technet.microsoft.com/en-us /library/word-online-service-description.aspx*.

## Word desktop version features

The desktop versions of Word have the most functionality. You can use Word 2011 on a Mac computer or Word 2013 on a computer running Windows to do the following:

- Create documents based on professionally designed templates from within the product.

- Copy and paste content without loss of formatting.

- Create custom bullet styles and numbering styles.

- Insert and format page borders and line numbers.

- Create and modify embedded objects, chart data, and SmartArt graphics.

- Create and modify captions and citations.

- Check spelling and grammar.

- Find and replace styles and special characters.

- Use gridlines and guides to align document content.

- Apply and modify document parts and thematic elements such as content controls, color schemes, font schemes, and preset graphic effects.

- Insert local and online videos into a document.

- Create and modify advanced document elements such as AutoText, cover pages, bibliographies, tables of contents, tables of authorities, indexes, equations, and watermarks.

- Compare, merge, and combine documents.

- Run macros and use advanced controls such as ActiveX controls, embedded OLE objects, and signature lines.

- Set and save zoom levels, display different views of documents, work in split windows, or open a single document in multiple windows.

- Install ancillary apps such as dictionaries, map generators, translation tools, search tools, templates, and image galleries.

- Create custom bullet styles and numbering styles.

- Perform mail merge operations.

- Use advanced document-protection features such as Information Rights Management (IRM) and password protection.

- Print documents with full printing options, and create and modify print styles.

# Create documents from templates

It's common to create new documents from scratch by first creating a new, blank document and then adding content.

If you're creating a more complicated document, you can often save time and effort by starting from a template. When working in Word for iPad you can create common documents such as brochures, letters, newsletters, resumes, invoices, flyers, and syllabi from any of the built-in templates.

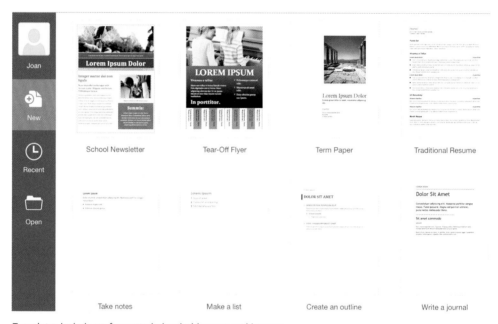

*Templates include preformatted placeholder text and images*

> **TIP** At the time of this writing, Word for iPad includes 23 built-in templates. Additional templates might be made available with later releases of Word for iPad.

The only templates available from the New page are those that are installed with the Word for iPad app. Hundreds of other templates are available for Word Online and the desktop versions of Word. If you create a document based on one of these templates and save the document to a shared storage location, you can then open and edit the document on your iPad.

You can access templates for Word Online from your iPad by using Safari or another web browser to visit *store.office.live.com/templates/templates-for-Word*.

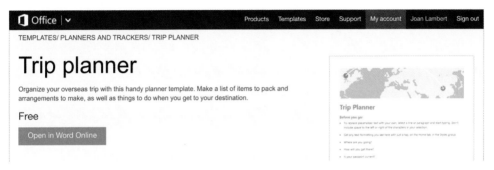

*You can preview information about any template by tapping its thumbnail*

Word Online and Word for iPad interact nicely on your iPad, so the process of creating a document from a Word Online template is reasonably simple. When you open a template, Word Online creates a document based on that template and automatically saves the document to the OneDrive associated with your user account. You can then open the document in Word for iPad by tapping a button in the Word Online window.

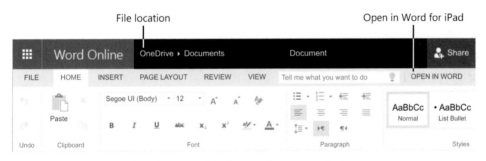

*You can open a document based on a Word Online template on your iPad*

> ⚠ **IMPORTANT** You perform many tasks in Word for iPad, Excel for iPad, and Power-Point for iPad by using the same processes. Common processes include those for giving commands in the Office user interface and for opening, saving, searching, and distributing files. For more information, see Chapter 3, "Create and manage files."

Templates for Word 2011 and Word 2013 are available from the New page of the Backstage view of those programs. To work with a document based on a desktop template on your iPad, you must create the document on a computer and save it to a shared storage location. Then you can browse to that location from the Open page of the Backstage view of Word for iPad.

**To create a blank document**

1. In the Backstage view, on the **File** bar, tap **New**.

2. On the **New** page, tap **New Blank Document**.

**To create a document from a built-in template**

1. In the Backstage view, on the **File** bar, tap **New**.

2. Locate and then tap the thumbnail of the document template you want to use.

**To create a document from an online template**

1. In Safari or another web browser, go to *office.microsoft.com*.

2. On the link bar at the top of the page, tap **Templates**. Then on the **Templates for Office Online** page, in the **Browse by Product** list, tap **Word**.

> **TIP** You can filter templates for Office Online either by product or by category. The steps for creating a workbook from an Excel Online template or creating a presentation from a PowerPoint Online template are the same as those described here.

3. On the **Templates for Word** page, locate the document template you want to use.

4. Tap the thumbnail of any document template to display its information page. On the information page of the template you want to use, tap **Open in Word Online**.

5. If prompted to do so, provide the credentials of the user account that is associated with your OneDrive.

   Word Online displays the location where it will save the document.

Start Word for iPad          Open document in Word Online

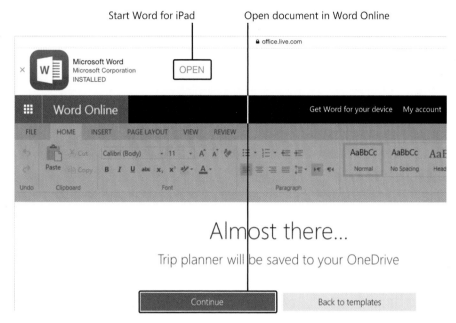

*Word Online automatically saves a document based on the template to your OneDrive*

>  **IMPORTANT** Word Online detects that Word for iPad is installed on your iPad. Tapping Open in the banner above the Word Online window opens the Word app window but doesn't provide a way of working with the template.

6. To save the document to the specified location and open it in Word Online, tap **Continue**.

7. On the Word Online ribbon, to the right of the tabs and the **Tell Me** box, tap **Open in Word**. If prompted to do so, enter your OneDrive credentials.

### To create a document based on a Word 2013 template

1. On a computer running Windows, start Word 2013.

2. On the **New** page of the Backstage view, tap or click the thumbnail of any template to display a preview and additional information.

*Desktop versions of Word provide access to hundreds of templates*

3. On the preview page of the template you want to use, tap or click **Create**.

4. Save the document to a shared storage location that you can access from Word for iPad, such as a OneDrive site or SharePoint site.

5. Open the document from within Word for iPad.

### To create a document based on a Word 2011 template

1. On a Mac computer, start Word 2011 and display the Document Gallery.

>  **TIP** You can open the Document Gallery by clicking New From Template on the File menu.

2. In the gallery, click the thumbnail of the template you want to use for your document. The template will appear in the preview pane to the right of the gallery.

3.  In the preview pane, choose a color scheme or a font scheme if you want to change the defaults, and then click **Choose**.

4.  On the **File** menu, click **Share**, choose a shared storage location that you can access from your iPad, and then complete the process of saving the document to that location.

5.  On your iPad, start Word and then open the document from the shared storage location.

> **TIP** If you're using an external keyboard with your iPad, you can perform many operations by using keyboard shortcuts. For a complete list of keyboard shortcuts, see the Appendix, "Touchscreen and keyboard shortcuts."

# Enter text in documents

The Office for iPad apps were specifically engineered for the screen area and touch-input capabilities of the iPad. There are many ways to add text content to a document when you are using Word for iPad. You can create new text by tapping the on-screen keyboard, typing on an external keyboard, or dictating text. By installing additional on-screen keyboards on your iPad, you can use the on-screen keyboard to enter letters from multiple languages, emoticons, and a huge variety of iconic images into a document.

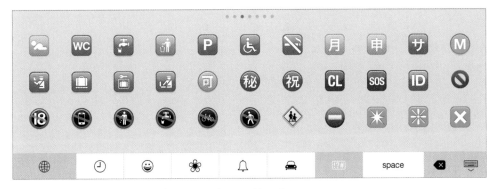

*The Emoji keyboard includes nearly 900 emoticon and icon images*

Entering a lot of text from the on-screen keyboard can be an arduous task. To simplify the process and tap fewer times to achieve the result you want, you can use the shortcuts described in the following table.

| Function | Action |
|----------|--------|
| Enter a period and trailing space | Double-tap the Spacebar twice at the end of a sentence |
| Enter a single quotation mark | Tap and hold the Comma key |
| Enter a double quotation mark | Tap and hold the Period key |
| Enter an accented vowel | Tap and hold a vowel to display a menu of accented vowels, then slide to the one you want to insert |
| Enter a single uppercase letter | Tap and slide from the Shift key to the letter |
| Turn on or release the Caps Lock function | Double-tap the Shift key |
| Enter a single character from the Number keyboard | Tap and slide from the Number key to the number or symbol |

*The on-screen keyboard has some handy shortcuts*

Given the limitations of tapping and typing text on a small-form device such as the iPad, the Siri dictation function partners smartly with Word for iPad to provide a simple method of quickly entering a lot of text. It doesn't take much time to become accustomed to dictating at the correct volume and speed, which you can determine by trial and error.

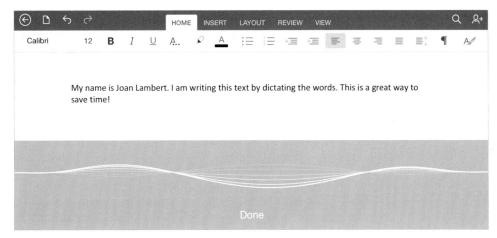

*In a Word document, the dictation pane replaces the on-screen keyboard and displays the level of audio input detected*

> ⚠ **IMPORTANT** The dictation function and the microphone key are available only when Siri is turned on and your iPad is connected to the Internet, and only in specific languages. You can turn on Siri from the General page of the Settings app. You can find a list of supported languages at *www.apple.com/ios/feature-availability/#quickType-keyboard-dictation*.

The following tips can help you successfully dictate text into a Word document:

- Speak clearly and enunciate each individual word.

- Don't worry about missing spaces or mistaken words while dictating. You can clean up errors manually after entering the text.

- Bookmark errors by speaking a specific word (such as *mistake*) or describing the required correction (such as *delete very*) so you can easily find them later.

- Control text input by speaking the specific commands shown in the following table, which are recognized by the dictation engine.

| Dictation command | Action |
| --- | --- |
| new paragraph | Start a new paragraph |
| new line | Wrap text to the next line without starting a new paragraph |
| cap | Capitalize the next word |
| caps on ... caps off | Capitalize the first character of each word between the commands |
| all caps | Make the next word all uppercase |
| all caps on ... all caps off | Make the words between the commands all uppercase |
| no caps on ... no caps off | Make the words between the commands all lowercase |
| no space on ... no space off | Run the words between the commands together |

- Insert non-alphanumeric characters by speaking these specific commands recognized by the dictation engine.

 **TIP** Speaking a punctuation mark command to end a word, phrase, or sentence inserts the punctuation mark and a space.

| Classification | Dictation commands | Character |
| --- | --- | --- |
| Punctuation marks | apostrophe | ' |
| | colon | : |
| | comma | , |
| | dash | - |
| | ellipsis | ... |
| | em dash | — |
| | en dash | – |
| | exclamation point | ! |
| | hyphen | - |
| | inverted question mark | ¿ |
| | period | . |
| | question mark | ? |
| | semicolon | ; |

| Classification | Dictation commands | Character |
|---|---|---|
| Symbols | ampersand | & |
| | asterisk | * |
| | at sign | @ |
| | caret | ^ |
| | copyright sign | © |
| | number sign | # |
| | percent sign | % |
| | registered sign | ® |
| | trademark sign | ™ |
| | underscore | _ |
| Mathematical operators | plus sign | + |
| | minus sign | - |
| | division sign | ÷ |
| | multiplication sign | × |
| | equal sign | = |
| Structural characters | open parenthesis and close parenthesis | ( and ) |
| | slash and backslash | / and \ |
| | quote and end quote | " and " |
| | left bracket and right bracket | [ and ] |
| | left brace and right brace | { and } |
| Currency symbols | cent sign | ¢ |
| | dollar sign | $ |
| | euro sign | € |
| | yen sign | ¥ |
| Emoticons | smiley | :-) |
| | frowny | :-( |
| | winky | ;-) |

**TIP** Of the symbol commands, only *end quote* (or *unquote*) enters a trailing space. Some symbols are produced by multiple commands, but others aren't. For example, *open paren*, *left paren*, *open parenthesis*, *left parenthesis*, *open parentheses*, and *left parentheses* all enter (, but only *percent sign* enters %. Speaking *percent symbol*, *percentage sign*, or *percentage symbol* enters the spoken words.

## Magnify the cursor position

Tapping to position the cursor can be an inexact practice, and it can be difficult to tap in exactly the right place. Word for iPad includes a convenient tool that can help with this. When you tap and do not lift your finger (tap and hold), a magnifying glass appears and displays a close-up view of the cursor location. When you lift your finger, a shortcut bar appears.

Flight delays or baggage-handling mishaps could result in your suitcase following you all the way home.
Make travel plans that ...ifference o arrive early.
If you have the oppor and whethe t the client site in advance, take it, and take notice of the details that make a di... ...ice:
processe

o   Where to park, and |whether you have to register your car

o   Building securi

If you hav... ...site in advance, take it,
the details...

| Select | Select All | Paste | Insert... |

o   Where to park, and |whether you have to register your car

o   Building security processes

*Magnifying the cursor location*

### To enter text from a keyboard

1.   Position the cursor where you want to insert the text.

2.   Enter text by tapping the on-screen keyboard.

   *Or*

   If you're using an external keyboard, enter text by typing on the keyboard.

**SEE ALSO**  For information about the on-screen keyboard, see "Configure iPad and Office app settings" in Chapter 1, "Office for iPad basics," and the sidebar "Reconfigure the on-screen keyboard" in Chapter 3, "Create and manage files."

**To switch among installed keyboards**

1. Near the lower-left corner of the on-screen keyboard, tap the **Globe** key until the keyboard you want appears.

>  **TIP** When you are switching to an alphabetic keyboard, the keyboard name appears briefly on the Spacebar.

4

**To dictate text into a document**

1. Display the on-screen keyboard.

2. On the on-screen keyboard, to the left of the Spacebar, tap the microphone key.

3. Speak clearly at a high enough volume to change the flat line in the dictation pane to a wave form.

4. When you finish, tap **Done**.

>  **TIP** Take care that you don't cover the iPad's microphone or microphones while dictating. These are located in different places depending on the model of your iPad. An iPad Air has dual microphones located on the edge and back of the iPad adjacent to the front-facing camera. An iPad Air 2 has dual microphones located on the edge and back of the iPad adjacent to the rear-facing camera.

## Check spelling

Even the most accurate typists occasionally make mistakes, and it's much easier to do so when you are entering text on a small on-screen keyboard or by using a method such as dictation. Word for iPad includes basic proofing tools to help ensure that your document content is free of spelling errors. These tools are available from the Review tab.

Tapping the Proofing Tools button located at the left end of the Review tab displays the Proofing Tools menu, from which you can select a proofing language and turn on or off the automatic checking of spelling as you enter text in the document.

# Move, copy, and delete text

During the process of entering text in a document, there will be times when you want to move or copy content from one area of a document to another, or repurpose content that you already created elsewhere. You can reuse existing text sourced from the same document, another file, a website, or any electronic resource from which content can be copied.

There are five standard operations involved in moving or reusing text and other document content:

- **Selecting** Choosing the content you want to work with

 **TIP** Selecting is often inaccurately referred to as *highlighting*, because of the colored shading that appears over the selected content. Highlighting is applying a translucent screen over text.

- **Dragging** Moving selected content by sliding your finger on the screen
- **Cutting** Storing selected content on the Clipboard and deleting it from its current location
- **Copying** Storing selected content on the Clipboard without deleting it from its current location
- **Pasting** Inserting content from the Clipboard into the file

You can also simply delete text that you no longer need.

## The Clipboard

The Clipboard is a storage area for cut and copied content. The Clipboard can store brief or lengthy content segments that can include text, images, formatted tables, worksheet data, and any other type of content you can cut or copy from an Office document. Unlike the Clipboard in the desktop versions of Office, in Office for iPad apps the Clipboard stores only one item at a time, and you can't display the Clipboard contents. You can, however, access the Clipboard contents from any Office for iPad app, which enables you to copy or move content from one app to another.

Word for iPad displays a handy shortcut bar when you select text. You can perform an operation on the selected text by tapping a command on the shortcut bar.

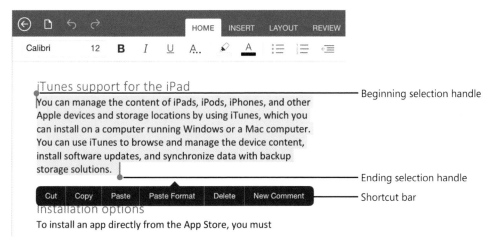

4

A document with a paragraph selected and the shortcut bar displayed

Because you can have only one document open at a time in Word for iPad, moving or copying content from one document to another isn't quite as simple as it is in the desktop versions of Word, but the basic process is the same.

**To select text**

1.  To select a word, double-tap the word.

2.  To select a paragraph, triple-tap anywhere in the paragraph.

> 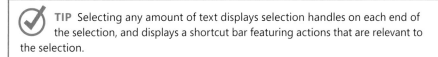 **TIP** Selecting any amount of text displays selection handles on each end of the selection, and displays a shortcut bar featuring actions that are relevant to the selection.

3.  To expand or contract a selection, drag the selection handles.

4.  To select all the content in a document, tap and hold anywhere in the document, and then tap **Select All** on the shortcut bar.

# Paste options

By default, when you paste text into another location, it retains its original formatting. To change the formatting of pasted text, tap the Paste Options button that appears when you paste the text.

The options on the Paste Options menu vary based on the content you're pasting and the destination formatting. The four primary options when pasting text are as follows.

- **Keep Source Formatting** This is the default option. It retains the original formatting of the pasted content.

- **Use Destination Theme** This option applies the theme, fonts, colors, and effects of the destination document to the pasted content.

- **Match Destination Formatting** This option merges the pasted content with the destination styles.

- **Keep Text Only** This option inserts unformatted text.

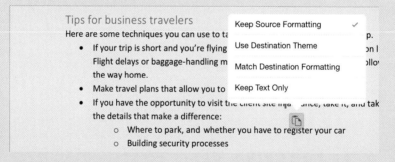

*The Paste Options button and menu*

Alternatively, you can paste only the formatting of the copied text by using the Paste Format command on the shortcut bar.

**To move text to a different location in the same document**

1. Select the text you want to move.

2. To move the text to a nearby location, tap and hold the selection and then slide your finger on the screen until the cursor is in the target location.

   *Or*

   To move the text to a farther location, tap **Cut** on the shortcut bar. Double-tap the target location, and then tap **Paste** on the shortcut bar.

> **TIP** If you're using an external keyboard with your iPad, you can press ⌘+C to copy the selected text to the Clipboard, ⌘+X to cut the selected text to the Clipboard, and ⌘+V to paste the most recent Clipboard content.

**To copy text to a different location in the same document**

1. Select the text you want to copy.

2. Tap **Copy** on the shortcut bar to copy the selected text to the Clipboard.

3. Double-tap the target location, and then tap **Paste** on the shortcut bar.

**To move or copy text to a different document**

1. Select the text you want to move or copy.

2. On the shortcut bar, tap **Cut** if you want to move the text, or **Copy** if you want to replicate it.

3. If the AutoSave feature is turned off, tap the **File** button, and then tap **Save**.

4. Tap the **Back** button. From the Backstage view, open the target document.

5. Double-tap the target location, and then tap **Paste**.

**To delete text**

1. Select the text you want to delete.

2. Do one of the following:

   - Tap **Delete** on the shortcut bar.

   - Tap the **Backspace** key on the on-screen keyboard.

   - If you're using an external keyboard, press the **Backspace** key.

# Align, space, and indent paragraphs

You create paragraphs by entering text and then tapping Return. A paragraph usually consists of at least three sentences but can be as short as a single sentence or even a single word. Every paragraph ends with a paragraph mark, which looks like a backward P (¶). Paragraph marks and other structural characters (such as spaces, line breaks, and tabs) are usually hidden, but you can display them by tapping the Show/Hide ¶ button (labeled with a paragraph mark) on the Home tab of the ribbon. Sometimes displaying these hidden characters makes it easier to accomplish a task or understand a structural problem.

 **SEE ALSO** For information about working with hidden structural characters, see "Structure content manually" later in this chapter.

You can change the appearance of a paragraph by modifying its left and right edge alignment and vertical spacing from the Home tab of the ribbon, and its left and right indents from the Home tab or from the ruler. The ruler is usually hidden to provide more space for the document content, but you can display it by tapping the Ruler slider on the View tab of the ribbon.

*The left indent can be set from the Home tab or the ruler*

 **SEE ALSO** For information about displaying the ribbon, see "Configure indents" later in this topic.

If you modify a paragraph and aren't happy with the changes, you can restore the original paragraph and character settings by resetting the paragraph to the Normal paragraph style.

## Configure alignment

The alignment setting controls the horizontal position of the paragraph text between the page margins.

There are four alignment options:

4

- **Align Left**  This is the default paragraph alignment. It sets the left end of each line of the paragraph at the left page margin or left indent. It results in a straight left edge and a ragged right edge.

- **Align Right**  This sets the right end of each line of the paragraph at the right page margin or right indent. It results in a straight right edge and a ragged left edge.

- **Center**  This centers each line of the paragraph between the left and right page margins or indents. It results in ragged left and right edges.

- **Justify**  This alignment adjusts the spacing between words so that the left end of each line of the paragraph is at the left page margin or indent and the right end of each line of the paragraph (other than the last line) is at the right margin or indent. It results in straight left and right edges.

The icons on the alignment buttons depict the effect of each alignment option.

**To set paragraph alignment**

1. Position the cursor anywhere in the paragraph, or select all the paragraphs you want to adjust.

2. On the **Home** tab, tap the **Align Left**, **Center**, **Align Right**, or **Justify** button.

**To reset a paragraph to the Normal paragraph style**

1. Select the paragraph you want to reset.

2. On the **Home** tab, tap the **Formatting** button, and then tap **Clear Formatting**.

## Configure vertical spacing

Paragraphs have two types of vertical spacing:

- **Paragraph spacing** The space between paragraphs, defined by setting the space before and after each paragraph. This space is usually measured in points.

- **Line spacing** The space between the lines of the paragraph, defined by setting the height of the lines in relation to the height of the text. This space is usually measured in lines.

Word for iPad provides options for setting the line spacing, but not the paragraph spacing. The default line spacing for documents created in Word for iPad is 1.0 lines. Other available options are 1.15 lines, 1.5 lines, 2 lines, 2.5 lines, and 3 lines. Changing the line spacing changes the appearance and readability of the text in the paragraph and, of course, also changes the amount of space it occupies on the page.

1.5 line spacing                                        1.0 line spacing

You don't have to sign in to a user account to start the app. You have the option to continue without signing in, but that option (Sign In Later) is shown in much smaller gray text and is far less noticeable than the Sign In and Create An Account options. If you choose the Sign In Later option, you can connect to an account either from within the app or when starting an app at a later time.

When you're connected to a user account, the Account button displays your name, and the Account menu that appears when you tap the Account button provides access to your connected storage resources and to account-specific settings.

*The effect of changing line spacing*

> **TIP** Word for iPad offers only the six preset line spacing options, and no paragraph spacing options. You can refine the line spacing and adjust the paragraph spacing in Word Online or a desktop version of Word.

**To adjust the space between the lines of a paragraph**

1. Position the cursor anywhere in the paragraph, or select all the paragraphs you want to adjust.

2. On the **Home** tab, tap the **Line Spacing** button, and then tap the preset line spacing option you want.

 **TIP** If the on-screen keyboard is displayed, you can hide the keyboard or flick through the Line Spacing list to display all the options.

**4**

## Configure indents

A paragraph indent is the space from the page margin to the text. When working with a document in Word for iPad, you can move the left indent by tapping buttons on the Home tab, or you can set the indents directly on the ruler. Three indent markers are always present on the ruler:

- **Left Indent** This defines the outermost left edge of each line of the paragraph.

- **Right Indent** This defines the outermost right edge of each line of the paragraph.

- **First Line Indent** This defines the starting point of the first line of the paragraph.

The ruler indicates the space between the left and right page margins in a lighter color than the space outside of the page margins.

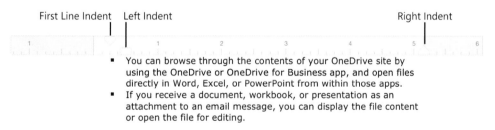

*The indent markers on the ruler*

The default setting for the Left Indent and First Line Indent markers is 0.0", which aligns with the left page margin. The default setting for the Right Indent marker is the distance from the left margin to the right margin. For example, if the page size is set to 8.5" wide and the left and right margins are set to 1.0", the default Right Indent marker setting is 6.5".

In Word for iPad, you can set the indent marker positions on the ruler only by dragging them; you can't enter a specific measurement for them as you can in Word Online and desktop versions of Word. However, when you drag the markers, the ruler position of the marker appears on the ruler as you drag it.

*Dragging a marker displays its position on the ruler*

You can arrange the Left Indent and First Line Indent markers to create a hanging indent or a first line indent. Hanging indents are most commonly used for bulleted and numbered lists, in which the bullet or number is indented less than the main text (essentially, it is *out*dented). First line indents are frequently used to distinguish the beginning of each subsequent paragraph in documents that consist of many consecutive paragraphs of text. Both types of indents are set by using the First Line Indent marker on the ruler.

>  **SEE ALSO** For information about setting page margins, see "Configure page layout" in Chapter 6, "Enhance document content."

**To display the ruler**

1. On the **View** tab, tap the **Ruler** slider to change its background to green.

**To indent or outdent the left edge of a paragraph**

1. Position the cursor anywhere in the paragraph, or select all the paragraphs you want to adjust.

2. To move the left edge of the paragraph in 0.25" increments, tap the **Increase Indent** or **Decrease Indent** button on the **Home** tab.

   *Or*

To move the left edge of the paragraph manually:

a. Display the ruler.

b. On the ruler, drag the **Left Indent** marker to the ruler measurement at which you want to position the left edge of the body of the paragraph.

 **TIP** You can't outdent a paragraph beyond the left page margin by tapping the Decrease Indent button. You can achieve this effect only by dragging the Left Indent marker on the ruler. Be aware, though, that content outdented beyond the page margin might not print.

**4**

## To create a hanging indent or first line indent

1. Set the left indent of the paragraph body.

2. On the ruler, drag the **First Line Indent** marker to the ruler measurement at which you want to begin the first line of the paragraph.

 **TIP** The First Line Indent marker is linked to the Left Indent marker. Moving the Left Indent marker also moves the First Line Indent marker, to maintain the first line indent distance. You can move the First Line Indent marker independently of the Left Indent marker to change the first line indent distance.

## To indent or outdent the right edge of a paragraph

1. Position the cursor anywhere in the paragraph, or select all the paragraphs you want to adjust.

2. Display the ruler.

3. On the ruler, drag the **Right Indent** marker to the ruler measurement at which you want to set the maximum right edge of the paragraph.

 **TIP** Unless the paragraph alignment is justified, the right edge of the paragraph will be ragged, but no line will extend beyond the right indent or outdent.

# Structure content manually

At times it's necessary to manually position text within a paragraph. You can do this by using two different hidden characters: line breaks and tabs. These characters are visible only when the option to show paragraph marks and formatting symbols is turned on. The hidden characters have distinctive appearances:

- A line break character looks like a bent left arrow: ↵

- A tab character looks like a right-pointing arrow: →

You can use a line break, also known as a *soft return*, to wrap a line of a paragraph in a specific location without ending the paragraph. You might use this technique to display only specific text on a line, or to break a line before a word that would otherwise be hyphenated.

A line break ends the line but not the paragraph

A tab character defines the space between two document elements. For example, you can separate numbers from list items, or columns of text, by using tabs. You can then set tab stops that define the location and alignment of the tabbed text.

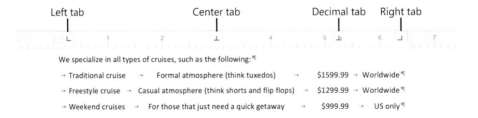

*You can align text in different ways by using tabs*

## To show or hide paragraph marks and formatting symbols

1. On the **Home** tab, tap the **Show/Hide ¶** button.

**To insert a line break**

1. Tap and hold until the magnifying glass appears. Confirm that the cursor is in the location where you want to insert the line break, and then release to display the shortcut bar.

2. On the shortcut bar, tap **Insert** and then tap **Line Break**.

**To insert a tab character**

1. Tap and hold until the magnifying glass appears. Confirm that the cursor is in the location where you want to insert the tab character, and then release to display the shortcut bar.

2. On the shortcut bar, tap **Insert** and then tap **Tab**.

**To align a tab and set a tab stop**

1. Tap the ruler once to add a left-aligned tab marker.

2. Double-tap the tab marker to change to the next tab alignment, in this order:

   - Left

   - Center

   - Right

   - Decimal

   - Bar

3. Drag the tab marker to the ruler measurement at which you want to set the tab.

**To remove a tab stop**

1. Drag the tab marker off the ruler.

# Change the appearance of text

The appearance of your document helps to convey not only the document's message but also information about the document's creator—you. A neatly organized document that contains consistently formatted content and appropriate graphic elements, and that doesn't contain spelling or grammatical errors, invokes greater confidence in your ability to provide any product or service.

Earlier in this chapter, you learned about methods of applying formatting to paragraphs. This topic covers methods of formatting the text of a document. Formatting that you apply to text is referred to as *character formatting*. In Word for iPad, you can apply three types of character formatting:

- Individual character formats including font, font size, bold, italic, underline, strikethrough, subscript, superscript, font color, and highlight color

- Artistic text effects that incorporate character outline and fill colors

- Preformatted styles associated with the document template, many of which not only affect the appearance of the text but also convey structural information (such as titles and headings)

 **SEE ALSO** For information about graphic elements, see Chapter 5, "Add visual elements to documents."

The commands you use to apply individual character formats and artistic text effects are grouped on the left end of the Home tab of the ribbon.

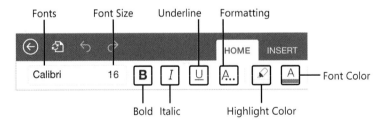

*Less frequently used formatting commands are available from the Formatting menu*

Tapping the Fonts box displays the Fonts menu, which is divided into groups: Theme Fonts, Recent Fonts, Office Compatible Fonts, and iOS Fonts. (The Theme Fonts and Recent Fonts groups exist only if the current document contains fonts associated with those groups.) As you flick through the Fonts menu, the name of the current group is shown at the top of the menu so you can select a font that is compatible with your intended usage.

Word for iPad includes 15 artistic text effects (sometimes referred to as *WordArt*). Applying a text effect retains the original font and font size but adds various font color, gradient, outline, dimensional, and reflection elements.

> **TIP** In the desktop versions of Word, you can apply these same text effects as a starting point and then customize the color, outline, shadow, reflection, and glow characteristics of the formatted text.

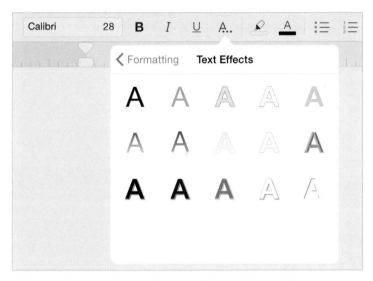

*The Text Effects menu displays the 15 available artistic text effects*

Each document template includes a selection of preformatted styles that control the appearance of entire paragraphs or selected characters. The most basic style, Normal, is the one that controls the appearance of unformatted text that you enter into the document. Common paragraph styles include Title, Subtitle, Heading 1, and Heading 2. Common character styles include Strong and multiple variations of Emphasis and Reference.

The styles are available from the menu that expands when you tap the Styles button at the right end of the Home tab. The available styles differ based on the document.

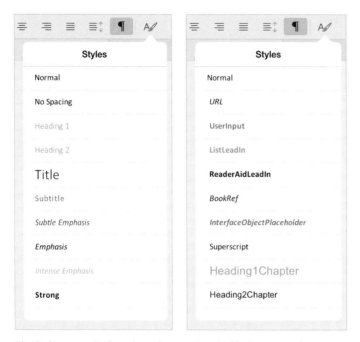

*The Styles menu displays the styles associated with the current document template*

The styles and characteristics of styles that are available in a document are linked to the document template. If you create a document from one of the prepopulated document templates, or if you're working in a document that is attached to a custom template, the styles will be different from those available when you create a new, blank document directly in Word for iPad.

> **IMPORTANT** The overarching concept behind styles is that you can entirely change the appearance of the document content by modifying the styles. Unfortunately, you can't directly modify styles in Word for iPad. However, you can modify the styles in a desktop version of Word, and they'll be available when you open the document on your iPad.

Word for iPad includes only a limited number of individual character formats and styles. However, if the document you're working in was created in Word Online or a desktop version of Word and contains formatting or styles that you want to reuse, you can easily copy existing formatting from one element to another.

**To change the font or size of text**

1.  Select the text you want to format.

2.  On the **Home** tab, tap the **Fonts** box.

3.  Flick through the **Fonts** menu to the font you want to apply, and then tap the font.

**To make text bold, italic, or underlined**

4

1.  Select the text you want to format.

2.  On the **Home** tab, tap the **Bold**, **Italic**, or **Underline** button.

**To strike through text**

1.  Select the text you want to strike through.

2.  On the **Home** tab, tap the **Formatting** button.

3.  On the **Formatting** menu, tap **Strikethrough**.

**To display superscript or subscript characters**

1.  Select the characters you want to reposition.

2.  On the **Home** tab, tap the **Formatting** button.

3.  On the **Formatting** menu, do one of the following:

    •   Tap **Subscript** to shift the characters to the bottom of the line.

    •   Tap **Superscript** to shift the characters to the top of the line.

**To apply artistic effects to text**

1.  Select the text you want to apply effects to.

2.  On the **Home** tab, tap the **Formatting** button.

3.  On the **Formatting** menu, tap **Text Effects**.

4.  On the **Text Effects** menu, tap the effect you want to apply.

**To apply preformatted styles to text**

1. Select the paragraphs or characters you want to format.

2. On the **Home** tab, tap the **Styles** button.

3. On the **Styles** menu, tap the style you want to apply.

**To copy formatting to other text**

1. Select the text that has the format you want to copy.

2. On the shortcut bar, tap **Copy**.

3. Select the text you want to apply the copied format to.

4. On the shortcut bar, tap **Paste Format**.

**To remove all character formatting**

1. Select the text you want to clear the formatting from.

> ⚠️ **IMPORTANT** If you select an entire paragraph, the process of clearing formatting will clear character formatting and paragraph formatting from the paragraph and reset it to the Normal paragraph style.

2. On the **Home** tab, tap the **Formatting** button, and then tap **Clear Formatting**.

# Skills review

In this chapter, you learned how to:

- Create documents from templates

- Enter text in documents

- Move, copy, and delete text

- Align, space, and indent paragraphs

- Structure content manually

- Change the appearance of text

# Practice tasks

The practice files for these tasks are located in the iPadOfficeSBS\Ch04 folder.

## Create documents and enter text

Start Word, and then perform the following tasks:

1. Create a blank new document, and save the document on your iPad as **My Practice Document**.

2. Create a new document based on a built-in template for a résumé.

3. By using either the on-screen keyboard or an external keyboard, enter your name, email address, phone number, and any other personal identification specified by the template in the space provided for that information.

4. By dictating to your iPad, enter information about your most current job.

5. Save the document on your iPad as **My Resume.docx**.

6. Create a document (in the default location on your OneDrive) based on any of the Word Online templates.

7. Open the document in Word Online and then in Word for iPad.

## Move, copy, and delete text

Open the ArrangeText document, and then perform the following tasks:

1. Select the bulleted paragraph that begins with *Character spacing*, and move it to the top of the bulleted list.

2. Select the last heading and the paragraph that follows it, cut the selected text to the Clipboard, and then paste it from the Clipboard to the area below the paragraph that follows the heading *Overview*.

3. In the heading *Manually changing the look of text*, select and copy the word *Manually*. In the *Changing the look of paragraphs* heading, make the first letter lowercase. Then paste the copied word at the beginning of the paragraph.

4. Select all the content in the **ArrangeText** document and copy it to the Clipboard. Then open the practice file named **PastePractice**.

5. In the **PastePractice** document, delete the heading *How to format text* and then paste the Clipboard contents into the document. Apply the formatting of the destination document to the pasted content.

## Align, space, and indent paragraphs

Open the FormatParagraphs document, display the ruler, display paragraph marks and formatting symbols, and then perform the following tasks:

1. Configure the alignment of the first paragraph so it has a ragged left edge and a straight right edge.

2. Compare the appearance and readability of the first two paragraphs. Then configure both paragraphs so the right and left edges of the paragraphs are straight.

3. Change the line spacing of the first paragraph to **1.15** and the line spacing of the second paragraph to **2.0**.

4. Compare the vertical height of the paragraphs and the readability of the paragraph content. Then change the line spacing of both paragraphs to **1.5**.

5. Using the markers on the ruler, increase the indent of the left edge of both paragraphs by 0.5".

6. Using the buttons on the ribbon, decrease the left indent of the first paragraph by 0.25".

7. Indent the first line of the second paragraph to the 0.5" mark.

8. Indent the right edge of both paragraphs to the 3" mark.

## Structure content manually

Open the StructureContent document, display the ruler, display paragraph marks and formatting symbols, and then perform the following tasks:

1. In the title, insert a line break before the word *The*.

2. Select the three paragraphs after the heading that begins *We specialize*.

3. Set the following tab stops:

   - A left tab stop at the 0.25" mark

   - A center tab stop at the 3" mark

   - A decimal tab stop at the 5.25" mark

   - A right tab stop at the right margin

4. In each of the three paragraphs, do the following:

   - Insert a tab at the beginning of the paragraph.

   - Replace the colon and the space that follows it with a tab.

   - Replace the comma and space before each dollar amount with a tab.

   - Replace the final comma and space with a tab.

5. Verify that the tabs align the text with the appropriate tab stops on the ruler.

## Change the appearance of text

Open the FormatText document, and then perform the following tasks:

1. Select all the text in the document and change the font to **Georgia**.

2. Select the words (including the periods after them) *Size*, *Style*, *Effects*, *Color*, and *Character spacing*, and then format them as **Bold**.

3. In the paragraph that begins with *Effects*, select the word *strikethrough*, and apply the **Strikethrough** character format.

4. In the same paragraph, select the word *subscript* and apply the **Subscript** character format. Then select the word *superscript* and apply the **Superscript** character format.

5. Select the first line of text in the document, *How to format text*, and apply the WordArt text effect that is blue and has a shadow below it (the second effect from the left in the second row). Then change the font size to **16**.

6. Select the *Overview* paragraph and the two paragraphs that begin with the word *Manually*, and apply the **Heading 2** to all of them.

7. Copy the strikethrough formatting you applied in step 3 to the paragraph that begins with *Character spacing*.

# Add visual elements to documents

Most Word documents consist primarily of text. In many instances, presenting that text within a clear visual structure is key to ensuring that readers can both discover the information you want them to read and locate the information they want to find. In larger documents and publications, such as this book, reader aids and reference materials provide structure and guidance. Typical elements include tables of contents, part openers that list the related chapters, chapter openers that list the chapter objectives, thumb tabs that indicate breaks between chapters, and, of course, the extensive index. It's not always possible or realistic to include those elements. You can, however, provide a navigable structure and improve the readability of certain types of content by using headings, lists, tables, and images.

The addition of visual or graphic elements such as pictures and drawings can enhance the content of a document, and the presentation of information within the structure of a list or table can more effectively convey information to the reader than if that information were provided in narrative format.

This chapter guides you through procedures related to creating lists and tables, inserting pictures and shapes, and formatting the appearance, position, and flow of text around those graphic elements.

## In this chapter

- Present content in lists
- Present content in tables
- Insert and format pictures
- Insert and format shapes
- Arrange images and text

## Practice files

For this chapter, use the practice files from the iPadOfficeSBS\Ch05 folder. For practice file download instructions, see the Introduction.

# Present content in lists

A list is an effective structure for communicating multiple related pieces of information. In Word for iPad, you can create bulleted lists and numbered lists, and you can combine these list types within multilevel lists. Each type of list serves a specific purpose.

The commands most frequently used when creating lists are located on the Home tab of the ribbon.

*The Bullets, Numbering, Decrease Indent, and Increase Indent commands*

## Create bulleted lists

Bulleted lists are appropriate for presenting information when the order of the information is not important. For example, bulleted lists can be used to present a set of related items (such as names, tasks, or groceries) or a series of informational paragraphs. Formatting multiple pieces of information as a bulleted list can help them stand out from the surrounding text as a cohesive set.

> **TIP** Bulleted lists are also referred to as *unordered lists* because the list structure doesn't connote a specific order, such as order of occurrence or priority. You can, however, introduce a bulleted list with a statement of order, such as "These are my favorite vacation destinations, in alphabetical order."

You can format existing paragraphs of text as a bulleted list or format an empty paragraph as a bulleted list item and then enter text. Each bulleted list item is one paragraph of text. You can choose from the seven bullet symbols that are available in Word for iPad.

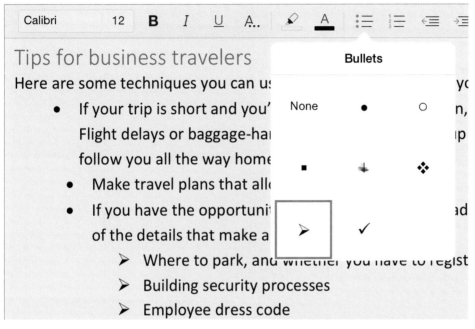

*Multilevel bulleted lists can use a variety of bullet symbols to indicate level and add meaning to list items*

>  **TIP** In the desktop versions of Word, you can choose any symbols, characters, or pictures as bullet symbols, and you can control the font, size, and color of the bullet symbols. If you need to designate a more complex bullet symbol, save the document to a shared location and open it in a desktop version of the program.

### To format existing text as a bulleted list

1. Select the paragraphs that you want to format as bulleted list items.

2. On the **Home** tab, tap the **Bullets** button, and then tap the bullet symbol you want to use at the beginning of each list item.

### To format a single paragraph as a bulleted list item

1. Position the cursor at the beginning of the paragraph.

2. Enter * (an asterisk) followed by a space.

> **TIP** If you want to start a paragraph with an asterisk rather than formatting it as a bulleted list item, tap the Undo button.

**To create a bulleted list as you type**

1. Create a blank paragraph where you want to start the list, and position the cursor in the paragraph.

2. Enter * (an asterisk) followed by a space to format the paragraph as a bulleted list item.

   *Or*

   On the **Home** tab, tap the **Bullets** button, and then tap the bullet symbol you want to use.

3. Enter the content of the first list item, and then tap the **Return** key to create the next bulleted list item.

4. Continue to enter content and tap **Return** to add subsequent list items.

5. To end the list, do one of the following:

   - To start the next paragraph at the left margin, tap **Return** twice.

   - To indent the next paragraph at the same level as the list, tap **Return** and then tap **Backspace**.

    **TIP** Starting the paragraph that follows a list item at the margin indicates that it is a continuation of the text that preceded the list. Indenting the paragraph indicates that it is a continuation of the list item.

**To change the bullet symbol of an existing bulleted list**

1. Tap anywhere in the bulleted list you want to change.

2. On the **Home** tab, tap the **Bullets** button, and then tap the symbol you want to use.

**To change the bullet symbol of one bulleted list item**

1. Select any text in the list item you want to change.

    **TIP** You can select from one character to the entire paragraph to change the bullet symbol for only the individual list item.

2. On the **Home** tab, tap the **Bullets** button, and then tap the symbol you want to use.

# Create numbered lists

Numbered lists are intended for the presentation of items in a specific order or quantity; for example, sequential steps for performing a process, or a "top 10" list.

> ✓ **TIP** Numbered lists are also referred to as *ordered lists* because the list structure does connote an order, such as order of operation, preference, or performance level. The sentence that introduces the list usually specifies the meaning of the order.

You can format existing paragraphs of text as a numbered list or format a blank paragraph as a numbered list item and then enter text. Each numbered list item is one paragraph of text.

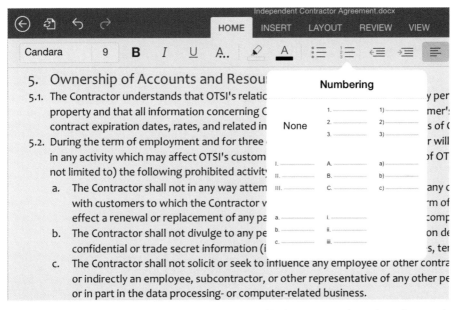

*Multilevel numbered lists present information in a hierarchical structure and permit readers to refer to specific information by item number*

### To format existing text as a numbered list

1. Ensure that each list item is in its own paragraph, and then select the paragraphs.

2. On the **Home** tab, tap the **Numbering** button, and then tap the number format you want to use.

>  **IMPORTANT** At the time of this writing, if you enter or format numbered list items and then separately format adjacent paragraphs as list items, the two lists do not merge; the numbering of each separately formatted set of items starts at 1. To resolve this issue, select all the list items that you want to number consecutively. Display the Numbering menu, tap None, redisplay the Numbering menu, and then tap the numbering style you want to use.

### To format a single paragraph as a numbered list item

1. Position the cursor at the beginning of the paragraph.

2. Enter the number 1 followed by a period and a space.

> ✓ **TIP** If you want to start a paragraph with a number rather than formatting it as a numbered list item, tap the Undo button.

### To create a numbered list as you type

1. Create a blank paragraph where you want to start the list, and position the cursor in the paragraph.

2. Enter the number 1 followed by a period and a space to format the paragraph as a numbered list item.

3. Enter the first list item, and then tap the **Return** key to create the next numbered list item.

4. Enter items and tap **Return** to add subsequent list items.

5. To end the list, do one of the following:

   - To start the next paragraph at the left margin, tap **Return** twice.

   - To indent the next paragraph at the same level as the list, tap **Return** and then tap **Backspace**.

### To change the numbering style of an existing numbered list

1. Tap anywhere in the numbered list you want to change.

2. On the **Home** tab, tap the **Numbering** button, and then tap the numbering style you want to use.

# Create multilevel lists

Bulleted and numbered lists can have multiple levels, each with a different bullet symbol or numbering style. You can create multilevel lists by increasing the indent of each lower-level list item. Increasing the indent automatically applies the hanging indent, tab stop, and bullet symbol or number style of the next level.

The standard bullet for a first-level list item is a black circle. By default, Word uses a hollow circle for second-level lists and a black square for third-level lists, and then it repeats that pattern for subsequent list levels.

- First-level list item
  - Second-level list item
  - Second-level list item
    - Third-level list item
    - Third-level list item
    - Third-level list item
  - Second-level list item
- First-level list item
- First-level list item

*A simple three-level bulleted list*

The standard numbering for a first-level list item is the number followed by a period. By default, Word uses lowercase letters for second-level list items and lowercase roman numerals for third-level list items.

1. First-level list item
   a. Second-level list item
   b. Second-level list item
      i. Third-level list item
      ii. Third-level list item
      iii. Third-level list item
   c. Second-level list item
2. First-level list item
3. First-level list item

*A simple three-level numbered list*

127

It is also common to provide information in bulleted (unordered) lists within numbered (ordered) lists—for example, when presenting options for a specific step of a procedure. In Word for iPad, you can assign any of the available bullet symbols or numbering styles to multilevel list items.

---

1. To remove a single row or column, do one of the following:
   - Position the cursor in any cell of the row or column you want to remove. On the **Table** tool tab, tap **Delete**, and then tap **Rows** or **Columns**.
   - Double-tap to select a cell in the row or column you want to remove. On the shortcut bar that appears, tap **Delete**, and then tap **Rows** or **Columns**.
2. To remove multiple rows or columns, do the following:
   a. Double-tap a cell adjacent to the insertion point, and then drag to select cells in the number of columns or rows you want to remove.
   b. On the shortcut bar or the **Table** tool tab, tap **Delete**, and then tap **Rows** or **Columns**.

---

*Multilevel lists can mix numbers and bullets*

### To demote multiple bulleted or numbered list items

1. Select the list items you want to demote.

2. On the **Home** tab, tap the **Increase Indent** button.

### To demote a single bulleted or numbered list item

1. Position the cursor anywhere in the list item, and then tap the **Increase Indent** button.

   *Or*

   If you're working with an external keyboard connected to your iPad, position the cursor at the beginning of a list item, and then press the **Tab** key.

### To promote multiple bulleted or numbered list items

1. Select the list items you want to promote.

2. On the **Home** tab, tap the **Decrease Indent** button.

---

 **TIP** Use the procedures described in the preceding sections of this topic for changing bullet symbols and numbering styles in multilevel and mixed-type lists.

---

**To promote a single bulleted or numbered list item**

1. Position the cursor anywhere in the list item, and then tap the **Decrease Indent** button.

   *Or*

   If you're working with an external keyboard connected to your iPad, position the cursor at the beginning of a list item, and then press the **Delete** key.

# Present content in tables                                            5

Tables provide a structure within which you can organize information into a series of columns and rows. Tables can contain text, numeric data, or images.

| Port | Destination | Days | Inside Cabin | Outside Cabin | Suite |
|------|-------------|------|--------------|---------------|-------|
| Tampa, FL | Eastern Caribbean | 7 | $500 | $1000 | $2000 |
| Miami, FL | Western Caribbean | 5 | $350 | $600 | $1500 |
| Galveston, TX | Western Caribbean | 7 | $600 | $1400 | $2400 |
| New Orleans, LA | Eastern Caribbean | 7 | $600 | $1500 | $2350 |
| Seattle, WA | Alaska | 14 | $1150 | $2400 | $4500 |
| Vancouver, BC | Alaska | 7 | $900 | $1250 | $3000 |

*A basic table with the default formatting and alignment settings*

In Word for iPad, you can create a table in a document by using any of these three methods:

- Insert a blank table, modify the table structure, and enter content.

- Convert existing text to a table.

- Paste a table from another document or source file, such as an Excel worksheet.

The intersection of each column and row is a cell. Each cell of the table can contain content. If appropriate, you can merge multiple cells within a row or column. Headings that classify the table data are usually presented in the first row of the table, and sometimes in the first column.

When you're working in a table, the Table tool tab appears on the ribbon. This tab contains commands for inserting and deleting table elements, formatting the appearance of the table, aligning content within cells (both vertically and horizontally), and sizing table columns to fit their content, to fit the page, or to be a specific width.

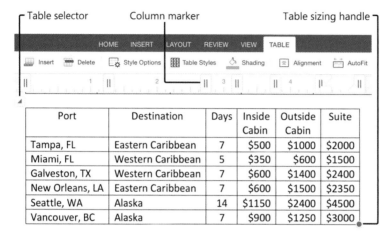

Changing column width and alignment makes a table look more professional

 **TIP** You can modify the left and right indents of the table and the width and padding of the columns by dragging the markers on the ruler. When a table, is active, the ruler displays markers for the table columns and the content of the current column.

**SEE ALSO** For information about configuring the alignment of text within tables, see "Align, space, and indent paragraphs" in Chapter 4, "Create professional documents."

Word for iPad provides options for formatting the appearance of a table by applying preset border and shading combinations. The placement of the border and shading helps to emphasize any of these table features that you select:

- Header row

- Banded rows

- Total row

- First column

- Banded columns

- Last column

> **IMPORTANT** Formatting a Total row in Word for iPad doesn't make any mathematical operations available within the row. You can insert mathematic formulas into table cells in the desktop version of Word. If you want to perform extensive calculations on the content of a table, you can create or work with the table content in Excel for iPad. For information about formulas and functions, see "Perform data-processing operations" in Chapter 8, "Process and present numeric data."

The available table color schemes are set by the document theme, so the table formatting will blend in with other colored elements in the document (such as headings and drawings) to give it a professional appearance. You can also select from the 10 standard colors available in all the Office for iPad apps or choose custom colors from a color spectrum.

5

Header row                                        Banded rows

| Port | Destination | Days | Inside Cabin | Outside Cabin | Suite |
|------|-------------|------|--------------|---------------|-------|
| Tampa, FL | Eastern Caribbean | 7 | $500 | $1000 | $2000 |
| Miami, FL | Western Caribbean | 5 | $350 | $600 | $1500 |
| Galveston, TX | Western Caribbean | 7 | $600 | $1400 | $2400 |
| New Orleans, LA | Eastern Caribbean | 7 | $600 | $1500 | $2350 |
| Seattle, WA | Alaska | 14 | $1150 | $2400 | $4500 |
| Vancouver, BC | Alaska | 7 | $900 | $1250 | $3000 |

*Style options such as banded shading can help readers locate information*

### To format existing text as a table

1. To create a multicolumn table, put the content of each row into one paragraph and insert a tab character to separate the content of each column.

   > **TIP** To insert a tab character, tap and hold. On the shortcut bar that appears, tap Insert, and then tap Tab.

2. Select the paragraphs.

3. On the **Insert** tab, tap **Table**.

> **IMPORTANT** To create a multicolumn table, ensure that every paragraph in the selection includes at least one tab character. If any paragraph doesn't contain a tab character, Word for iPad creates a single-column table with one row for each paragraph and retains the tab characters within the content.

**To create an empty table**

1. Position the cursor in the location where you want to insert the table.

2. On the **Insert** tab, tap **Table**.

   Word creates a page-width table that has three columns of equal width and three rows.

**To select a table**

1. Position the cursor anywhere in the table, or select any table content.

2. Tap the table selector that appears outside the upper-left corner of the table.

**To insert rows or columns in a table**

1. To insert a single row or column, do one of the following:

   - Tap to position the cursor in any cell adjacent to which you want to insert the column or row. On the **Table** tool tab, tap **Insert**, and then tap **Rows Above**, **Rows Below**, **Columns Left**, or **Columns Right**.

   - Double-tap to select any cell adjacent to which you want to insert the column or row. On the shortcut bar that appears, tap **Insert**, and then tap **Rows Above**, **Rows Below**, **Columns Left**, or **Columns Right**.

2. To insert multiple rows or columns, do the following:

   a. Double-tap any cell adjacent to which you want to insert the columns or rows, and then drag to select cells in the number of columns or rows you want to insert.

   b. On the shortcut bar or the **Table** tool tab, tap **Insert**, and then tap **Rows Above**, **Rows Below**, **Columns Left**, or **Columns Right**.

3. To double the number of rows or columns, do the following:

   a. Position the cursor or select content anywhere in the table.

   b. Tap the table selector.

   c. On the shortcut bar, tap **Insert**, and then tap **Rows Above**, **Rows Below**, **Columns Left**, or **Columns Right**.

## To remove rows or columns from a table

1. To remove a single row or column, do one of the following:

   - Tap to position the cursor in any cell of the row or column you want to remove. On the **Table** tool tab, tap **Delete**, and then tap **Rows** or **Columns**.

   - Double-tap to select a cell in the row or column you want to remove. On the shortcut bar that appears, tap **Delete**, and then tap **Rows** or **Columns**.

2. To remove multiple rows or columns, do the following:

   a. Double-tap any cell in the range you want to remove, and then drag to select cells in each column or row you want to remove.

   b. On the shortcut bar or the **Table** tool tab, tap **Delete**, and then tap **Rows** or **Columns**.

> ⚠ **IMPORTANT** Word for iPad doesn't prompt you to confirm the deletion of a table or any of its rows or columns. If you mistakenly delete a table or its content, tap the Undo button to restore the deleted content.

## To control the width of table columns

1. Position the cursor anywhere in the table.

2. Drag the table sizing handle to increase or decrease the width of the table and all its columns.

   *Or*

   Display the ruler, and drag the column markers on the ruler.

   *Or*

   On the **Table** tool tab, tap **AutoFit**, and then do one of the following:

   - To set each column to the minimum width required to contain its content, tap **AutoFit Contents**.

   - To set the width of the table to the page width and maintain the existing relationship between column widths, tap **AutoFit Page**.

**To change the height of all rows of a table**

1. Position the cursor anywhere in the table.

2. Drag the table sizing handle.

   *Or*

   Tap the table selector. On the **Home** tab, tap the **Line Spacing** button, and then tap a line spacing setting.

**To change the height of specific table rows**

1. Position the cursor or select content in the row or rows you want to change.

2. On the **Home** tab, tap the **Line Spacing** button, and then tap a line spacing setting.

**To format text in tables**

1. Select the text you want to format; the cells, rows, or columns that contain the text; or the entire table.

2. Use the character-formatting and paragraph-formatting commands on the **Home** tab.

 **SEE ALSO** For information about formatting text, see "Change the appearance of text" in Chapter 4, "Create professional documents."

**To apply preset table formatting options**

1. Position the cursor anywhere in the table.

2. On the **Table** tool tab, tap **Style Options**.

3. On the **Style Options** menu, tap to select or clear the table elements you want to emphasize.

4. On the **Table** tool tab, tap **Table Styles**.

 **TIP** The thumbnails on the Table Styles menu depict the available table styles and selected style options.

5. Flick through the available table styles and tap the style you want to apply.

**To apply a different table style**

1. Position the cursor anywhere in the table.

2. On the **Table** tool tab, tap **Table Styles**.

3. On the **Table Styles** menu, tap the style you want to apply.

**To apply shading to specific cells**

1. Position the cursor in the cell you want to shade, or select multiple cells.

2. On the **Table** tool tab, tap **Shading**.

3. On the **Shading** menu, tap any color block.

**To format specific table elements**

1. Position the cursor anywhere in the table.

2. On the **Style Options** menu, tap to select or clear the table elements you want to emphasize.

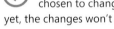 **TIP** If a style has been applied to the table, the formatting of the elements you have chosen to change will change immediately. If no style has been applied to the table yet, the changes won't appear until you apply a table style.

**To remove table styling**

1. Position the cursor anywhere in the table.

2. On the **Table** tool tab, tap **Table Styles**.

3. In the **Plain Tables** section near the top of the **Table Styles** menu, do one of the following:

   • To remove colors applied by the table style and formatting applied by the style options, tap the first, second, or sixth thumbnail in the row.

     Tapping the first thumbnail displays black gridlines, tapping the second thumbnail displays gray gridlines, and tapping the sixth thumbnail hides the gridlines.

   • To remove colors applied by the table style but retain formatting applied by the style options, tap the third, fourth, fifth, or last thumbnail in the row.

**To repeat table headings when a table runs onto multiple pages**

1. Position the cursor anywhere in the table.

 **IMPORTANT** Do not select table content. The Repeat Headers command will be unavailable (dimmed) if table content is selected.

2. On the **Table** tool tab, tap **Style Options**.

3. On the **Style Options** menu, tap **Repeat Headers**.

**To delete a table**

1. Position the cursor anywhere in the table.

2. On the **Table** tool tab, tap **Delete**, and then tap **Table**.

*Or*

Tap the table selector. On the shortcut bar, tap **Delete**, and then tap **Table**.

*Or*

1. Select content anywhere in the table.

2. On the shortcut bar, tap **Delete**, and then tap **Table**.

# Insert and format pictures

Photographs and other digital images can enhance, supplement, or replace text content in documents. In Word for iPad, you can insert an image into a document, apply a variety of picture formats and effects to the image, and control the layout of the image and surrounding text on the page.

## Insert and modify pictures

By using Word for iPad, you can insert images into a document from a variety of iPad and iCloud sources, including your iPad Camera Roll and Photo Stream albums.

> **TIP** In other versions of Word, you can insert images from external online sources. It's possible that as Microsoft releases additional updates to Word for iPad, other sources will become available. Until then, you can get external images to your iPad by saving them to your iPad from email messages or from another computer to your Photo Stream.

5

*Use pictures to enhance and expand on text content*

You can insert a picture in its own paragraph or within another paragraph. The best location is somewhat dependent on how you want text to flow around the image on the page. When you insert an image, it is associated with a paragraph, which is referred to as an *anchor*. When paragraph marks and formatting symbols are displayed and the image is selected, an anchor symbol indicates the anchor paragraph.

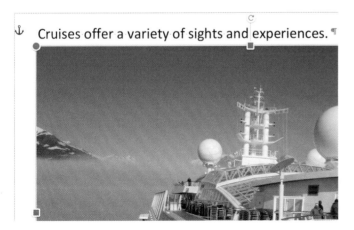

*Each image is anchored to a paragraph*

 **SEE ALSO** For information about flowing text around images, see "Arrange images and text" later in this chapter.

## About Photo Streams

A Photo Stream is an online storage folder that is hosted on iCloud. You can configure your iPad and other devices to automatically copy images that you capture on the devices to the Photo Stream. This creates a backup version of the locally stored image and also makes the image available from other devices (including computers running Windows). You can store up to 1,000 images for up to 30 days each in your Photo Stream.

To turn on the Photo Stream feature for your Apple account, follow these steps:

1. Open iCloud on your Mac or PC.

2. Enter your Apple ID if required, and select either or both photo options: **My Photo Stream** or **Photo Sharing**.

To configure your iPad to automatically upload photos to your Photo Stream, follow these steps:

1. Open the Settings app.

2. In the **Settings** list, tap **Photos & Camera**, or tap **iCloud** and then tap **Photos**.

3. On the **Photos & Camera** or **Photos** page, tap the **My Photo Stream** slider to change its background color to green.

Your Photo Stream is automatically available on the devices that upload images to it—in other words, the devices you sign in to by using your Apple ID. You can also access it from other computers by installing iCloud.

For information about setting up iCloud on an iPad, a Mac computer, or a computer running Windows, visit *www.apple.com/icloud/setup/ios.html*.

Inserting or selecting a picture activates its sizing handles and the Picture tool tab. This tab contains commands for formatting the appearance of a picture and controlling its position relative to text, images, and other page elements.

If a picture depicts more content than you want to show—for example, if the background dwarfs the primary subject of the picture or the picture contains content that isn't pertinent to your purpose, you can crop it. Cropping an image simulates cutting away parts of the image to display only a portion of it.

You have several different options when you crop an image. For example, you can:

- Specify or disregard the aspect ratio of the cropped image.

- Move the picture to position the intended subject within the cropped image.

- Adjust the size of the cropped image to fit the picture content.

- Adjust the size of the picture to fit the content to the cropped size.

*A picture cropped to display a portion of the image at a 1:1 aspect ratio*

Resizing, rotating, or cropping a picture affects the appearance of the picture in the document; it doesn't make any permanent changes to the original picture. You can undo your changes at any time.

You can make several types of changes to pictures that are embedded in documents. Some of these changes appear to change the picture itself; others apply effects to the picture.

You can modify the height and width of a picture by dragging the handles that appear when you tap the picture to select it or activate it for editing. You can also rotate the picture so that it appears at a different angle than the original.

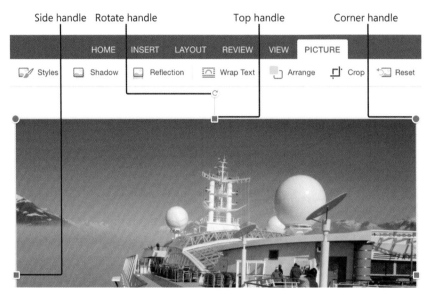

You resize and rotate an image by dragging its handles

> **TIP** Rotating a picture can make it appear that the picture was taken with the camera held at a different angle—you can use this method to straighten a picture that isn't properly aligned.

### To insert a picture in a document

1. Position the cursor in the location where you want to insert the picture.

2. On the **Insert** tab, tap **Pictures** to display the **Photos** menu.

   The content of the Photos menu varies depending on your device, the installed version of iOS, and the storage locations you've configured. The Photos menu might display the contents of your local Camera Roll album, your Photo Stream album, your iCloud photo library, or shared albums that you've created or subscribed to.

3. On the **Photos** menu, tap the storage location from which you want to insert the picture. Then locate and tap the picture you want to insert.

## To change the size of a picture

1.  Tap the picture to select it.

    >  **IMPORTANT**  Selecting a picture activates its sizing handles and the Picture tool tab.

2.  Drag the handles to resize the picture in any of the following ways:

    -   To resize the picture and maintain its aspect ratio, drag any round corner handle.

    -   To change only the picture height, drag the square handle on the top or bottom of the picture.

    -   To change only the picture width, drag the square handle on the left or right side of the picture.

## To crop a picture

1.  Select the picture.

2.  On the **Picture** tool tab, tap **Crop**.

    Crop handles appear in the corners and on all four sides of the picture. A shortcut bar displays aspect ratio options.

3.  To crop the image without a fixed aspect ratio, do any of the following:

    -   To change the size of the cropped image while maintaining the original aspect ratio, drag the corner crop handles.

    -   To change the size and aspect ratio of the cropped image, drag the side crop handles.

    -   To make the image larger or smaller in the active crop preview, drag the sizing handles.

    -   To move the image behind the active crop preview, drag it.

4.  When you finish adjusting the picture and crop handles, tap the **Crop** button to implement the changes.

5. To crop the image to a specific aspect ratio, do the following:

   a. On the shortcut bar, tap the aspect ratio you want.

   b. Drag the image to move it behind the fixed-aspect crop preview.

   c. Drag the sizing handles to make the image larger or smaller while keeping the crop size the same.

   d. Drag the corner crop handles to change the size of the cropped image while maintaining the selected aspect ratio.

 **TIP** You can repeat the cropping process to change the aspect ratio, picture size, or magnification, or to remove the cropping effect. For information about resetting an image to its original size and aspect ratio, see "Replace and reset pictures" later in this topic.

**To rotate a picture**

1. Select the picture.

2. Drag the **Rotate** handle in a clockwise or counterclockwise direction until the picture is at the angle of rotation you want.

## Apply styles and effects to pictures

You can apply preset combinations of visual effects, called picture styles, to a picture. Picture styles incorporate elements such as frames, shapes, edges, shadows, reflections, and angles. Some of these combinations of effects cause the image to appear three-dimensional.

 **TIP** Word for iPad supports the same 28 picture styles as the full desktop versions of Word.

If you want to enhance a picture without quite as many special effects, you can add a shadow or reflection to it.

You can choose from 23 different shadow effects: nine outer shadows (each emphasizing the outside of one corner or side of the picture, or placed directly behind the picture); nine inner shadows that emphasize the inside of the same locations; and five "perspective" shadows that give the picture a three-dimensional appearance. There are nine reflection variations, presented in three rows. Each row includes the same three options: Tight, which reflects the bottom third of the picture; Half, which reflects the bottom half of the picture; and Full, which reflects the entire picture. The first row positions the reflection touching the picture, the second row positions the reflection 4 points below the picture, and the third row positions the reflection 8 points below the picture.

**5**

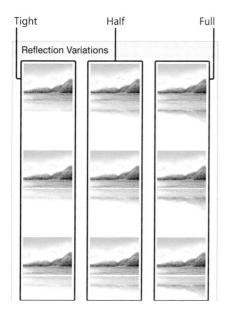

Tight      Half      Full

Reflection Variations

*The available reflection variations represent three levels of reflection at varying distances from the picture*

### To apply a style to a picture

1. Tap the picture to select it.

2. On the **Picture** tool tab, tap **Styles**.

3. On the **Styles** menu, tap the style you want to apply to the picture.

 **TIP** You can repeat the process of applying a picture style, shadow effect, or reflection effect to apply a different variation of the same type of effect.

**To add a shadow to a picture**

1. Tap the picture to select it.

2. On the **Picture** tool tab, tap **Shadow**.

3. On the **Shadow** menu, do one of the following:

   - To make the picture appear slightly raised above the document content, tap one of the **Outer** shadow thumbnails.

   - To make the picture appear slightly sunken into the background of the document, tap one of the **Inner** shadow thumbnails.

   - To make the picture appear even more raised above or sunken into the document, tap one of the **Perspective** shadow thumbnails.

 **TIP** You can add a shadow effect or reflection effect to a picture that has a picture style applied to it.

**To remove a shadow applied to a picture**

1. Tap the picture to select it.

2. On the **Picture** tool tab, tap **Shadow**.

3. On the **Shadow** menu, tap the thumbnail in the **No Shadow** section.

**To display a reflection of a picture**

1. Tap the picture to select it.

2. On the **Picture** tool tab, tap **Reflection**.

3. On the **Reflection** menu, in the **Reflection Variations** section, tap the level of reflection you want to display.

**To remove a reflection applied to a picture**

1. Tap the picture to select it.

2. On the **Picture** tool tab, tap **Reflection**.

3. On the **Reflection** menu, tap the thumbnail in the **No Reflection** section.

# Replace and reset pictures

After you insert and format a picture, you might find that another picture is more appropriate for the situation. You can replace an embedded picture with another, without losing the changes you've made.

When you replace a picture, Word applies the changes you made to the original picture to the replacement picture. You can take advantage of this if you want to display multiple pictures with the same sizing and effects—insert and format the first picture, copy the picture and paste as many copies as you need into the document, and then replace each of the copies with another picture.

When you apply a style or effect to a picture in a document, the appearance of the picture changes, but the original picture doesn't. You can change or remove effects that you apply to the picture at any time.

> ⚠ **IMPORTANT** If a picture is significantly larger than the page you insert it on, Word adjusts the proportions of the picture to fit it onto the page. Resetting the size of a picture returns it to its actual dimensions, which will not necessarily be the size it was when you inserted it. You might, therefore, need to resize the picture again to fit the page.

**To replace a picture**

1. Tap the picture to select it.

2. On the shortcut bar that appears, tap **Replace**.

3. On the **Photos** menu that appears, tap the storage location of the replacement photo, locate the photo, and then tap it.

**To remove all changes made to a picture**

1. Tap the picture to select it.

2. On the **Picture** tool tab, tap **Reset**.

3. On the **Reset** menu, do one of the following:

   • To remove styles and effects from the picture, tap **Reset Picture**.

   • To revert the picture to its original size but retain styles and effects, tap **Reset Size**.

   • To undo all modifications to the picture, tap both options in turn.

# Insert and format shapes

If you want to add visual interest and impact to a document but don't need anything as specific as a picture, you can use shapes.

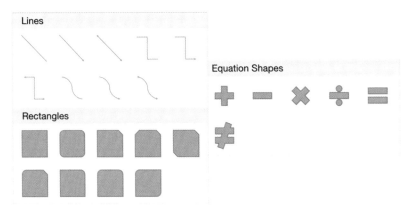

*The Shapes menu includes a wide variety of shapes*

You can choose from many different shapes, which are grouped by category: Lines, Rectangles, Basic Shapes, Block Arrows, Equation Shapes, Flowchart Shapes, Stars and Banners, and Callouts. All the shapes other than those in the Lines category support the addition of text, although some display it better than others.

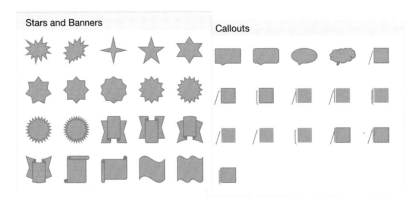

*Many shapes are designed to display text*

Word for iPad inserts each shape into the document at the default size and aspect ratio, and anchors it to a paragraph. You can then change the shape's dimensions, angles, and rotation to create exactly the shape you want. You can arrange multiple shapes to draw iconic images.

> **TIP** You can add text to any shape other than a simple line. You can format the text on a shape by using the same methods you would to format document text. For more information, see "Insert and animate shapes" in Chapter 9, "Create compelling presentations."

Nine shapes arranged to create a recognizable image

When you insert a new shape it has a blue outline and, depending on the shape, might be filled with blue. You can modify the outline color and fill color independently, or you can apply any of the 42 preformatted shape styles.

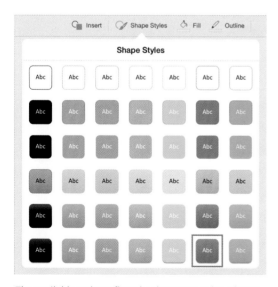

The available styles reflect the document color scheme

Shape styles combine fill color, outline color, transparency, and shadows to create a professional palette of options based on the color scheme of the document.

You modify the height, width, and rotation of a shape in the same way that you modify those aspects of a picture.

> **SEE ALSO** For information about resizing and rotating images, see "Insert and format pictures" earlier in this chapter. For information about controlling the position and order of shapes, see "Arrange images and text" later in this chapter.

*A happy fan cheering her team to victory!*

> **TIP** At the time of this writing, Word for iPad doesn't support managing multiple shapes by grouping them as one object or placing them on a drawing canvas.

### To draw a shape

1. Position the cursor in the paragraph where you want to insert the shape.

2. On the **Insert** tab, tap the **Shapes** button. Then on the **Shapes** menu, tap the shape you want to insert.

   Word for iPad inserts the shape on the page and anchors it to the paragraph.

**TIP** When you insert a shape, the Shape tool tab becomes active. You can insert additional shapes in the same location from the Insert menu on the Shape tool tab, and then arrange them the way you want.

## To select a shape and activate the Shape tools

1. Tap the shape to select it.

   Selecting a shape activates its sizing handles and the Shape tool tab.

## To change the size of a shape

1. Select the shape.

2. Drag the sizing handles to resize the shape in any of the following ways:

   - To resize the shape and maintain its aspect ratio, drag any round corner handle.

   - To change only the height, drag the square handle on the top or bottom of the shape.

   - To change only the width, drag the square handle on the left or right side of the shape.

## To rotate a shape

1. Select the shape.

2. Drag the **Rotate** handle in a clockwise or counterclockwise direction until the shape is at the angle of rotation you want.

## To apply preset fill and outline colors to a shape

1. Select the shape.

2. On the **Shape** tool tab, tap **Shape Styles**.

3. On the **Shape Styles** menu, tap the style you want to apply to the picture.

 **TIP** You can change the style that is applied to a shape by repeating the process of applying a style; it isn't necessary to remove the style.

**To change the interior color of a shape**

1. Select the shape.

2. On the **Shape** tool tab, tap **Fill**.

3. On the **Fill** menu, do one of the following:

   - In the **Theme Colors** section at the top of the menu, tap any one of the six hues of the 10 theme colors.

   - In the **Standard Colors** section, tap one of the 10 standard colors or a recent custom color (if shown).

   - At the bottom of the menu, tap **Custom Color**, locate the color you want by dragging on the spectrum, and then tap **Apply**.

**To make the interior of a shape transparent**

1. Select the shape.

2. On the **Shape** tool tab, tap **Fill**. Then on the **Fill** menu, tap **No Fill**.

**To change the outline color of a shape**

1. Select the shape.

2. On the **Shape** tool tab, tap **Outline**.

3. On the **Outline** menu, tap the theme color or standard color you want to apply.

   *Or*

   At the bottom of the menu, tap **Custom Color**, locate the color you want by dragging on the spectrum, and then tap **Apply**.

**To remove the outline from a shape**

1. On the **Shape** tool tab, tap **Outline**.

2. On the **Outline** menu, tap **No Outline**.

---

 **SEE ALSO** For more information about inserting and formatting shapes, see "Add visual elements to slides" in Chapter 9, "Create compelling presentations."

# Arrange images and text

In a text-heavy document, the relationship of pictures or shapes (collectively referred to in this section as *images*) to the text on the page can make a significant difference in the readability and professional appearance of the document. You can move images within the document to change their relationship to the document text. You can also configure an image to control the way that text wraps around it.

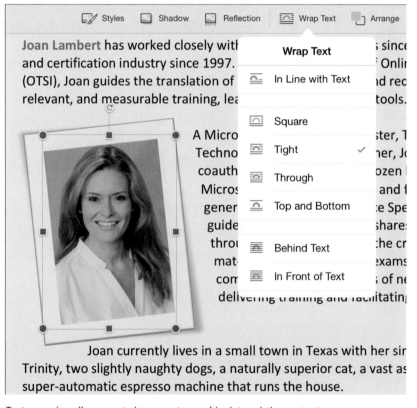

*Text wrapping allows you to incorporate graphics into existing content*

The text wrapping options have descriptive names and icons that accurately depict the application of each option. The options are:

- **In Line with Text**  The image is placed directly within a paragraph.

- **Square**  Text wraps around all four sides of the image. The image sits within a rectangular space that is the maximum height and width of the image.

- **Tight**  Text wraps around all four sides of the image, but no space is reserved on the left and right sides; the text flows to the edge of the image.

- **Through**  Text wraps around all four sides of the image, including through any open space on the top or bottom of the image.

- **Top and Bottom**  Text flows above and below the image, but not on either side. This is the default text wrapping for a picture or shape you insert in Word for iPad.

- **Behind Text**  The text flow is not affected by the image, which appears behind the text. The text might interfere with the reader's view of the image.

- **In Front of Text**  The text flow is not affected by the image, which appears in front of the text and might block the reader's view of the text.

If you insert several images and then position them so that they overlap, they are said to be "stacked." The stacking order (which object appears on top of which) is initially determined by the order in which you inserted the images, but it can also be determined by other factors such as the text wrapping setting of each image. If all the images use the same text wrapping style, you can change the order of the images by moving them toward (or to) the top or bottom of the stack.

If you can't find a way to make an image work within a document, you can, of course, delete it.

**To move an image within a document**

1. Tap the image to select it.

2. Drag the image to the target location.

   *Or*

   On the shortcut bar that appears, tap **Cut**. Display the target location, double-tap to position the cursor and display the shortcut menu, and then tap **Paste**.

**To wrap text around an image**

1. Tap the image to select it.

2. On the **Shape** tool tab, tap the **Wrap Text** button.

3. On the **Wrap Text** menu, tap the text wrapping option you want.

4. If necessary, move the image on the page to adjust its position to account for the change in alignment.

**To set the order of overlapping images**

1. Tap the image you want to move forward or backward in the image stack.

2. On the **Picture** or **Shape** tool tab, tap **Arrange**.

3. On the **Arrange** menu, do one of the following:

    • To move the picture to the top of the stack, tap **Bring to Front**.

    • To move the picture one position closer to the top of the stack, tap **Bring Forward**.

    • To move the picture to the bottom of the stack, tap **Send to Back**.

    • To move the picture one position closer to the bottom of the stack, tap **Send Backward**.

**To delete an image**

1. Tap the image to select it.

2. On the shortcut bar that appears, tap **Delete**.

# Skills review

In this chapter, you learned how to:

■ Present content in lists

■ Present content in tables

■ Insert and format pictures

■ Insert and format shapes

■ Arrange images and text

# Practice tasks

The practice files for these tasks are located in the iPadOfficeSBS\Ch05 folder.

## Present content in lists

Open the CreateLists document, and then perform the following tasks:

1. In the *Tips for business travelers* section, select the paragraphs from *If your trip is short* to the end of the section, and then style the paragraphs as bulleted list items.

2. Add a travel tip of your own as a new list item at the end of the list.

3. Select the first bulleted list item and try different bullet symbols. Choose a bullet symbol other than the default and apply it to the entire list.

4. Select the fourth through seventh bulleted list items and demote them to a second-level list.

5. Select the paragraphs in the *Don't forget!* section, and then style them as a bulleted list.

6. In the third-to-last item in this bulleted list, convert *school*, *doctor*, *vet*, and *alarm company* to separate second-level bulleted list items. Then delete the em dash.

7. In the blank paragraph near the beginning of the *Snack idea* section, enter 1. Take out three bowls, a cookie sheet, a large spoon, and all the ingredients. Notice that the entry becomes a numbered list item.

8. Select all the paragraphs that follow the numbered list item other than the final paragraph. Format these paragraphs as a numbered list. If the two lists don't automatically merge, take the necessary action to merge the lists.

## Present content in tables

Open the CreateTables document, and then perform the following tasks:

1. Select the paragraphs at the top of the document. Note that they contain entries separated by tab characters. Convert the paragraphs to a table.

2. In the blank paragraph at the end of the page, create a table that has two columns and eight rows. Then add the following headers:

   - Nearby places I want to visit

   - International places I want to visit

3. Add two more rows to the table, and then populate the empty cells by entering names of local and international destinations that you want to travel to.

4. Identify the table row that contains the places you least want to travel to. Delete that row.

5. Use the AutoFit function to size each column and row to fits its content.

6. Apply a table style of your choice.

7. Select the entries of the local and international destinations that you are most interested in visiting, and style them as italic.

8. Format the header row so that it is shaded, and then configure it to repeat at the top of each page if the table runs onto multiple pages.

9. Shade the cells that contain your second-favorite destinations.

10. Remove the table styling from the table above the one you created.

11. Select the table below the table you converted from text, and then delete it.

## Insert and format pictures

Open the FormatPictures document, display the ruler, and then perform the following tasks:

1. Crop the image to display an area of the lower-left corner that is approximately 3.5 inches high and 5 inches wide.

2. Resize the picture to about half its height and width, keeping the same aspect ratio.

3. Rotate the picture 90 degrees clockwise.

4. Apply a frame style to the picture.

5. Add various shadow and reflection styles to the picture, and then remove either the shadow or the reflection style, depending on the look you want.

6. Replace the picture with one of your own, and then, if you want to, remove all the changes that are applied to the picture.

## Insert and format shapes

Open the FormatShapes document, and then perform the following tasks:

1. Draw a heart shape above the word *love*.

2. Rotate the heart shape so that it's leaning on its left side.

3. Resize the heart shape so that it's wide enough to fit the text displayed below the heart.

4. Change the outline color of the heart to one you like, and then make the interior of the heart transparent.

5. Add the text that is below the heart to the shape, and then make any additional formatting changes that you want.

## Arrange images and text

Open the ArrangeImages document, and then perform the following tasks:

1.  Wrap the text squarely around the image of the train.

2.  Move the image of the plane to the right side of the page, under the *Tips for business travelers* heading.

3.  Wrap the text on the top and bottom of the trail mix image.

4.  Move the trail mix image and the train image below the *Don't forget*! heading.

5.  Overlap the images with the train on the top and the trail mix behind it.

# Enhance document content

Chapter 5, "Add visual elements to documents," discussed the various graphic elements you can add to a document to convey information, brand the document, or simply provide decoration. Beyond these visual elements, there are ways that you can format the content of a document to put the finishing touches on it.

You can lay out long segments of text in columns to make them more readable, or long lists of items in columns to fit more on the page. You can draw attention to a quotation by displaying it in a text box that floats on the page. You can provide ancillary text in text boxes or in footnotes, or you can provide a link from within the document directly to a reference webpage.

When the document content is ready, you can specify the dimensions of the printable space and add headers, footers, and page numbers if appropriate. You can then invite other people to review the document, provide feedback, and make edits for your review and approval.

This chapter guides you through procedures related to laying out text in columns or text boxes, linking to external content, creating footnotes, controlling the layout of content on the page, tracking changes, and working with comments.

## In this chapter

- Configure text in columns
- Draw and format text boxes
- Reference additional information
- Configure page layout
- Collaborate on content development

## Practice files

For this chapter, use the practice files from the iPadOfficeSBS\Ch06 folder. For practice file download instructions, see the Introduction.

# Configure text in columns

You can configure a section of text to display in two or three columns, rather than a single page-width column. You can use columns for different purposes. For example, long sections of text (such as newspaper articles) are often formatted in partial-page columns so that people can more easily read the content. Columns are also useful for displaying more than one page of short entries (such as a word list) on one page.

been released that support or resemble the Office apps, so you might have to scroll through a lot of search results to identify the actual app you want to install.

## iTunes support for the iPad

You can manage the content of iPads, iPods, iPhones, and other Apple devices and storage locations by using iTunes, which you can install on a computer running Windows or a Mac computer. You can use iTunes to browse and manage the device content, install software updates, and synchronize data with backup storage solutions.

When you connect your iPad to a computer that has iTunes installed, iTunes starts automatically. Selecting the iPad displays information about the device, including the iOS version, total storage space, and available storage space.

This book primarily provides information about managing Office apps and files directly from your iPad, but be aware that iTunes also provides methods for accessing content that is stored on the iPad, and if you're accustomed to using that program you can also use it to manage and synchronize Office files stored on your iPad.

A more direct path to the Office apps is through the Office for Mobile Devices website. You can learn about and install all the Office apps that are available for a specific mobile device

*The ruler displays the margins and indents for the active column*

By default, Word divides the columns as evenly as possible. If you don't like the location of the column breaks—for example, if you don't want to break a column in the middle of a paragraph—you can set them manually.

# Display column-related marks and tools

Columnar text is set off from the surrounding text by dividers called *section breaks*, which are visible when you display paragraph marks, spaces, tabs, and other hidden formatting symbols in the document. It can be useful to display the section breaks when you want to modify the content of the columns or remove them.

been released that support or resemble the Office apps, so you might have to scroll through a lot of search results to identify the actual app you want to install. ¶

- iTunes support for the iPad ¶ ———————— Section Break (Continuous) ————————

You can manage the content of iPads, iPods, iPhones, and other Apple devices and storage locations by using iTunes, which you can install on a computer running Windows or a Mac computer. You can use iTunes to browse and manage the device content, install software updates, and synchronize data with backup storage solutions. ¶

When you connect your iPad to a computer that has iTunes installed, iTunes starts automatically. Selecting the iPad

displays information about the device, including the iOS version, total storage space, and available storage space. ¶

This book primarily provides information about managing Office apps and files directly from your iPad, but be aware that iTunes also provides methods for accessing content that is stored on the iPad, and if you're accustomed to using that program you can also use it to manage and synchronize Office files stored on your iPad. ¶ ——— Section Break (Continuous) ———

A more direct path to the Office apps is through the Office for Mobile Devices website. You can learn about and install all the Office apps that are available for a specific mobile device

*Continuous section breaks mark the beginning and end of the columnar content*

Another tool that is useful for working with columns, but not shown by default, is the ruler. You can modify the margins and indents of the active column by dragging the markers on the ruler.

To display hidden formatting symbols, tap the Show/Hide ¶ button located at the right end of the Home tab. To display the ruler, tap the Ruler slider on the View tab to change the slider background to green.

**SEE ALSO** For information about using page and section breaks to structure document content, see "Configure page layout" later in this chapter. For information about indent and tab markers on the ruler, see "Align, space, and indent paragraphs" in Chapter 4, "Create professional documents."

### To display text in columns

1. Select the text that you want to display in columns.

>  **SEE ALSO** For information about selecting text in Word documents, see "Move, copy, and delete text" in Chapter 4, "Create professional documents."

2. On the **Layout** tab, tap **Columns**, and then do one of the following:

   - Tap **Two** or **Three** to format the selected text in two or three columns of equal width.

   - Tap **Left** or **Right** to format the selected text in two columns, with a narrow column on the specified side and a wide column on the other side.

### To manually set the column break location

1. Position the cursor at the beginning of the content you want to start the next column with.

2. On the **Layout** tab, tap **Breaks**, and then tap **Column**.

>  **TIP** If you're using an external keyboard with your iPad, you can set the column break location by pressing Shift+Return.

### To change the number or width of columns

1. Position the cursor anywhere in the columnar text.

2. On the **Layout** tab, tap **Columns**, and then tap the column layout you want.

### To change the content included within the columns

1. To add text from outside of the current column content, move the text to the position you want it to appear within the column area.

2. To expand or contract the content that is included in the columns, first display hidden characters.

3. To move the starting point of the column content, tap to position the cursor at the beginning of the section break that precedes the columns.

   *Or*

To move the ending point of the column content, tap to position the cursor at the beginning of the section break that follows the columns.

4.  Tap the same location again to display the shortcut bar. On the shortcut bar, tap **Select**, and then tap **Cut**.

5.  Double-tap at the new starting point or ending point of the content you want to include in the columns, and then on the shortcut bar, tap **Paste**.

**To change the space between columns**

1.  Display the ruler.

2.  Select the content of a column adjacent to the space you want to modify.

3.  On the ruler, drag the left margin marker or right margin marker of the column to change its width and adjust the space between it and the next column.

4.  Repeat the process if necessary to adjust another space.

 **SEE ALSO** For information about markers on the ruler, see "Align, space, and indent paragraphs" in Chapter 4, "Create professional documents."

**To revert from multiple columns to one column**

1.  Position the cursor anywhere in the columnar text.

2.  On the **Layout** tab, tap **Columns**, and then tap **One**.

*Or*

1.  Display hidden characters.

2.  Tap the section break that precedes or follows the columns, and then tap again to display the shortcut bar.

3.  On the shortcut bar, tap **Select**, and then tap **Delete**.

4.  Repeat steps 2 and 3 to delete the other section break.

 **TIP** Formatting multiple columns as one column retains the section breaks that start and end the columnar text. Deleting the section breaks is a more complete process.

# Draw and format text boxes

When you want to display text that is independent of the standard flow of content on a page, you can do so by inserting the content in a text box. Text boxes are containers that you can position either in a specific location on a page or relative to other page elements. Common uses for text boxes are as containers for sidebars and quotes that you pull from the content (referred to as *pull quotes*).

## Installation options

You always install the Office apps from the App Store. To install an app directly from the App Store, you must first locate it by searching for the app and then identifying the actual app from among the related results. This approach seems straightforward, but many apps have been released that support or resemble the Office apps, so you might have to scroll through a lot of search results to identify the actual app you want to install.

A more direct path to the Office apps is through the Office for Mobile Devices website. You can learn about and install all the Office apps that are available for a specific mobile device (in this case, the iPad) from the Office for Mobile Devices website at *office.microsoft.com/mobile*.

### iTunes support for the iPad

You can manage the content of iPads, iPods, iPhones, and other Apple devices and storage locations by using iTunes, which you can install on a computer running Windows or a Mac computer. You can use iTunes to browse and manage the device content, install software updates, and synchronize data with backup storage solutions.

When you connect your iPad to a computer that has iTunes installed, iTunes starts automatically. Selecting the iPad displays information about the device, including the iOS version, total storage space, and available storage space.

When you start an app installation, the app icon is automatically added to the iPad Home Screen. Until the app is ready to use, the icon is screened (dark) and labeled with the installation status rather than the app name.

*Sidebars can contain ancillary content that you want readers to notice*

If the text you want to feature in a text box already exists in the document you can select the text and create a text box around it. Otherwise, you can insert a blank text box and enter content into it. Then you can move, resize, and format the text box.

You format the content of a text box independently of the surrounding text. You can define the outline color, fill color, and text effects (referred to on the Shape tool tab as *WordArt Styles*).

Text boxes that you create in Word for iPad are always square or rectangular, although you can make the text box appear to be a different shape by placing a shape on top of an unformatted text box.

You control the way that text flows around a text box in the same way that you control the flow of text around a graphic. You can position the text box in line with other text, wrap text around the text box, or position the text box behind or in front of the document content.

 **SEE ALSO** For information about working with shapes, see "Insert and format shapes" and "Arrange images and text" in Chapter 5, "Add visual elements to documents," and "Add visual elements to slides" in Chapter 9, "Create compelling presentations."

You can apply a thematic style to the text box or format the text box outline and fill colors independently. You can also apply a WordArt text effect to the text within the text box. (The WordArt effects could be appropriate when placing a title or short slogan in the text box, but aren't well-suited to longer sections of text.)

 **SEE ALSO** For information about text effects, see "Change the appearance of text" in Chapter 4, "Create professional documents."

The commands that you use to format text boxes are on the Shape tool tab, which is visible when the text box or its content is active.

*Each command on the Shape tool tab displays a menu of options*

**To create a text box that contains existing text**

1. Select the text you want to move.

2. On the **Insert** tab, tap **Text Box**.

 **TIP** You can create a text box from existing text in Word for iPad but not in Excel for iPad, PowerPoint for iPad, or OneNote for iPad.

**To insert a blank text box**

1. On the **Insert** tab, tap **Text Box** to insert a basic square text box.

2. Display the ruler. Using the markers on the ruler as a guide, do the following:

   a. Drag the text box to the location where you want it.

   b. Drag the handles to roughly resize the text box.

    **TIP** You can most precisely finalize the text box size after you insert the content.

3. On the **Shape** tool tab, tap **Wrap Text**.

4. On the **Wrap Text** menu, tap the wrapping option you want.

**To insert text into a text box**

1. If you're moving or copying existing text into the text box, cut or copy the text to the Clipboard.

2. Double-tap inside the text box to position the cursor.

   *Or*

   Tap the text box, and then on the shortcut bar, tap **Edit Text**.

3. Enter the text you want or paste the text from the Clipboard.

**To change the way text fits into a text box**

1. If you want to change the text box to fit the text:

   a. Tap the text box to select it.

   b. Resize the text box by dragging the handles.

2. If you want to change the text to fit the text box:

   a. Select all or part of the text.

   b. Drag the margin markers on the ruler to set the inside margins.

   c. Tap the formatting commands on the **Home** tab to change the size and alignment of the text.

**To apply preset fill and outline colors to a text box**

1. Tap the text box to select it.

2. On the **Shape** tool tab, tap **Shape Styles**.

3. On the **Shape Styles** menu, tap one of the 42 preset color combinations.

**To fill a text box with color**

1. On the **Shape** tool tab, tap **Fill**.

2. On the **Fill** menu, do one of the following:

   - In the **Theme Colors** section at the top of the menu, tap any one of the 6 hues of the 10 theme colors.

   - In the **Standard Colors** section, tap one of the 10 standard colors or a recent custom color (if shown).

   - At the bottom of the menu, tap **Custom Color**, locate the color you want by dragging on the spectrum, and then tap **Apply**.

**To remove the fill color from a text box**

1. On the **Shape** tool tab, tap **Fill**.

2. On the **Fill** menu, tap **No Fill**.

**To outline a text box with color**

1. On the **Shape** tool tab, tap **Outline**.

2. On the **Outline** menu, do one of the following:

   - In the **Theme Colors** section at the top of the menu, tap any one of the 6 hues of the 10 theme colors.

   - In the **Standard Colors** section, tap one of the 10 standard colors or a recent custom color (if shown).

   - At the bottom of the menu, tap **Custom Color**, locate the color you want by dragging on the spectrum, and then tap **Apply**.

6

**To remove the outline from a text box**

1. On the **Shape** tool tab, tap **Outline**.

2. On the **Outline** menu, tap **No Outline**.

> ✓ **TIP** Text normally flows from left to right. You can change the direction of the text to read sideways, from top to bottom, as though you were changing the orientation of the page. To do so, first select the text you want to rotate. Then, on the **Layout** tab, tap **Text Direction**, and tap **Rotate All Text 90°**. When working with text in a text box, you also have the option to rotate text 270° so that it reads from bottom to top.

# Reference additional information

When you are creating a document, it is sometimes useful to be able to refer the reader to external content on the Internet. You can make that content easily available to readers by inserting a hyperlink from a location in your document to the web content. It is customary to hyperlink from a word or short phrase (such as *click here*), but you can also hyperlink from images and other content elements. The hyperlinked text or object (the anchor) appears underlined. The reader taps or clicks the underlined content to open the webpage you've specified, in his or her default web browser.

If you want to provide only a small amount of ancillary information and make it quickly available within the context of the document, you can insert a footnote at a specific location in the document that refers the reader to the related supporting content at the bottom of the page. Footnotes are often used to attribute quoted information to its original source.

Footnotes that you insert in Word for iPad are identified by numbers, starting with 1, rather than by letters, roman numerals, or symbols. If you want to use something other than consecutive numbers to identify footnotes in a document, or if you want the footnotes to appear immediately after the text on the page or at the end of the document, rather than at the bottom of the page, you can configure those from a desktop version of Word.

**To create a hyperlink from document content to a webpage**

1. Select the text or object you want to anchor the hyperlink to.

2. On the **Insert** tab, tap **Link**.

3. In the **Insert Hyperlink** box, do the following:

   a. In the **Address** box, enter the URL of the webpage you want to link to.

   b. Verify that the information in the **Display** box is correct.

   >  **TIP** Display the webpage you want to link to. Copy the address from the Address bar of the web browser, and paste it into the Insert Hyperlink box.

4. Tap away from the **Insert Hyperlink** box to close it.

**6**

**To create a footnote**

1. Position the cursor at the location in the document content where you want the footnote reference mark to appear.

2. On the **Insert** tab, tap **Footnote** to insert a footnote reference mark in the content and move to the corresponding footnote area.

3. In the footnote area, enter the ancillary information you want to provide to readers.

4. Tap in the document area to return to the document content.

**To change footnote content**

1. Tap in the footnote area at the bottom of the page.

2. Edit the footnote content.

3. Tap in the document area to return to the document content.

**To delete a footnote**

1. Position the cursor in the document content, after the superscript number that identifies the footnote you want to delete.

2. Tap **Delete** on the on-screen keyboard or a connected external keyboard one time to select the number and a second time to delete the number and the associated footnote content.

# Configure page layout

Page layout is the way that text and other content fits onto the pages of a document. You can define the basic layout of a document by specifying the dimensions of the content area and the document information that appears outside of the content area. You can control the amount of content that falls on each page. If necessary, you can divide a document into sections and define the characteristics of each section.

## Specify the dimensions of the content area

When you are configuring the presentation of a document, the primary boundaries are defined by three settings: the dimensions of the page (the page size), the direction of the page (the page orientation), and the space between the content boundaries and the edge of the page (the page margins).

The commands that are most frequently used to define the content area are available from the Layout tab of the ribbon.

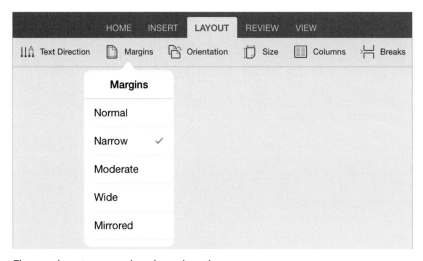

*The page layout commands and margin options*

There are two page orientation options: Portrait and Landscape. These options are appropriately named for the type of content that would be printed at each orientation. In practice, most documents have a portrait orientation (with the page higher than it is wide). Landscape orientation (with the page wider than it is high) is standard for content that requires a greater width to display appropriately, such as documents with complex tables, worksheets with many columns of data, and full-page slides.

The page size is almost always defined by the paper you're planning to print on. Word for iPad supports seven page sizes: Letter (8.5 by 11 inches), Legal (8.5 by 14 inches), A3, A4, A5, B4 JIS, and B5 JIS.

- The Letter and Legal paper sizes are part of a group of paper size standards known as "loose" standards, which don't follow any specific guidelines but are the official paper standards of the United States, Canada, and Mexico.

- The A series of paper sizes has an aspect ratio of one to the square root of two (approximately 1:1.4) and is the official paper standard of most European countries and regions.

- The JIS-B series represents the Japan Industrial Standard (JIS) paper size standard and has an area approximately 1.2 times that of the corresponding A series paper sizes.

**6**

The most common paper sizes are 8.5-by-11 inches in the United States and Canada, and A4 in most other countries and regions. Your installation of Word for iPad is probably set to default to the common paper size for your country or region. Sometimes, though, you'll create a document that you intend to print at a different size, such as a legal contract, and you'll need to change the page size.

The page margins define the space around the outside edge of the page that is blank other than any headers, footers, or page numbers you choose to display. The following table details the six margin options that Word for iPad supports.

| Margin name | Top | Bottom | Left | Right |
|---|---|---|---|---|
| Normal | 1" | 1" | 1" | 1" |
| Narrow | 0.5" | 0.5" | 0.5" | 0.5" |
| Moderate | 1" | 1" | 0.75" | 0.75" |
| Wide | 1" | 1" | 2" | 2" |
| Mirrored | 1" | 1" | 1.25" (Inside) | 1" (Outside) |

The Mirrored margin settings are intended for use in documents with pages that are printed on both sides of the paper and turned like those of a book.

 **TIP** These are the same standard margins supported by the desktop versions of Word. The desktop versions also allow you to set custom margins.

**To set page margins**

1. On the **Layout** tab, tap the **Margins** button.

2. On the **Margins** menu, tap **Normal**, **Narrow**, **Moderate**, **Wide**, or **Mirrored**.

**To set page orientation**

1. On the **Layout** tab, tap the **Orientation** button.

2. On the **Orientation** menu, tap **Portrait** or **Landscape**.

**To set page size**

1. On the **Layout** tab, tap the **Size** button.

2. On the **Size** menu, tap **Letter**, **Legal**, **A3**, **A4**, **A5**, **B4 JIS**, or **B5 JIS**.

## Add page headers and footers

As previously mentioned, document margins are empty of any content other than headers, footers, and page numbers.

The header is a defined area within the top page margin, and the footer is a defined area within the bottom page margin. You can insert text and images in the page headers and footers. By default, the header and footer content appears on every page of the document. You can configure different header and footer content for the first page and for all subsequent pages, and for odd pages and even pages. Here are some examples of when you might want to configure different headers and footers:

- If your document has a cover page, leave the header and footer of the cover page blank, and display information only in the headers and footers of subsequent pages.

- If your document will be printed double-sided and page-turned like a book, configure different headers and footers for odd and even pages, and position the information on the outside margin of each.

You can turn on both options (different first page and different odd and even pages) for documents that have a cover page and will be printed double-sided.

Page Numbers    Footnotes

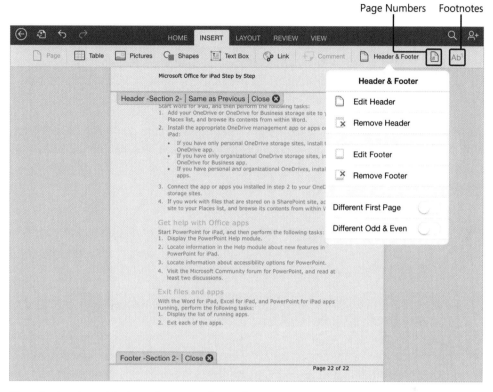

*The active header and footer and corresponding options*

The header and footer areas have preset tab stops to position content at the left margin, in the center, and at the right margin. Inserting one tab character aligns the subsequent content with the horizontal center of the page; inserting two tab characters right-aligns the subsequent content with the right margin.

*You can format the header content and adjust the tab stops to fit your needs*

> **SEE ALSO** For information about tabs, see "Align, space, and indent paragraphs" in Chapter 4, "Create professional documents."

As you flick through a document vertically in Word for iPad, the page number appears temporarily near the bottom of the app window. The page number shown corresponds to the page of the document when it is printed at the current page layout settings. You can also display the page number in the header or footer so that it is visible in the printed document. You don't have to enter the correct number on each page; Word enters it for you and keeps it up to date.

The default setting when you turn on page numbers is for the number to appear at the right end of the footer on every page of the document. You can configure the position, alignment, and format of the page number, and whether the page number is shown on the first page. (When a document has a cover page, it is standard practice to omit the page number from that cover page.)

### To activate the document header or footer area for editing

1. Double-tap the document header area or document footer area.

*Or*

1. On the **Insert** tab, tap the **Header & Footer** button.

2. On the **Header & Footer** menu, tap **Edit Header** or **Edit Footer**.

### To display information in a document header or footer

1. Activate the document header or footer.

2. Enter and format the content.

3. Tap the **Close** button below the header or above the footer to return to the document.

### To display a unique header and footer on the first page

1. On the **Insert** tab, tap the **Header & Footer** button.

2. On the **Header & Footer** menu, tap the **Different First Page** slider to change its background to green. Then tap **Edit Header**.

3. Move to the first page of the document. Enter the content in the header and footer that you want to display on only that page (or leave them blank).

4. In the second page header and footer, enter the content you want to display on the second and subsequent pages.

**To display different headers and footers on odd and even pages**

1. On the **Insert** tab, tap the **Header & Footer** button.

2. On the **Header & Footer** menu, tap the **Different Odd & Even** slider to change its background to green. Then tap **Edit Header**.

3. In the second page header and footer, enter the content you want to display on even-numbered pages.

4. In the third page header and footer, enter the content you want to display on odd-numbered pages.

> ✓ **TIP** When you turn the pages of a document that is printed double-sided, the odd-numbered pages appear on the right (recto) and even-numbered pages on the left (verso). You can ensure that header or footer content is always on the outside edge of the page by positioning it on the left side of even pages and on the right side of odd pages.

**6**

**To remove all content from the header or footer**

1. On the **Insert** tab, tap the **Header & Footer** button.

2. On the **Header & Footer** menu, tap **Remove Header** or **Remove Footer**.

**To display page numbers**

1. On the **Insert** tab, tap the **Page Numbers** button (represented by a page icon with a number sign [#] on it).

2. On the **Page Numbers** menu, tap the **Numbering** slider to change its background to green and display the page numbering options.

3. On the **Page Numbers** menu, do any of the following:

   - To remove the number from the first page of the document, tap the **Show # on First Page** slider to change its background to white.

   - To change the location of the page number, tap **Position**. On the **Position** menu, tap **Top of page (Header)** or **Bottom of page (Footer)**.

   - To change the horizontal position of the page number, tap **Alignment**. On the **Alignment** menu, tap **Left**, **Center**, **Right**, **Inside**, or **Outside**.

   - To change the page number format, tap **Format**. On the **Format** menu, tap the numbering format you want.

**To remove page numbers**

1. On the **Insert** tab, tap the **Page Numbers** button.

2. On the **Page Numbers** menu, tap the **Numbering** slider to change its background to white.

## Manage page and section breaks

When the content of a document doesn't fit between the top and bottom margins of one page, Word inserts soft page breaks to create additional pages. If you don't like the location of a page break, you can break the page earlier by inserting a manual page break. (Or you can change the margins, but that will affect the layout of the entire document.)

>  **TIP** Word for iPad doesn't provide access to paragraph line and page break settings that permit you to specify whether or where paragraphs can break across pages. For this finer level of control, edit the document in a desktop version of Word.

If you want to change more than a page break, you can divide a document into sections. For each section of the document, you can configure the page layout differently. For example:

- If you're working in a document that has the usual portrait page orientation (with the page higher than it is wide) and you need to display a large table or graphic, or other content that is wider than the page, you can put that content in its own section and configure the section to display and print in a landscape orientation (with the page wider than it is high).

- If you want specific document content to have wider or narrower page margins than the rest of the document, you can put that content in its own section and configure the margins of each section separately.

- If you plan to print a multipage document double-sided and want to make sure that a specific page (such as the beginning of a new chapter of a book) prints on the "front" side of the page, you can start a new section and configure the section to start on the next odd-numbered page.

> **TIP** Section breaks are also used to start and end columnar formatting. For more information, see "Configure text in columns" at the beginning of this chapter.

The type of section break you insert determines the starting location of the content immediately following the section break. The section break options are Continuous (which doesn't force a page break), and Next Page, Even Page, and Odd Page (which forces the content that follows the section break onto the next page, the next even-numbered page, or the next odd-numbered page.

 **TIP** Section breaks are also used to start and end columnar formatting. For more information, see "Configure text in columns" at the beginning of this chapter.

### To start a new page

1. Position the cursor at the beginning of the content that will start the next page.

2. On the **Layout** tab, tap the **Breaks** button.

3. On the **Breaks** menu, tap **Page**.

### To create a section without affecting page breaks

1. Position the cursor at the beginning of the content that will start the next section.

2. On the **Layout** tab, tap the **Breaks** button.

3. On the **Breaks** menu, tap **Continuous**.

### To create a section that starts on the next page

1. Position the cursor at the beginning of the content that will start the next section.

2. On the **Layout** tab, tap the **Breaks** button. Then on the **Breaks** menu, tap **Next Page**.

### To create a section that starts on the next even-numbered page

1. Position the cursor at the beginning of the content that will start the next section.

2. On the **Layout** tab, tap the **Breaks** button. Then on the **Breaks** menu, tap **Even Page**.

### To create a section that starts on the next odd-numbered page

1. Position the cursor at the beginning of the content that will start the next section.

2. On the **Layout** tab, tap the **Breaks** button. Then on the **Breaks** menu, tap **Odd Page**.

6

# Collaborate on document content

Teams of people frequently work together to develop business documents. Gone are the days of passing around printouts and trying to figure out what changes to enter—by using Word, you and your colleagues can collaborate directly within the document file. Word has many features to simplify the process of collaborating on documents. Chief among these are change tracking and comments.

## Track and review changes

During the writing and reviewing processes, document authors can track the changes they make to content, either for their own reference or for other people to review. When change tracking is turned on, Word tracks the insertion, deletion, and movement of text, and changes to formatting. You can turn off the tracking of each of these elements individually.

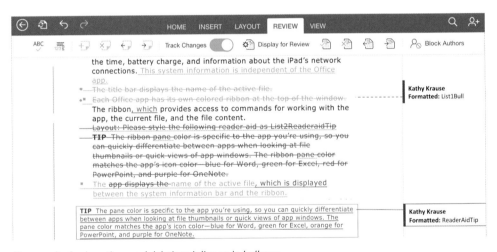

*You can display insertions and deletions inline or in balloons*

The commands that you use to manage change tracking and tracked changes are located on the Review tab.

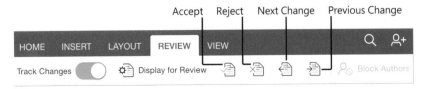

*The change tracking management buttons*

# Simultaneous coauthoring

Within the Office 365 structure, it is increasingly easy for Word users to collaborate with other document authors while developing content. Word for iPad, Word Online, and the desktop versions of Word all support coauthoring of documents that are stored in shared locations such as SharePoint or One-Drive. Multiple people who have access to the document storage location can open the document on their own computers or iPads, review the document content, and make changes to the document content simultaneously.

Coauthoring of files stored in a SharePoint document library works only for files that aren't checked out for the exclusive use of any one person.

When multiple people are editing a document, the Share icon at the right end of the ribbon changes to display the number of concurrent authors. You can tap the Share icon to display the user account names of the people who currently have the file open.

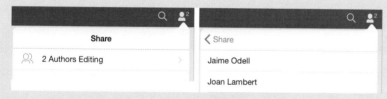

*You can coauthor documents with colleagues who are using Word on any device*

Word locks the content of any paragraph for the exclusive use of the person who is editing that paragraph. Depending on the version of Word an author is working in, changes are available to other document authors as soon as they're made or when the document is saved.

When reviewing a document, you can display it with the tracked changes visible, display the document as it would look if all the changes were incorporated, or display the original version without any of the changes. A vertical gray line in the left margin indicates each line of text that contains changes.

Word assigns a color to each reviewer for the purpose of tracking changes and inserting comments. In Word for iPad the color is based on your user account.

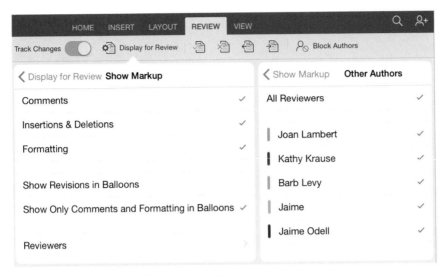

*Each user account has a specific color for revisions*

Changes can be shown either inline or in balloons in the margin. You can accept or reject individual changes or all changes in the document at one time.

### To turn on change tracking

1. On the **Review** tab, tap the **Track Changes** slider to change its background to green.

### To move among visible changes and comments

1. On the **Review** tab, tap the **Previous Change** or **Next Change** button.

### To switch among different views of revisions

1. On the **Review** tab, tap the **Display for Review** button.

2. On the **Display for Review** menu, tap one of the following to specify the visible changes:

   - **All Markup** to display the final content with changes and comments visible

   - **No Markup** to display the final content with changes and comments hidden as though they have all been accepted

   - **Original with Markup** to display the original content with changes and comments visible

   - **Original** to display the original content without any changes

**To show or hide specific types of changes or comments**

1. On the **Review** tab, tap the **Display for Review** button.

2. On the **Display for Review** menu, tap **Show Markup**.

3. On the **Show Markup** menu, tap to select or clear any of the following:

   - Comments

   - Insertions & Deletions

   - Formatting

**To show or hide revisions by specific reviewers**

1. On the **Review** tab, tap the **Display for Review** button.

2. On the **Display for Review** menu, tap **Show Markup**.

3. On the **Show Markup** menu, tap **Reviewers**.

4. On the **Other Authors** menu, tap **All Reviewers** to select or cancel the selection of all reviewers. Then tap any reviewer's name to display or hide that reviewer's revisions and comments.

**To display insertions, deletions, and formatting changes in the page margins**

1. On the **Review** tab, tap the **Display for Review** button.

2. On the **Display for Review** menu, tap **Show Markup**.

3. On the **Show Markup** menu, tap **Show Revisions in Balloons**.

**To display insertions and deletions within the text**

1. On the **Review** tab, tap the **Display for Review** button.

2. On the **Display for Review** menu, tap **Show Markup**.

3. On the **Show Markup** menu, tap **Show Only Comments and Formatting in Balloons**.

> **TIP** When displayed within the text, insertions are underlined and deletions are struck through. This is not an actual application of character formatting; it is visible only within the context of the tracked changes.

6

**To accept one or more changes**

1. On the **Review** tab, tap the **Accept** button.

2. On the **Accept** menu, tap one of the following:

   - **Accept & Move to Next** to accept the selected insertion, deletion, or formatting change and move to the next insertion, deletion, formatting change, or comment

   - **Accept Change** to accept the selected insertion, deletion, or formatting change and remain at that location in the document

   - **Accept All Shown** to accept all the types of changes that are currently selected on the **Show Markup** menu

   - **Accept All** to accept all insertions, deletions, and formatting changes in the document

   - **Accept All & Stop Tracking** to accept all insertions, deletions, and formatting changes in the document and turn off change tracking

**To reject one or more changes**

1. On the **Review** tab, tap the **Reject** button.

2. On the **Reject** menu, tap one of the following:

   - **Reject & Move to Next** to reject the selected insertion, deletion, or formatting change and move to the next insertion, deletion, formatting change, or comment

   - **Reject Change** to reject the selected insertion, deletion, or formatting change and remain at that location in the document

   - **Reject All Shown** to reject all the types of changes that are currently selected on the **Show Markup** menu

   - **Reject All** to reject all insertions, deletions, and formatting changes in the document

   - **Reject All & Stop Tracking** to reject all insertions, deletions, and formatting changes in the document and turn off change tracking

> **TIP** To accept or reject all revisions of a specific type, hide the changes you want to remain tracked by clearing their check marks on the Show Markup menu, and then tap Accept All Shown on the Accept menu or Reject All Shown on the Reject menu.

**To turn off change tracking**

1. On the **Review** tab, tap the **Track Changes** slider to change its background to white.

*Or*

1. On the **Review** tab, tap the **Accept** button.
2. On the **Accept** menu, tap **Accept All & Stop Tracking**.

*Or*

1. On the **Review** tab, tap the **Reject** button.
2. On the **Reject** menu, tap **Reject All & Stop Tracking**.

## Insert and manage comments

While reviewing a document in Word for iPad, you can insert comments in the document. Comments are useful for making suggestions, asking questions, explaining changes, or providing additional information. When comments are displayed, they appear in balloons at the right edge of the page.

Create, open, and save files

Start Excel for iPad, and then perform the following tasks:
1. Create a new workbook based on the **Household Budget** template.
2. Delete the new workbook instead of saving it for the first time.
3. Create a new workbook based on the **Simple To-Do List** template.
4. Name the workbook **My To-Do List** and save it in the **IPadOfficeSBS\Ch03** practice files folder.
5. Pin the **My To-Do List** workbook to the **Recent** page.
6. From the **Open** page of the Backstage view, browse to the practice files folder and open the **OpenFiles** workbook.
7. Save a copy of the **OpenFiles** workbook in the practice files folder as **My Expenses**.
8. From the **Recent** page, open the **My To-Do List** workbook.

Use common Office interface features

Open the NavigateOffice Word document, and then perform the following tasks:
1. Display each tab of the ribbon and familiarize yourself with the available commands.

**Joan Lambert**
This is complete and the practice file has been created.

**Kathy Krause**
Joan/Jaime: These should be IO as well as intPracticeFile, shouldn't they? Or does the intPracticeFile style automatically make things IO in InDesign?

> **Jaime**
> Good catch. Yes, they s/b IO in steps when we're interacting with them.

**Joan Lambert**
Tasks not yet covered:
• Undo and redo recent changes
• Restore previous file versions
Practice file has not been created.

> **Jaime Odell**
> Done. One file created/posted.

*Each user's comments are shown in the same color as his or her tracked changes*

The buttons used for inserting and managing comments are located near the left end of the Review tab.

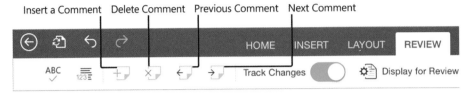

*The comment management buttons*

You can also attach a comment to text when you select it, by tapping the New Comment button on the shortcut bar.

You can attach comments to specific text or simply tap to position the cursor in the area where you'd like to insert the comment. Comments can contain elements such as formatted text, graphics, hyperlinks, and lists.

You can review comments as you flick through the text, or move directly from one comment to the next. When using Word for iPad, you can respond to comments by adding text to the existing comment balloon. (Desktop versions of Word have a Reply To Comment feature that is not available in Word for iPad.)

 **TIP** When responding inline to a comment, start your response with your name or initials to indicate that your response isn't part of the original comment.

**To insert a comment**

1. Select the text you want to attach the comment to, and then do one of the following:

   - On the shortcut bar that appears, tap **New Comment**.

   - On the **Review** tab, tap the **Insert a Comment** button.

   *Or*

   Tap to position the cursor where you want to insert the comment. Then on the **Review** tab, tap the **Insert a Comment** button.

2. Enter your comment in the active comment balloon.

3. Tap away from the balloon to return to the text.

**To move among comments**

1. On the **Review** tab, tap the **Previous Comment** or **Next Comment** button.

**To show or hide comments by specific reviewers**

1. On the **Review** tab, tap the **Display for Review** button.

2. On the **Display for Review** menu, tap **Show Markup**.

3. On the **Show Markup** menu, tap **Reviewers**.

4. On the **Other Authors** menu, tap **All Reviewers** to select or cancel the selection of all reviewers. Then tap any reviewer's name to display or hide that reviewer's revisions and comments.

**To delete one or more comments**

1. On the **Review** tab, tap the **Delete Comment** button.

2. On the **Delete** menu, tap one of the following:

   - **Delete Comment** to delete the active comment

   - **Delete All Shown** to delete all comments from the reviewers who are currently selected on the **Other Authors** menu

   - **Delete All** to delete all comments in the document

> **TIP** To delete all comments inserted by specific reviewers, hide the comments of the reviewers you don't want to process by clearing their check marks on the Other Authors menu, and then tap Delete All Shown on the Delete menu.

# Skills review

In this chapter, you learned how to:

- Configure text in columns

- Draw and format text boxes

- Reference additional information

- Configure page layout

- Collaborate on content development

# Practice tasks

The practice files for these tasks are located in the iPadOfficeSBS\Ch06 folder.

## Configure text in columns

Open the CreateColumns document, and then perform the following tasks:

1. Select the text from the heading *Parents' night out and open gym* through the end of the paragraph before the heading *Movie night in the park*.

2. Split the selected text into two columns, and start the second column with the *Community Theater and art contest/auction* section.

3. Add the *Movie night in the park* and *Potluck/game night* sections to the end of the first column.

4. Move the *Farmers' Market park games* section to the end of the first column.

5. Set the right indent of each column to 2.5 inches.

6. Configure the modified column content as a single column and ensure that the method you use removes the section breaks.

## Draw and format text boxes

Open the CreateTextBoxes document, and then perform the following tasks:

1. At the end of the document, insert a text box that is anchored to the blank paragraph.

2. Resize the text box to approximately 5 inches wide and 4 inches high.

3. Move the text that follows the first paragraph of the *Community chalkboard creation and a bouncy house* section into the text box.

4. Resize the text box to fit its contents.

5. Outline and fill the text box with standard colors of your choice.

6. Change the text box fill color to one of the 10 theme colors, and outline the text box with a variation of the same color.

7. Remove the outline and fill color from the text box if you want to.

## Reference additional information

Open the InsertReferences document, and then perform the following tasks:

1. Display the *Pre-festival marketing and fundraising ideas* section.

2. In the bulleted item that begins with *Scavenger hunt*, insert a hyperlink from the word *website* to a charitable foundation of your choice.

3. In the bulleted item that begins with *Potty Protection Insurance*, insert a footnote after the word *ideas*. In the footnote area, suggest possible variations on this fundraiser (for example, using garden gnomes instead of toilets).

4. Edit the footnote you created in the first step in any way you want.

## Configure page layout

Open the ConfigurePages document, and then perform the following tasks:

1. Configure the page settings to print the document on A4 paper with a horizontal orientation and wide margins.

2. Display the following information in the page headers:

   - On only the first page, display Trey Research Event Highlights.

   - On the second page (and any subsequent even pages), display Upcoming events.

   - On the third page (and any subsequent odd pages), display Event recap.

3. Display the following information in the page footers:

   - On only the first page, display Copyright 2015.

   - On all other pages, display the page number.

4. Insert a page break to start the *Movie night in the park* section on a new page.

5. Insert a section break that doesn't affect the page breaks before the *COMING SOON* section.

6. Insert a section break to start the *Event recaps* section on a new page.

## Collaborate on content development

Open the ReviewContent document, and then perform the following tasks:

1. Turn on change tracking. At the end of the document, in the blank paragraph after the *For more information* paragraph, enter your name.

2. Display the next revision in the document. Jump to each next revision until you arrive back at your name.

3. Display the revisions in balloons, or inline if they are already in balloons.

4. Hide all the revisions and comments in the document.

5. Redisplay the comments, and then hide only the comments made by Robin Wood.

6. Redisplay all revisions and comments.

7. Accept all the revisions in the paragraph that begins *The garden is an asset* at one time.

8. Accept all the formatting changes in the document at one time.

9. Display all remaining revisions and comments, and then turn off change tracking.

10. In the paragraph that begins *The garden needs your help*, select *$15*, and then insert a comment that says $10 might entice more people to attend.

11. In the last full paragraph of the document, reject the change from *children* to *kids*.

12. Display the next comment in the document. Jump to each next comment until you have reviewed them all.

13. Delete all the comments entered by Robin Wood.

# Part 3

# Microsoft Excel for iPad

# Store and retrieve data

Excel provides a practical yet powerful data management framework. You can store massive quantities of data within this deceptively simple structure, analyze that data, and present the resulting information in a variety of structures. The key ingredient in all of these tasks is the original data. The final presentation or analysis is only as good as the data it's based on. This "garbage in, garbage out" rule is true for many business tools, programs, and processes; Excel is no exception.

A worksheet can contain a vast amount of static and calculated data. You can structure worksheet content so that data is presented correctly on the screen and when printed, and you can format data so that it is easier for readers to locate and understand specific categories of information.

This chapter guides you through procedures related to creating workbooks and worksheets, managing worksheets and worksheet elements, populating worksheets with text or numeric data, modifying worksheet structure, and formatting data for presentation. It also includes procedures for efficiently displaying, filtering, and sorting data to provide specific information and perspectives.

## In this chapter

- Create workbooks
- Create and manage worksheets
- Enter and edit data on worksheets
- Modify columns and rows
- Modify cells and cell content
- Manage the display of data

## Practice files

For this chapter, use the practice files from the iPadOfficeSBS\Ch07 folder. For practice file download instructions, see the Introduction.

# The Excel feature set

Excel for iPad has only a subset of the features of the full program. Here is a brief comparison of the features in each version. You can save and edit workbooks in a shared storage location by using multiple versions.

## Excel for iPad features

After you sign in by using a Microsoft account, you can do the following:

- Create, manage, and print workbooks and worksheets.
- Format, find, replace, sort, and filter content.
- Insert pictures that are available on your iPad.
- Create formulas, Excel tables, and charts.
- Display conditional formatting and interact with data validation options, PivotTables, and comments.

The following premium features require that you sign in by using an account that is associated with a qualified Office 365 subscription:

- Insert and edit WordArt.
- Customize PivotTable styles and layouts.
- Add custom colors to shapes, and add shadows and reflection styles to pictures.

## Excel Online features

You can use Excel Online to do the following:

- Coauthor workbooks in real time and edit macro-enabled workbooks.
- Display three-dimensional charts, slicers, Power Pivot tables and charts, and Power View sheets.
- Embed workbooks on webpages.
- Send and compile surveys.

For more information about Excel Online, visit *technet.microsoft.com/en-us/library/excel-online-service-description.aspx*.

## Excel desktop version features

The desktop versions of Excel have the most functionality. For example, you can use Excel 2013 on a computer running Windows to do the following:

- Display multiple views of worksheets, split windows, multiple windows, and very large workbooks.
- Display and edit workbooks from remote storage locations offline.
- Insert equations and symbols.
- Insert pictures from local and online sources.
- Create SmartArt diagrams, and capture screen images.
- Copy and paint formatting.
- Insert header and footer content.
- Configure page layout options.
- Use apps and web resources to enhance content.
- Apply conditional formatting and sparklines.
- Sort and filter data by using slicers and timelines.
- Create and edit three-dimensional charts.
- Define named ranges.
- Audit formulas and require manual calculation of formulas.
- Analyze data by using the Quick Analysis tool.
- Create data validation rules, consolidate data, and perform conditional analysis.
- Group, subtotal, and outline data.
- Create PivotTables, Power Pivot data models, and Power View sheets.
- Create, save, and run macros.
- Use Office proofing tools.
- Protect workbook elements.
- Track changes, insert comments, and respond to comments.

**7**

# Create workbooks

As with other Office files, you can create a blank Excel workbook or a workbook that contains content from a template. Excel templates focus more on purpose than on appearance; they provide structure and functionality for specific types of information.

The templates that are available from within Excel for iPad range from a simple to-do list to a complex financial report and include expense reports, sales reports, household budgets, marketing budgets, time sheets, invoices, loan calculators, and ledgers. Most of the templates include basic calculations; some include advanced calculations and visual representations of data. Even if these don't meet your specific needs, they can serve as a good example of ways to collect, track, process, or present data.

*Excel for iPad has 16 built-in templates, including the blank workbook*

Only the templates that are installed with Excel for iPad are available from the New page. Other workbook templates are available for Excel Online, and hundreds are available from within the desktop versions of Excel. If you create a workbook based on one of these templates and save the workbook to a shared storage location, you can then open and edit the workbook on your iPad.

You can access templates for Excel Online from your iPad by using Safari or another web browser to visit *store.office.live.com/templates/templates-for-Excel*.

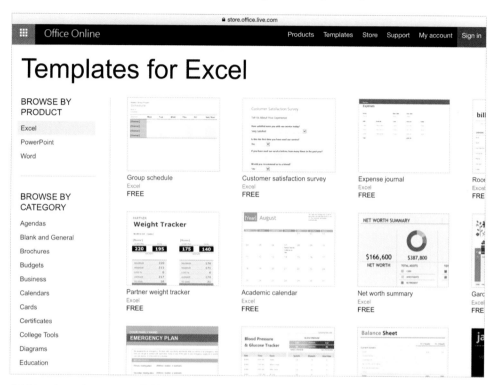

*Additional templates are available online*

### To create a blank Excel workbook

1. In the Backstage view, on the **File** bar, tap **New**.

2. On the **New** page, tap **New Blank Workbook**.

### To create a workbook from a built-in template

1. In the Backstage view, on the **File** bar, tap **New**.

2. Locate and then tap the thumbnail of the workbook template you want to use.

> **TIP** The processes of creating workbooks from Excel and Excel Online templates for use in Excel for iPad are the same as those of creating documents from Word and Word Online templates for use in Word for iPad. For step-by-step instructions, see "Create documents from templates" in Chapter 4, "Create professional documents." For general information about creating files in Excel for iPad and other Office apps, see "Create, open, and save files" in Chapter 3, "Create and manage files."

# Create and manage worksheets

Workbooks provide structure for the storage of information, but you store the information on worksheets within the workbook. A worksheet provides a seemingly simple cellular structure that can store more than 17 billion data points.

 **TIP** The current worksheet size limitation is 16,384 columns by 1,048,576 rows (which won't be a limitation for most Excel users). A single cell can contain up to 32,767 characters.

You don't have to store all your data on one worksheet. You can organize information on separate worksheets so that the content of each worksheet is easier to review and manage. You don't even have to store all related data on the same worksheet—you can easily reference data on other worksheets for purposes such as performing calculations or creating reports. You can also reference data in other workbooks, so it isn't necessary to have a copy of a worksheet that you reference from multiple workbooks in each of those workbooks.

*Scroll sideways to access worksheet tabs that don't fit in the sheet tab area*

 **SEE ALSO** For information about referencing other worksheets and workbooks, see "Perform data-processing operations" in Chapter 8, "Process and present numeric data."

## Add, rename, and remove worksheets

A new, blank Excel workbook contains one worksheet named *Sheet1*. You can add more worksheets to the workbook for the purpose of storing or displaying data, and give each worksheet a meaningful name. If you want to use an existing worksheet as a starting point for another, you can make a copy of the worksheet, rename the copy, and then modify the data on the copy. The data on the copy is not linked to the data on the original worksheet.

**To select or display a worksheet**

1. In the sheet tab area, tap the worksheet tab.

**To add a worksheet to a workbook**

1. In the sheet tab area, to the right of the existing worksheet tabs, tap the **Insert Worksheet** button, which is labeled with a plus sign (+).

**To create a copy of a worksheet**

1. Display the worksheet that you want to copy.

2. Tap the active worksheet tab to display the shortcut bar.

3. On the shortcut bar, tap **Duplicate**.

**To rename a worksheet**

1. Display the worksheet that you want to rename.

2. Double-tap the active worksheet tab to activate the worksheet name for editing and display the on-screen keyboard.

3. Enter the new worksheet name, and then do one of the following:

   - Tap anywhere on the worksheet.

   - On the on-screen keyboard, tap **Done** or tap the **Keyboard** key.

> ⚠ **IMPORTANT** The Undo command does not reverse actions such as renaming, hiding, and deleting that you perform on worksheet tabs.

**To delete a worksheet from a workbook**

1. Display the worksheet that you want to delete.

2. Tap the active worksheet tab. Then on the shortcut bar, tap **Delete**.

>  **TIP** You can display charts and other visual representations of data on worksheets with their supporting data, or you can move them onto their own worksheets. In some versions of Excel, you can export a chart from a worksheet to its own chart sheet. For more information, see "Display data in charts" in Chapter 8, "Process and present numeric data."

**7**

## Move and hide worksheets

Many workbooks contain multiple worksheets. The data you store or display on individual worksheets might exist independently or interact with content on other worksheets. For example, you might:

- Store data for individual time periods or projects on separate worksheets.
- Store static information such as resources, list options, and holiday dates on one worksheet and reference that information in calculations on several other worksheets.
- Display a chart on a worksheet that is separate from the data that supports it.
- Display data from multiple worksheets on a summary worksheet.

You can organize worksheets in a workbook by reordering them.

If you don't need to have the information on a worksheet immediately available, or if you want to protect or conceal a worksheet, you can hide it. Hiding a worksheet removes the worksheet tab from the sheet tab area on the status bar but doesn't remove any data.

**To move a worksheet within a workbook**

1. Display the worksheet that you want to move.
2. In the sheet tab area, tap and hold the active worksheet tab, and then drag it to its new location.

**To hide a worksheet**

1. Display the worksheet that you want to hide.
2. In the sheet tab area, tap the active worksheet tab. Then on the shortcut bar, tap **Hide**.

**To unhide a worksheet**

1. Tap the active worksheet tab.
2. On the shortcut bar, tap **Unhide** to display a list of the hidden worksheets in the workbook.
3. In the list, tap the name of the worksheet that you want to unhide.

# Show and hide worksheet elements

Data stored in an Excel worksheet is organized in columns and rows. The junction of each column and row is a cell, and this is where you enter data.

An empty worksheet resembles a piece of graph paper, with each cell outlined so you can easily locate it. Lettered headings across the top of the worksheet identify specific columns, and numbered headings down the left side of the worksheet identify specific rows. Worksheet tabs at the bottom of the window identify worksheets within the workbook.

You can hide all these user interface elements to display more of a worksheet or to focus on the worksheet content. You can also hide the Formula Bar when it isn't required, so that it appears only temporarily while you edit cell content.

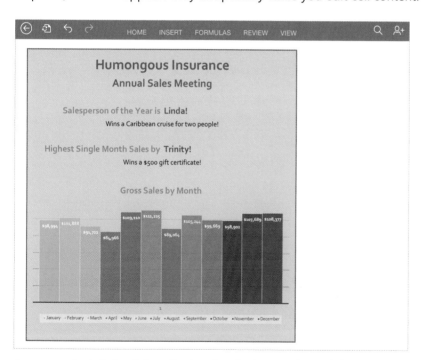

*A summary sheet displays information based on the data on other worksheets*

Hiding the Formula Bar or worksheet tabs affects all the worksheets in a workbook. Hiding the gridlines or headings affects only the active worksheet. Excel preserves the gridline and heading settings, so if you exit and reopen a workbook the gridlines and headings on each worksheet will be as you left them.

**To hide Excel user interface elements**

1.  On the **View** tab, tap the **Formula Bar**, **Gridlines**, **Headings**, or **Sheet Tabs** slider to change its background to white.

**To temporarily display the Formula Bar**

1.  Double-tap a worksheet cell to activate it for editing.

**To permanently redisplay Excel user interface elements**

1.  On the **View** tab, tap the **Formula Bar, Gridlines, Headings,** or **Sheet Tabs** slider to change its background to green.

 **TIP** Exiting and reopening a workbook redisplays the Formula Bar and worksheet tabs if they've been hidden.

# Enter and edit data on worksheets

Excel for iPad has a Ready mode and an Edit mode. When you're working with the structural aspects of cells, Excel is in Ready mode and the active cell or cell range has selection handles. When you're working with cell content, Excel is in Edit mode and there are no selection handles.

When you enter Edit mode, the Formula Bar opens above the worksheet, and the on-screen keyboard opens below the worksheet. This compresses the workspace significantly. You can orient your iPad horizontally to display more columns or vertically to display more rows.

 **TIP** If your iPad is connected to an external keyboard, the on-screen keyboard doesn't open in Edit mode. You can perform many operations by using keyboard shortcuts on an external keyboard. For a complete list of keyboard shortcuts, see the Appendix, "Touch-screen and keyboard shortcuts."

When Excel is in Edit mode, you can select individual cells, columns, or rows, but you can't expand the selection directly on the iPad. (You can do so from a connected external keyboard.) Selecting a column or row activates the first cell in the column or row for editing.

# Select cells, columns, and rows

A key step in the process of entering, modifying, or formatting worksheet content is selecting the cell or cells you want to work with. You can use these selection methods in the Excel for iPad touch interface:

- To select a cell, tap it once.

  **TIP** Selecting a cell or range of cells displays selection handles in the upper-left and lower-right corners of the selection and a related statistic on the status bar. For more information, see the sidebar "Quickly display statistics" in Chapter 8, "Process and present numeric data."

- To select a range of cells, select the upper-left cell in the range, and then drag the lower-right handle to the lower-right cell of the range or flick the handle down or to the right to select all populated cells in that direction (from the current cell to the next blank cell).

- To select a column, tap the column heading (the colored block above the worksheet that is labeled with a letter). Selecting a column displays selection handles on the left and right sides of the column and the content of the first visible cell of the column in the Formula Bar.

- To select a row, tap the row heading (the colored block to the left of the worksheet that is labeled with a number). Selecting a row displays selection handles on the top and bottom of the row and the content of the first visible cell of the row in the Formula Bar.

  **TIP** Selecting a column or row displays a shortcut bar of relevant commands. To close the shortcut bar and maintain the selection, tap an empty area of the ribbon.

- To select multiple columns or rows, select one column or row and then drag the handles to select adjacent columns or rows.

  **TIP** When an Excel table is active, tapping the column or row heading might select only the corresponding column or row of the table.

- To select an entire worksheet, tap the Select All button, which is located at the junction of the column headings and row headings and is labeled with a triangle that points toward the worksheet.

7

When you enter Edit mode from a cell that already contains content, or switch to a cell that contains content while you're in Edit mode, Excel displays and selects the cell content in the Formula Bar.

*The content of the active cell shifts to the far left when Excel is in Edit mode*

>  **TIP** It's easy to forget that you're in Edit mode. If you can't select cells, columns, or rows in the worksheet, check the Formula Bar for the telltale Cancel and Finish buttons.

In Excel for iPad, you enter and edit all text in the Formula Bar. The cell immediately displays the text, but the cursor is never active in the cell as it is in the desktop versions of Excel. In addition to the standard letters and numbers, you can enter the special characters that are available from the standard, number, and function online keyboards. Most notably, you can insert a line break within text to manually wrap cell content in a specific location.

If the data you want to enter follows a specific pattern such as 5, 10, 15, 20 or Monday, Tuesday, Wednesday, Thursday, you can establish the pattern and then have Excel continue the pattern and fill in the rest of the cells for you.

If the data you want to store in a worksheet already exists in another location, you can copy it from the source and paste it into the worksheet. This avoids the errors that can occur when entering data manually. The process of pasting content in Excel is the same as in other Office for iPad apps. If you paste a table into a worksheet, the table cells will map to the worksheet cells so that the table retains its structure.

>  **TIP** You can locate information within a workbook by searching for values, formula elements, or named objects. For information about searching Excel workbooks, see "Search file content" in Chapter 3, "Create and manage files."

# Display and hide the shortcut bar

Regardless of your experience with Excel, it can take some practice to master the techniques for selecting and manipulating content by touch on an iPad rather than by using a mouse. When you are working with content in Excel for iPad, the shortcut bar can be very convenient because it provides access to the most frequently used commands for a selected entity. It can also be inconvenient because sometimes it opens on top of content or tools that you want to work with.

Tapping a cell and then tapping it again displays the shortcut bar for the cell. (This action of tapping twice isn't the same as double-tapping; it's slower and has a different result.) Tapping a column or row heading once selects the column or row and also displays the shortcut bar.

*You can perform most common tasks from the context-specific shortcut bar*

You can hide the shortcut bar and still maintain the selection by tapping a colored part of the ribbon.

> ⚠ **IMPORTANT** You perform many tasks in Word for iPad, Excel for iPad, and Power-Point for iPad by using the same processes. Common processes include those for giving commands in the Office user interface and for opening, saving, searching, and distributing files. For more information, see Chapter 3, "Create and manage files."

### To switch from Ready mode to Edit mode

1. Do any of the following:

   - Double-tap a cell.

   - Select a cell and then tap the Formula Bar.

   - Begin typing on a connected external keyboard.

   - Press **Ctrl+2** on a connected external keyboard.

### To switch from Edit mode to Ready mode

1. Do any of the following:

   - To complete the edit and move to the next cell, tap the **Return** key on the on-screen keyboard or press the **Enter** key on a connected external keyboard.

   - To complete the edit and stay in the current cell, tap the **Finish** button (labeled with a check mark) at the right end of the Formula Bar or the **Keyboard** key on the on-screen keyboard.

   - To complete the edit and expand the selection, hold down the **Shift** key and press an arrow key.

   - To discard the edit, tap the **Cancel** button (labeled with an X) at the right end of the Formula Bar.

### To enter or edit cell content

1. Switch to Edit mode, and then enter text from the on-screen keyboard.

   *Or*

   From Ready mode or Edit mode, enter text from a connected external keyboard.

### To insert a line break in cell content

1. In Edit mode, position the cursor where you want the line break.

2. In the upper-right corner of the on-screen keyboard, tap the **Function** button (labeled **123**) to display the function keyboard.

 **SEE ALSO** For more information about the function keyboard, see "Perform data-processing operations" in Chapter 8, "Process and present numeric data."

3. On the function keyboard, press and hold the **Return** key (labeled with a curved arrow) to display the **Line Break** key, and then slide your finger to the **Line Break** key.

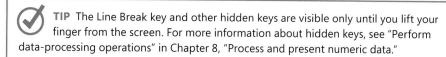 **TIP** The Line Break key and other hidden keys are visible only until you lift your finger from the screen. For more information about hidden keys, see "Perform data-processing operations" in Chapter 8, "Process and present numeric data."

### To move the content of one or more cells

1. Select the cell or cells.

2. Tap and hold the selection until an animated dotted line outlines the selection. Then without lifting your finger, drag the selected content to the new location.

### To fill cells with data that matches a pattern

1. In Edit mode, enter the first two items of the data series into adjacent cells.

2. Switch to Ready mode.

3. Tap the first cell and then drag the selection handle to select the second cell.

4. Tap the selection to display the shortcut bar.

5. On the shortcut bar, tap **Fill**. Note the arrows that appear on the right and bottom sides of the selected cell.

6. Drag the right-pointing arrow to the right to fill the series over, or drag the downward-pointing arrow down to fill the series down.

 **TIP** You can automatically fill series containing days of the week, months of the year, numbers, text, dates, times, and more.

### To delete cell content

1. Select the range of cells you want to clear.

2. On the shortcut bar, tap **Clear**.

   *Or*

   On the on-screen keyboard or a connected external keyboard, tap or press the **Delete** key.

# Modify columns and rows

A new worksheet has columns of equal width and rows of equal height. A standard letter-size printed page displays approximately 9 columns and 47 rows at the default sizes. The number of columns and rows visible on screen varies based on the dimensions and resolution of your screen. The content that you enter in a worksheet will rarely fit perfectly in the default structure, especially if you're entering text content.

*You can vary the size and visibility of columns and rows to suit your data*

## Resize columns and rows

After you enter data in a worksheet, you can easily modify the structure of the worksheet to fit the content. You can change the size of columns and rows so their content is visible on screen and when printed. You can change the width of a column or height of a row manually or by using the AutoFit feature to size the column or row to fit its contents.

 **TIP** You can't display or set the specific column width or row height measurements in Excel for iPad; you can adjust them only by dragging or by using the AutoFit feature.

**To fit a column or row to its contents**

1. Double-tap the column or row heading.

   *Or*

   Select the column or row, and then tap **AutoFit** on the shortcut bar.

**To change the width of a column**

1. Select the column. Notice the handle that appears on the right side of the column heading.

2. Drag the handle to the left to make the column narrower or to the right to make the column wider.

**To change the height of a row**

1. Select the row. Notice the handle that appears below the row heading.

2. Drag the handle upward to make the row shorter or downward to make the row taller.

# Insert and delete columns and rows

After you populate a data range or table, you can easily insert additional columns or rows into the range or table without overwriting existing data; existing columns shift to the right and rows shift down. Excel automatically updates any references in the workbook to the cells that shift to accommodate the insertion.

 **SEE ALSO** For information about referencing cells and cell ranges, see "Perform data-processing operations" in Chapter 8, "Process and present numeric data."

You can specify the insertion location for columns or rows, or the columns or rows you want to delete, by selecting them, or by selecting only representative cells.

If a column or row containing the data you want to insert already exists, you can move that column or row to a different location or copy it to another location. When you delete columns or rows, Excel shifts the remaining content to fill the gap and updates any cell references in the workbook to reflect the change.

 **TIP** Note the difference between *deleting* and *clearing* cells. When you delete a cell, it is completely removed from the worksheet, and other cells move to replace it. When you clear a cell, the content of the cell is deleted, but the cell structure remains in place.

**To insert a blank column**

1. Select the column, or any cell in the column, that is in the position where you want to insert the blank column.

    **TIP** If you want to insert multiple columns in one location, drag the selection handle to the right to select the number of columns you want to insert.

2. On the shortcut bar, tap **Insert Left**.

   *Or*

   On the **Home** tab, tap the **Insert & Delete Cells** button, and then tap **Insert Sheet Columns**.

**To move or copy a column to another location**

1.  Select the column you want to move or copy.

     **TIP** If you want to move or copy multiple contiguous columns, drag the selection handles to select the adjacent columns.

2.  On the shortcut bar, do one of the following:

    -   If you want to move the selected column, tap **Cut**.

    -   If you want to duplicate the selected column, tap **Copy**.

3.  Select the column that is in the position where you want to place the column.

4.  On the shortcut bar, tap **Insert Left**.

    *Or*

    On the **Home** tab, tap the **Insert & Delete Cells** button, and then tap **Insert Sheet Columns**.

**To insert a blank row**

1.  Select the row, or any cell in the row, that is in the position where you want to insert the blank row.

     **TIP** If you want to insert multiple rows in the same location, drag the selection handle down to select the same number of rows that you want to insert.

2.  On the shortcut bar, tap **Insert Above**.

    *Or*

    On the **Home** tab, tap the **Insert & Delete Cells** button, and then tap **Insert Sheet Rows**.

**To move or copy a row to another location**

1. Select the row you want to move or copy.

 **TIP** If you want to move or copy multiple contiguous rows, drag the selection handles to select the adjacent rows.

2. On the shortcut bar, do one of the following:

   - If you want to move the selected row, tap **Cut**.

   - If you want to duplicate the selected row, tap **Copy**.

3. Select the row that is in the position where you want to place the cut or copied rows.

4. On the shortcut bar, tap **Insert Above**.

   *Or*

   On the **Home** tab, tap the **Insert & Delete Cells** button, and then tap **Insert Sheet Rows**.

**7**

**To delete a column**

1. Select the column, or any cell in the column, that you want to delete.

 **TIP** If you want to delete multiple contiguous columns, drag the selection handles to select the adjacent columns or cells.

2. On the **Home** tab, tap the **Insert & Delete Cells** button, and then tap **Delete Sheet Columns**.

**To delete a row**

1. Select the row, or any cell in the row, that you want to delete.

 **TIP** If you want to delete multiple contiguous rows, drag the selection handles to select the adjacent rows or cells.

2. On the **Home** tab, tap the **Insert & Delete Cells** button, and then tap **Delete Sheet Rows**.

## Hide and unhide columns and rows

If a data range includes a column or row of information that you either don't want to display or don't want to include in a chart, but that you don't want to delete, you can hide it instead. The headings of a hidden column or row don't change, so you can identify locations of hidden columns and rows by the missing headings and the thick lines that replace them.

> ⚠ **IMPORTANT** You can't hide columns or rows of Excel tables when you are working with a workbook in Excel for iPad. If you need to hide a table column or row, you can convert the table to a data range, hide the column or row, and then convert the data range to a table. For more information about Excel tables, see "Create and manage Excel tables" in Chapter 8, "Process and present numeric data."

**To hide a column or row**

1.  Tap the heading of the column or row you want to hide.

>  **TIP** If you want to hide multiple contiguous columns or rows, drag the selection handles to select the adjacent columns or rows.

2.  On the shortcut bar, tap **Hide**.

**To unhide a hidden column or row**

1.  Tap the column heading to the left of the hidden column, then drag the right selection handle to the right to select the next visible column.

    *Or*

    Tap the row heading above the hidden row, then drag the lower selection handle down to select the next visible row.

2.  On the shortcut bar, tap **Unhide**.

# Modify cells and cell content

Sometimes you need to modify the structure of a worksheet on the cell level rather than modifying an entire column or row. For example, you might need to remove only one entry from a column that contains a list of entries. Deleting (clearing) the cell content would leave a gap—you must delete the entire cell to close the gap.

# Insert and delete cells

When you insert or delete individual cells from a worksheet, you must stipulate the direction in which Excel should shift the worksheet content that is below and to the right of the cell.

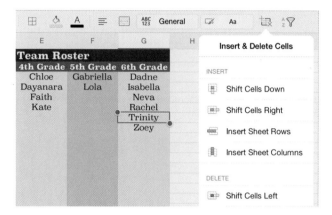

*You choose the direction to shift content when inserting or deleting cells*

## To insert a blank cell in a populated range

1. Select the cell that is located where you want the blank cell.

2. On the **Home** tab, tap the **Insert & Delete Cells** button, and then tap **Shift Cells Down** or **Shift Cells Right**, depending on where you want to move the adjacent cells.

## To insert multiple cells

1. Select the range of cells that occupy the space in which you want to insert the new blank cells.

2. On the **Home** tab, tap the **Insert & Delete Cells** button, and then tap **Shift Cells Down** or **Shift Cells Right**, depending on where you want the surrounding cells to be moved.

## To delete a cell

1. Select the cell (or range of cells) that you want to delete.

2. On the **Home** tab, tap the **Insert & Delete Cells** button, and then tap **Shift Cells Left** or **Shift Cells Up**, depending on where you want the surrounding cells to be moved.

## Modify cell structure

By default, text content that exceeds the width of its column extends across adjacent columns if they are empty. If the adjacent column contains content, only the text that fits in the first column is visible. If you don't want to resize the column to fit the text, you can wrap the text to display it on multiple lines.

 **TIP** In Excel for iPad, you can wrap the content of a single cell or multiple cells, but not of an entire column.

If a number is too wide to be displayed in a column, Excel displays the result in scientific notation, or displays number signs (#) instead of the number. You can't wrap a long number, but you can widen the column or change the font size to fit the number in the cell.

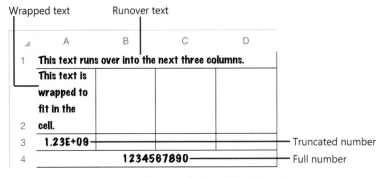

*Methods of handling content that exceeds the width of the cell*

Sometimes it is appropriate to merge the content of multiple cells into one cell; for example, to indicate that a heading or label applies to multiple columns or rows. A merged cell occupies the space of the original cells.

⚠ **IMPORTANT** When you merge multiple cells, Excel keeps only the data from the upper-left cell, and discards the other values. If the other cells contain data that you want to keep, move the data before merging the cells.

Merged cells

| | D | E | F | G | H | I | J | K | L | M |
|---|---|---|---|---|---|---|---|---|---|---|
| 15 | | | | | | | | | | |
| 16 | | | | | | | Costs | | | |
| 17 | Provider | Level | Plan | | Premium | Deductible | OOP max | Coinsurance | Copay 1st 3 | Copay > 3 |
| 18 | | Bronze | Basic 5 | | $ 351.28 | $ 3,750 | $ 6,250 | 70% | $ 150 | $ 150 |
| 19 | | Gold | Premier 1 | | $ 551.37 | $ 1,000 | $ 2,750 | 80% | $ 25 | $ 25 |
| 20 | Company B | Gold | Premier 2 | | $ 543.53 | $ 500 | $ 4,000 | 80% | $ 30 | $ 30 |
| 21 | | Silver | Solution 3 | | $ 431.63 | $ 4,500 | $ 6,350 | 80% | $ 30 | $ 30 |
| 22 | | Silver | Solution 4 | | $ 414.67 | $ 6,250 | $ 6,250 | 100% | $ 40 | $ 40 |

*You can merge cells vertically, horizontally, or both*

> **TIP** Merged cells can interfere with some types of operations on the surrounding columns or rows, such as filling cell data. If this happens, you can unmerge the cells, perform the operation, and then remerge the cells.

## To wrap or unwrap text

1. Select the cell you want to format, and then tap the selected cell.

   *Or*

   Select multiple contiguous cells that you want to format.

2. On the shortcut bar, tap **Wrap** or **Unwrap**.

## To merge a range of cells

1. Select the cells you want to combine.

2. On the **Home** tab, tap the **Merge & Center** button.

# Format cell appearance

You can format worksheet content to help people identify key information. Beyond the standard font formatting options, you can add shading (also called *fill color*) and borders to cells. You can fill cells and apply borders independently or as part of a preset cell style. Some of the cell styles available in Excel are intended to convey specific information and others are linked to the workbook theme.

> **TIP** Conditional formatting is an incredibly useful tool for exposing trends in numeric data. You can't apply or modify conditional formatting rules in Excel for iPad, but you can open worksheets that include conditional formatting rules created in other versions of Excel, and the rules function correctly in Excel for iPad.

All the cell styles are purely decorative. None of the styles that are designated as titles and headings actually affect the structure of the content or link to an outline level, as headings in a Word document do.

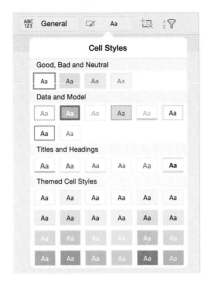

*You can use cell styles to add visual interest and meaning to a cell*

 **SEE ALSO** For information about changing the font, size, color, and style of text, see "Change the appearance of text" in Chapter 4, "Create professional documents."

A workbook can store many types of numeric data, and not all of these numbers should be displayed or processed in the same way. You can format specific types of numbers to display correctly and so that Excel correctly recognizes whether to process the number as a value or as something else (such as a date).

Excel for iPad includes 11 categories of number formats:

- **General** This is the default format for numbers. It permits Excel to process numbers in mathematic operations and to display numbers by using scientific notation if necessary to fit within the cell.

- **Text** This number format instructs Excel to display and process the number exactly as you enter it. It is particularly useful for numbers with leading zeros and long numbers, such as credit card numbers, that Excel would otherwise change to scientific notation.

- **Accounting**  This format allows you to display a specific number of decimal places and a currency symbol, which is left-aligned in the cell so the values are easier to read.

- **Currency**  This format allows you to display a specific number of decimal places and a currency symbol, which is flush against the numbers. You can also specify the format of negative values.

- **Date**  This format allows you to choose from among many standard options for displaying short and long dates to regional standards.

- **Fractions**  This format expresses a decimal number as the equivalent fraction. You can specify the denominator or degree of precision up to 1/999.

- **Number**  This format allows you to display a specific number of decimal places and specify whether to display the thousands separator and how to format negative numbers.

- **Percentage**  This format displays a decimal number as the equivalent percentage followed by the percent symbol. If you want to display more precise percentages, you can specify the number of decimal places.

- **Scientific**  This format expresses a number in scientific notation. You can specify the number of decimal places of the expression.

- **Time**  This format allows you to choose from among many standard options for displaying times or date/time combinations to regional standards.

- **Special**  This category includes region-specific formats for numbers such as ZIP codes, postal codes, phone numbers, and Social Security numbers.

**To add, change, or remove cell borders**

1. Select the cell or cell range for which you want to format borders.

2. On the **Home** tab, tap the **Cell Borders** button.

3. On the **Cell Borders** menu, do one of the following:

   - To apply a border to only one side of the selection, tap **Bottom Border**, **Top Border**, **Left Border**, or **Right Border**.

   - To apply borders to multiple sides of the selection, tap **All Borders**, **Outside Borders**, or **Thick Box Border**.

   - To remove all cell borders, tap **No Border**.

**TIP** Additional border styles and customization options are available in the desktop versions of Excel. If a worksheet cell has a border style that is unavailable in Excel for iPad, you can apply the border to other cells by copying the cell and then pasting only the format to the other cells.

### To specify or remove a cell background color

1. Select the cell or cell range you want to format.

2. On the **Home** tab, tap the **Fill Color** button.

3. On the **Fill Color** menu, do one of the following:

   - Tap the color you want to apply.

   - Tap **No Fill** to remove any applied color.

**TIP** The Fill Color dialog box displays six variations of each theme color, 10 standard colors, and a Custom Color link that displays a spectrum you can select a color from.

### To apply a preset cell style

1. Select the cell or cell range you want to format.

2. On the **Home** tab, tap the **Cell Styles** button.

3. On the **Cell Styles** menu, tap the style you want to apply.

### To specify a number format

1. Select the cell or cell range you want to format.

2. On the **Home** tab, tap the **Number Formatting** button.

3. On the **Number Formatting** menu, do one of the following:

   - To apply the default format for a category, tap the category name.

   - To apply a specific number format, tap the **i** (the information symbol) to the right of the category name. Set the format-specific options, and then tap away from the menu to close it.

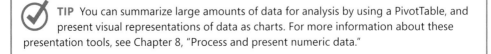 **TIP** You can summarize large amounts of data for analysis by using a PivotTable, and present visual representations of data as charts. For more information about these presentation tools, see Chapter 8, "Process and present numeric data."

# Manage the display of data

When a worksheet contains a large amount of data, it can be challenging to review the data, especially on a small screen such as that of the iPad. If you need to keep all the data at hand, you can rotate the iPad to display more columns or more rows at the same magnification; hide headings, worksheet tabs, and other user interface elements to increase the space available for the worksheet; or zoom out to display more content in the app window. You can freeze the column and row labels so they stay visible—and identify the on-screen content—while you flick through the data range.

If you're focusing on specific data, you can hide columns and rows that you don't need to review. To really narrow things down, you can hide data that isn't relevant to your needs by filtering it, and then present different aspects of the data for evaluations by changing the sort order.

7

 **SEE ALSO** For information about hiding user interface elements, columns, and rows, see "Create and manage worksheets" and "Modify columns and rows" earlier in this chapter.

## Freeze panes

When a worksheet contains more data than you can display on one screen, you must scroll vertically or horizontally to display additional fields and entries. When you scroll a worksheet that contains a data range, the lettered column headings and numbered row headings can help you to identify the visible data, but it's easy to lose track of specific fields or entries. To simplify this process, you can "freeze" the columns and rows that contain labels so they stay in place when you flick through a worksheet.

For a typical data range that starts in the upper-left corner of a worksheet (cell A1), the top row contains the column labels and the first column contains the row labels. Because this is common, Excel provides options to freeze the top row and the first column. Alternatively, you can select the first cell that you want to scroll and then choose the option to freeze the worksheet panes above and to the left of that.

Frozen panes are indicated by thin lines on the worksheet that start between the column headings or row headings. When the display of gridlines is turned off, the lines are visible in the worksheet background.

Frozen panes

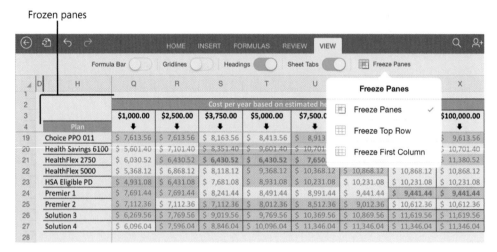

*You can freeze panes at any location in a worksheet*

## To freeze the panes to the left of and above a specific cell

1. Position the worksheet so that the rows you want to have visible after you freeze the panes are the first rows in the window.

> 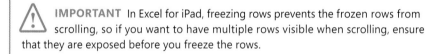 **IMPORTANT** In Excel for iPad, freezing rows prevents the frozen rows from scrolling, so if you want to have multiple rows visible when scrolling, ensure that they are exposed before you freeze the rows.

2. Select the first cell that you want to scroll (this cell will not be frozen).

3. On the **View** tab, tap **Freeze Panes**. Then on the **Freeze Panes** menu, tap **Freeze Panes**.

## To freeze the first visible column

1. Position the worksheet so that the one column you want to freeze as you scroll horizontally is the first column in the window.

2. On the **View** tab, tap **Freeze Panes**. Then on the **Freeze Panes** menu, tap **Freeze First Column**.

## To freeze the first visible row

1. Position the worksheet so that the one row you want to freeze as you scroll vertically is the first row in the window.

2. On the **View** tab, tap **Freeze Panes**. Then on the **Freeze Panes** menu, tap **Freeze Top Row**.

**To unfreeze panes**

1. On the **View** tab, tap **Freeze Panes**.

2. On the **Freeze Panes** menu, tap the current selection, and then tap a blank area of the ribbon to close the menu.

## Sort and filter data

A key feature of Excel is the ability to locate specific data or data that meets specific requirements. You can use the search function to locate specific text or characteristics and then move among the results one by one. For many purposes, however, it's more useful to manipulate the data range to display data in a certain arrangement or to display only (and all) the records that share specific characteristics.

You can sort a data range or Excel table by the entries in any column to present the data in different ways. For example, if you have a list of products offered by different companies at different prices, you can sort the data by company name, by product name, or by price. Then you can narrow down the options by filtering the data to display only (and all) the records that share specific characteristics.

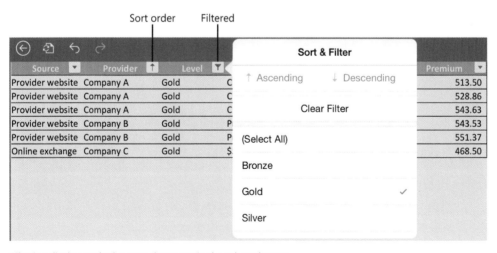

*Filtering displays only the rows that contain the selected entry*

**TIP** You can filter a data range by more than one column to display only entries that meet multiple criteria. In Excel for iPad, you can sort a data range by only one column at a time; you can't perform multilevel sorts from the Sort & Filter menu.

Filtering is off by default for data ranges, but you can easily turn it on. When you do, Excel evaluates the data and displays a Sort & Filter button at the right edge of each data column heading. The button label changes to indicate the column status, as follows:

- When a column is neither sorted nor filtered, the button is labeled with a downward-pointing triangle.

- When data is sorted by a specific column, the button is labeled with an arrow that points up to indicate an ascending sort order from smallest to largest (or A to Z) or down to indicate a descending sort order from largest to smallest (or Z to A).

- When the data range is filtered by a specific column, the button is labeled with a funnel-shaped symbol that represents a filter.

Filtering a data range by one or more columns displays the entire entry (row) that matches the filter criteria specified for the columns.

**To display the Sort & Filter buttons for a data range**

1. Select any cell in the data range.

2. On the **Home** tab, tap the **Sort & Filter** button, and then tap the **Filter** slider to change its background to green.

 **TIP** It isn't necessary to display the Sort & Filter buttons to sort data, but if you're going to perform more than one sort it's convenient to have them there.

**To sort a data range by a specific column**

1. In the heading of the column that contains the sort criteria, tap the **Sort & Filter** button, and then tap **Ascending** or **Descending**.

*Or*

1. Select any cell in the column that contains the sort criteria.

2. On the **Home** tab, tap the **Sort & Filter** button.

3. On the **Sort & Filter** menu, tap **Ascending** or **Descending**.

**To filter a data range by a specific column entry**

1. Display the **Sort & Filter** buttons for the data range.

2. In the heading of the column that contains the filter criteria, tap the **Sort & Filter** button.

3. On the **Sort & Filter** menu, tap to select or clear the selection of values to be displayed.

>  **TIP** A check mark indicates the filter values. Tap (Select All) to quickly select or clear the selection of all available values.

**To clear a filter**

1. In the heading of the column that contains the filter criteria, tap the **Sort & Filter** button.

2. On the **Sort & Filter** menu, tap **Clear Filter**.

# Skills review

In this chapter, you learned how to:

- Create workbooks
- Create and manage worksheets
- Enter and edit data on worksheets
- Modify columns and rows
- Modify cells and cell content
- Manage the display of data

# Practice tasks

The practice files for these tasks are located in the iPadOfficeSBS\Ch07 folder.

## Create workbooks

Start Excel, and then perform the following tasks:

1. Create a blank workbook, and then save the workbook on your iPad as My Blank Workbook.

2. Create a new workbook based on the built-in **Movie List** template.

3. Starting in cell C9, add information about your three favorite children's movies to the table. Notice that Excel continues the banded row striping automatically.

4. Save the workbook on your iPad as My Movie Workbook.

5. Create a new workbook based on any of the Excel Online templates.

6. After Excel saves the workbook to your OneDrive, open it in Excel for iPad and notice the file name.

7. Save a duplicate copy of the workbook on your iPad as My Online Workbook. Then navigate from the **Open** page of the Backstage view to the **Documents** folder on your OneDrive and open the workbook that has the name you identified in step 6.

8. Verify that the open workbook is the one you created from the Office Online website.

9. On the **Open** page of the Backstage view, tap the **File Actions** button next to the workbook name and then follow the process to delete the open workbook from your OneDrive.

## Create and manage worksheets

Open the ManageWorksheets workbook, and then perform the following tasks:

1. Review the information on the *Month 1* worksheet.

2. Create a new worksheet after the *Month 2* worksheet. Name the new worksheet **Our Goals**.

3. Insert two copies of the *Month 1* worksheet as the last worksheets in the workbook. Name the worksheets **Month 3** and **Month 4**.

4. Move the *Our Goals* worksheet to the right end of the sheet tab area, and then hide it.

5. On the *Month 1* worksheet, hide the Formula Bar, gridlines, and headings. Then verify that the gridlines and headings are still visible on the other worksheets.

6. Redisplay the hidden worksheet, and then redisplay the Formula Bar.

## Enter and edit data on worksheets

Open the EnterData workbook, and then perform the following tasks:

1. Review the information on the *January* worksheet. Then display the *February* worksheet.

2. In cell A9, add a new employee to the schedule by replacing *Employee 5* with the name **Jean**.

3. Without leaving Edit mode, move to cell AG4 and insert a line break immediately before the word *Days*. Then complete the edit and return to Ready mode.

4. Move the content of cells M7:N7 to Q7:R7 so there are only two people out of the office on February 13th.

5. Extend Kathy's vacation for the rest of the week by filling the pattern from Q7:R7 through to cell U7.

6. On the *March* worksheet, update cell A9 to add Jean to the schedule. Schedule an offsite training for Jean on the first weekday of the month by entering a **T** in cell C9 and completing the edit.

7. Cancel two of Susie's vacation days by deleting the content of cells Q5:R5.

## Modify columns and rows

Open the ManageStructure workbook, and then perform the following tasks:

1. Manually change the width of column B and the height of row 2 to more closely fit their content. Then use the AutoFit feature to make the column and row exactly the right sizes to fit their content.

2. Insert a new column to the left of column C. Enter Teacher in the column header.

3. Insert a copy of column E in columns F and G. Change the new column headers to Quarter 3 and Quarter 4, and then delete the grades from the new columns without clearing the formatting.

4. Move the *Teacher* column so it is between the *Period* and *Class* columns.

5. Insert two new rows above row 5. Enter Lunch in B5 and Recess in B6.

6. Hide the *Lunch* row. Then unhide the *Lunch* row and hide the *Recess* row instead.

## Modify cells and cell content

Open the ManageCells workbook, and then perform the following tasks:

1. Review the *Team Jerseys* worksheet. This worksheet contains a list of team members, the number that appears on the back of each player's uniform shirt, and a space to indicate the person who picked up the shirt from the coach. The entries are split into two sets of columns.

2. Change the number format in columns B and F to display whole numbers (without any decimal places).

3. The numbers printed on the players' shirts are all two digits. Apply a number format that won't remove leading zeros. Then enter a 0 before each number from 1 through 9.

4. Select the three cells that contain information about *Jane*. Insert a set of three cells above Jane's (without deleting Jane's information), and then enter the name Jaime in the new *Player Name* cell.

5. Cells E16:G17 contain two entries for the same girl, as evidenced by the matching names and shirt numbers. Delete the three cells in row 16 that contain information for Presley K, and shift the cells upward to fill the gap.

6. In the second set of columns, create space for two new entries in rows 14 and 15, below the entry for *Mallory*. Enter **Marcella** in row 14 and **Mary** in row 15.

7. Format cells C1 and G1 so that the column headings no longer wrap within the cells. Then use the AutoFit feature to size the columns to the minimum width required to fit the text.

8. Merge cells G10:G11, and enter **Lola's mom** in the merged cell to indicate that she picked up both girls' shirts. Then format the cell so its content is left-aligned like those above and below it.

9. Select cells A1:G31, and add a thick border around the outside of the selection.

10. Apply a cell fill color that you like to cells A1:G1. Then remove the fill from cell D1 so only the headings are shaded.

## Manage the display of data

Open the DisplayData workbook, and then perform the following tasks:

1. Freeze rows 1 and 2. Then flick down and up through the worksheet to confirm that the two rows remain visible.

2. Freeze column A. Then flick right and left through the worksheet to confirm that the column remains visible.

3. Unfreeze the frozen rows and column, and then move the worksheet up in the app window so that cell A10 is the first cell visible in the upper-left corner of the worksheet. Freeze the panes to the left of and above cell B13, and then move around the worksheet to see the effect.

4. Select any cell in the *Daily Living* data range, and then display the **Sort & Filter** buttons for that data range.

5. Sort the *Home* data in ascending alphabetical order.

6. Filter the *Daily Living* data range to display only data related to child care, dining out, and dog walking.

# Process and present numeric data

One of the primary purposes of storing numeric data in Excel is so that you can process that data programmatically. You can create simple to complex equations to perform calculations based on the numeric content of specific cells or data ranges. By using the many and varied functions built in to Excel, you can interpret raw data stored in a workbook in meaningful ways. You can increase the consistency and reliability of the information you extract from the data by using formulas to calculate, evaluate, and express it.

It is sometimes difficult to comprehend or draw conclusions from raw or processed data, especially when there is a lot of it. You can organize data in tables that provide added functionality, and visually represent data in charts. You can create many types of charts in Excel for iPad, and easily give tables and charts a consistent and professional appearance by applying styles.

This chapter guides you through procedures related to creating Excel tables, using formulas and functions to perform calculations, creating charts from worksheet data, and working with PivotTables and comments that other people create in shared workbooks.

## In this chapter

- Create and manage Excel tables
- Perform data-processing operations
- Display data in charts
- Display data from PivotTables
- Collaborate on workbook content

## Practice files

For this chapter, use the practice files from the iPadOfficeSBS\Ch08 folder. For practice file download instructions, see the Introduction.

# Create and manage Excel tables

An Excel table is a series of contiguous cells that have been formatted as a named Excel object that has functionality beyond that of a simple data range. When work-ing with data in an Excel table, you can do things that you can't do with a data range, such as automatically apply and update purpose-specific formatting and quickly insert column totals and other statistics.

| PRODUCT | Q1 | Q2 | Q3 | Q4 | TOTAL |
|---|---|---|---|---|---|
| Frames | 4,000 | 4,500 | 5,000 | 5,000 | 18,500 |
| Disc Brakes, Front | 294 | 250 | 323 | 368 | 1,235 |
| Caliper Brakes, Front | 200 | 170 | 220 | 250 | 840 |
| Disc Brakes, Rear | 400 | 340 | 440 | 500 | 1,680 |
| Caliper Brakes, Rear | 294 | 250 | 323 | 368 | 1,235 |
| Saddles | 235 | 200 | 32 | 294 | 761 |
| Forks | 100 | 85 | 110 | 125 | 420 |
| Brake Cables | 300 | 255 | 330 | 375 | 1,260 |
| Shifter Cables | 250 | 213 | 275 | 313 | 1,050 |
| Rear Sprockets | 400 | 340 | 440 | 500 | 1,680 |
| Front Sprockets | 200 | 170 | 220 | 250 | 840 |
| Handle Bars | 1,895 | 1,611 | 3,445 | 3,333 | 10,284 |
| Brake Levers | 544 | 462 | 598 | 680 | 2,285 |
| Pads | 30 | 26 | 33 | 38 | 126 |
| Chains | 208 | 177 | 229 | 260 | 874 |
| Derailers | 356 | 303 | 392 | 445 | 1,495 |
| Quick Release Hubs | 258 | 219 | 284 | 323 | 1,084 |
| Standard Hubs | 414 | 352 | 455 | 518 | 1,739 |
| Pedals | 369 | 314 | 406 | 461 | 1,550 |
| Chain Guards | 324 | 275 | 356 | 405 | 1,361 |
| Mirrors | 87 | 74 | 96 | 109 | 365 |
| Total | | | | | 50,662 |

*Excel tables have added functionality*

The simplest way to create a table is by converting an existing data range. Alterna-tively, you can create a blank table and then add data to it. (Adding data to a table is often referred to as *populating the table*).

Regardless of the method you use to create a table, Excel displays Sort & Filter but-tons in each column header and applies thematic formatting (a table style). The table style defines the shading, borders, and font colors used in the table. It also incor-porates formatting and functionality based on the default style options. After you create the table, you can apply a different table style and specify the style options you want to use.

As with other object styles in the Office for iPad apps, the available table styles are governed by the color scheme of the file you're working in. Excel table styles are divided into Light, Medium, and Dark categories. These designators refer to the color and coverage of the table cell shading. The default table style in a new workbook is near the middle of the Medium category and incorporates several shades of blue.

When you create a table from existing data, Excel evaluates the table content to identify the cells that are included in the table and to define functional table elements (such as header rows and Total rows). You can specify the table elements you want to emphasize by selecting the following style options:

- **Header Row** This option emphasizes the first row of the table and is intended for use in tables that have column headings.

- **First Column** and **Last Column** These options emphasize the first or last column of the table by applying font effects or shading.

- **Banded Row** and **Banded Column** These options shade every other row of the table to help readers track horizontal entries, or every other column of the table to help readers track vertical entries.

- **Total Row** This option adds a row at the bottom of the table that is preconfigured to display common statistics. By default, the Total row displays either the sum of numeric values or count of nonempty cells in the final column of the table. Tapping any cell in the row displays an arrow. Tapping the arrow displays the following list of statistics and options for you to choose from:

  - **None** The default option for all cells in the row other than the last column in which Excel locates numeric values, this option leaves the cell blank.

  - **Average** This function displays the average of the numeric values in the table column.

  - **Count** This function displays the number of nonempty cells in the table column.

  - **Count Numbers** This function displays the number of cells in the table column that contain numbers.

  - **Max** This function displays the largest numeric value in the table column.

  - **Min** This function displays the smallest numeric value in the table column.

**8**

- **Sum** The default option for the last column in the row in which Excel locates numeric values, this function displays the sum of all numeric values in the table column.

- **StdDev** This statistical function estimates the amount of variation from the average within the table column, ignoring logical values and text.

- **Var** This statistical function estimates the spread of values within the table column, ignoring logical values and text.

>  **TIP** The StdDev and Var functions are available for compatibility with Excel 2007 and earlier. More-specific functions were introduced in Excel 2010.

- **More Functions** Tapping this option activates the Formula Bar. If the cell already contains a formula, it's shown in the Formula Bar and the function's arguments are color-coded in the table. If the cell is currently blank, Excel inserts an equal sign (=), and activates the on-screen keyboard so you can enter a formula that uses any function you want.

*Style options emphasize or enable table features*

> **TIP** The format-related style options available for Excel tables (such as banded columns and rows) are the same as those for Word tables. For more information, see "Present content in tables" in Chapter 5, "Add visual elements to documents."

When you're working in an Excel table, the Table tool tab appears on the ribbon. You can manage the table structure and styles from this tab and from the shortcut bar that appears when you double-tap a table cell.

| | | | | HOME | INSERT | FORMULAS | REVIEW | VIEW | **TABLE** |
|---|---|---|---|---|---|---|---|---|---|

| Insert | Delete | Style Options | Table Styles | Convert To Range |
|---|---|---|---|---|

| | | Cut | Copy | Paste | Clear | Insert... | Delete... | Auto Fill | Wrap | |
|---|---|---|---|---|---|---|---|---|---|---|
| Joan | $ | | | | | | | | | 8 |
| Kay | $ | 4,572 | $ | 6,103 | $ | 7,129 | $ | 2,879 | $ | 4,494 |
| Linda | $ | 5,311 | $ | 7,380 | $ | 1,897 | $ | 5,736 | $ | 7,267 |
| Max | $ | 1,082 | $ | 4,404 | $ | 5,274 | $ | 1,903 | $ | 7,196 |
| Nancy | $ | 5,261 | $ | 4,742 | $ | 7,706 | $ | 4,557 | $ | 4,627 |

*Table management tools*

> **TIP** Excel assigns a name to each table based on its order of creation in the workbook (Table1, Table2, and so on). The table name isn't exposed in Excel for iPad but is available when you open the workbook in a desktop version of Excel. You can reference tables and fields by name in formulas.

Inserting, deleting, or moving columns or rows in the table automatically updates the table formatting to gracefully include the new content. For example, adding a column to the right end of a table extends the formatting to that column, and inserting a row in the middle of a table that has banded rows updates the banding. You can modify the table style options at any time.

> **TIP** Filters are turned on by default when you create a table or format a data range as a table. If you want to copy or cut an existing table from a worksheet and paste it into a different worksheet, first clear any filters that have been applied, to ensure that all the table content is copied. For more information about filters, see "Manage the display of data" in Chapter 7, "Store and retrieve data."

When a table includes formulas, Excel automatically copies a new formula to the rest of the table column. If you make a change to a formula, Excel updates the other instances of the formula so you don't have to. When you create a formula that references data stored in a table, you can refer to the table and the data in each column of the table by name rather than by columns and rows.

8

For example, the following formula returns the total of the December column of an Excel table named *SalesTable*.

*=SalesTable[[#Totals],[December]]*

If you want to remove the table functionality from a table, you can easily convert it to a data range. Note that the conversion does not remove formatting (such as cell colors and fonts) from the data range. You can retain the formatting or clear it.

**To format a data range as a table**

1. Select the data range.

   *Or*

   If the data range is clearly defined, tap anywhere in the data range.

2. On the **Insert** tab, tap the **Table** button.

**To create a blank table**

1. To create a single-column table with a header row and one content row, tap the cell you want to designate as the upper-left corner of the table.

   *Or*

   To create a table of a specific size, select the cells you want to convert to a table.

2. On the **Insert** tab, tap the **Table** button.

**To select a table**

1. Tap any cell in the table.

2. Tap the table selector that appears outside the upper-left corner of the table.

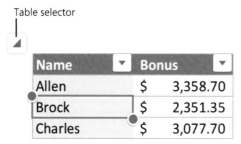

*The table selector appears when the table is active*

**To specify the style options for a table**

1.  Tap any cell in the table.

2.  On the **Table** tool tab, tap the **Style Options** button.

3.  On the **Style Options** menu, tap to select each of the table elements you want to format, and tap to clear the selection of each element you want to remove formatting from.

4.  Tap away from the **Style Options** menu to return to the worksheet.

> 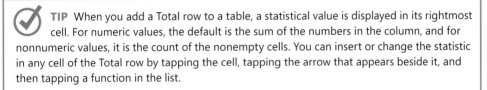 **TIP** When you add a Total row to a table, a statistical value is displayed in its rightmost cell. For numeric values, the default is the sum of the numbers in the column, and for nonnumeric values, it is the count of the nonempty cells. You can insert or change the statistic in any cell of the Total row by tapping the cell, tapping the arrow that appears beside it, and then tapping a function in the list.

**To apply a different style to a table**

1.  Tap any cell in the table.

2.  On the **Table** tool tab, tap the **Table Styles** button.

3.  On the **Table Styles** menu, tap the style you want to apply.

>  **TIP** To return to the worksheet without changing the style, tap outside the **Table Styles** gallery.

**To extend a table by dragging**

1.  Move the table in the app window so the lower-right corner of the table is displayed in the content area. Then tap any cell in the table.

2.  Drag the table sizing handle that appears outside the lower-right corner of the table in one of the following directions:

    -   To add rows, drag down.

    -   To add columns, drag to the right.

    -   To add columns and rows, drag diagonally down and to the right.

**8**

Table sizing handle

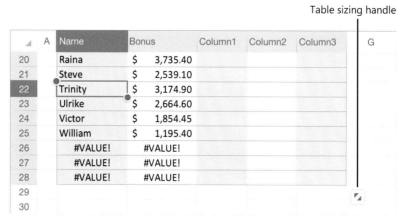

| ◢ A | Name | Bonus | Column1 | Column2 | Column3 | G |
|---|---|---|---|---|---|---|
| 20 | Raina | $ 3,735.40 | | | | |
| 21 | Steve | $ 2,539.10 | | | | |
| 22 | Trinity | $ 3,174.90 | | | | |
| 23 | Ulrike | $ 2,664.60 | | | | |
| 24 | Victor | $ 1,854.45 | | | | |
| 25 | William | $ 1,195.40 | | | | |
| 26 | #VALUE! | #VALUE! | | | | |
| 27 | #VALUE! | #VALUE! | | | | |
| 28 | #VALUE! | #VALUE! | | | | |
| 29 | | | | | | |
| 30 | | | | | | |

*Excel attempts to fill the new rows with content*

**To extend a table by adding columns or rows to the edges**

1. To extend the table by only one column, do one of the following:

   - Select the cell to the right of the rightmost column header and switch to Edit mode. Enter the new column heading, and then tap the **Return** key.

   - Tap any cell in the rightmost column of the table, or select the column. On the **Table** tool tab, tap the **Insert** button, and then on the **Insert** menu, tap **Insert Columns Right**.

2. To extend the table by multiple columns, do the following:

   a. Select the same number of cells or columns as you want to insert, with one end of the selection in the last column of the table.

   b. On the **Table** tool tab, tap the **Insert** button, and then tap **Table Columns Right**.

3. To extend the table by only one row, tap any cell in the last row of the table, or select the row. On the **Table** tool tab, tap the **Insert** button, and then tap **Table Rows Below**.

4. To extend the table by multiple rows, do the following:

   a. Select the same number of cells or rows as you want to insert, with one end of the selection in the last row of the table.

   b. On the **Table** tool tab, tap the **Insert** button, and then tap **Table Rows Below**.

**To insert blank columns or rows inside a table**

1. To specify the number and location of columns or rows to insert, do one of the following:

   - To insert a single column, tap a cell to the right of the insertion location.

   - To insert multiple columns, select that number of cells or rows to the right of the insertion location.

   - To insert a single row, tap a cell below the insertion location.

   - To insert multiple rows, select that number of cells or rows below the insertion location.

2. On the **Table** tool tab, tap the **Insert** button.

3. On the **Insert** menu, tap **Table Columns Left** or **Table Rows Above**.

**To remove columns or rows from a table**

1. Tap the heading of the column or row you want to remove, or any cell in the column or row.

2. On the **Table** tool tab, tap the **Delete** button.

3. On the **Delete** menu, tap **Table Columns** or **Table Rows**.

*Or*

1. With the lower-right corner of the table displayed on the screen, tap any cell in the table.

2. Drag the table sizing handle that appears outside the lower-right corner as follows:

   - To remove rows, drag up.

   - To remove columns, drag to the left.

> ⚠ **IMPORTANT** Resizing a table to remove columns or rows doesn't delete the contents of the columns or rows; it only converts those columns or rows to normal worksheet cells.

**To convert a table to a data range**

1. Tap any cell in the table.

2. On the **Table** tool tab, tap the **Convert to Range** button.

# Perform data-processing operations

You process data by creating formulas that take the input from one or more cells and perform calculations. You can create formulas that evaluate independent data points or entire data series stored in data ranges or Excel tables.

Every formula begins with an equal sign (=) to indicate to Excel that it must perform a calculation. The equal sign can precede a simple equation, a function that evaluates the arguments defined by a series of parameters, or a formula that combines both elements.

Excel for iPad automatically builds formulas for five common mathematical functions —SUM, AVERAGE, COUNT, MAX, and MIN—and leads you through the process of building formulas that use other functions.

When you create a formula in a table, Excel automatically copies the formula that you enter in one cell to the other cells in that column, and to new rows that you add to the table later. When you reference data stored in an Excel table, you can reference the content of an entire column by name rather than specifying the range of cells within the column. For example, if column C of a table has the heading Cost in row 1 and rows 2 through 98 contain data, a formula that calculates values based on the cost data can reference *Cost* instead of *C2:C98*. The benefit of this is that adding or removing rows won't invalidate the formula; the Cost reference will always include all and only the cells in that column.

> **TIP** This book provides basic information about formulas and the mechanics of creating formulas in Excel for iPad. Hundreds of functions are available for use in formulas. The Formula Builder leads you through the process of constructing a formula with the correct syntax for the function you're using. To learn about specific functions in more depth, consult a book such as *Microsoft Excel 2013 Inside Out* by Craig Stinson and Mark Dodge (Microsoft Press, 2013), or *Microsoft Excel 2010 Formulas and Functions Inside Out* by Egbert Jeschke, Helmut Reinke, Sara Unverhau, and Eckehard Pfeifer (Microsoft Press, 2011).

## Create simple formulas

The most basic formulas involve only operands (numbers or cell references) and operators. For example, the formula *=A2+B2* returns the sum of the numbers in cells A2 and B2.

$fx$    =A2+B2

| ◢ | A | B | C | D | E |
|---|---|---|---|---|---|
| 1 | **Hourly wages** | **Piecework** | **Hours worked** | **Total pay** | |
| 2 | 1260 | 768 | 40 | 2028 | |
| 3 | | | | | |

*The formula adds the hourly wages and piecework compensation to calculate the total pay*

You can perform simple calculations by using basic mathematical operators, such as those in the following table.

| Operator | Represents | Action | Precedence |
|---|---|---|---|
| ^ (caret) | Exponent | Raise to a power | 1 |
| * (asterisk) | Multiplication sign | Multiply | 2 |
| / (forward slash) | Division sign | Divide | 2 |
| + (plus sign) | Plus sign | Add | 3 |
| - (minus sign) | Minus sign | Subtract or negate | 3 |

A simple formula can include one operation or multiple operations. Formulas that involve multiple operations can include suboperations enclosed in parentheses. For example, the formula *=(A2+B2)/C2* divides the sum of the numbers in cells A2 and B2 by the number in cell C2.

$fx$    =(A2+B2)/C2

| ◢ | A | B | C | D | E |
|---|---|---|---|---|---|
| 1 | **Hourly wages** | **Piecework** | **Hours worked** | **Net hourly rate** | |
| 2 | 1260 | 768 | 40 | 50.7 | |
| 3 | | | | | |

*The formula divides the total pay by the hours worked to calculate the hourly rate*

> ✓ **TIP** Excel processes operations of equal precedence in order from left to right and operations that include multiple parenthetical calculations from the innermost parentheses to the outermost.

8

After performing parenthetical calculations, Excel processes operations in the order of precedence indicated in the preceding table. For example, the formula =A2+B2/C2 first divides the number in cell B2 by the number in cell C2, and then returns the sum of A2 and the result of the first operation.

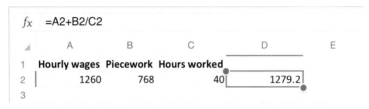

*The formula incorrectly calculates the hourly rate*

When you begin entering a formula in a cell, the Formula Bar opens automatically if it isn't already open, and the formula appears both in the cell and in the Formula Bar. If you prefer, you can enter the formula directly into the Formula Bar. While you're entering a formula that includes cell references, Excel color-codes the cells and the corresponding references so you can easily verify the data used by the formula.

*fx* = A2 + B2

|   | A | B | C | D | E |
|---|---|---|---|---|---|
| 1 | **Hourly wages** | **Piecework** | **Hours worked** | | |
| 2 | 1260 | 768 | 40 | =A2+B2 | |
| 3 | | | | | |

*Cell references and selectors are color-coded so you can more easily parse long formulas*

You can enter formula components from the standard on-screen keyboard or from an external keyboard if your iPad is connected to one. Excel also has a version of the on-screen keyboard called the *function keyboard* that contains the non-text characters most commonly used in formulas. Green corners indicate multifunction keys on the function keyboard. Pressing a multifunction key displays a list of other characters; you can insert one of these characters by sliding from the multifunction key to the character in the list. You can easily switch between the standard keyboard and the function keyboard by tapping the toggle button located at the right end of the status bar.

The standard keyboard also has multifunction keys, but they aren't labeled.

 **SEE ALSO** For information about multifunction keys on the standard on-screen keyboard, see "Enter text in documents" in Chapter 4, "Create professional documents."

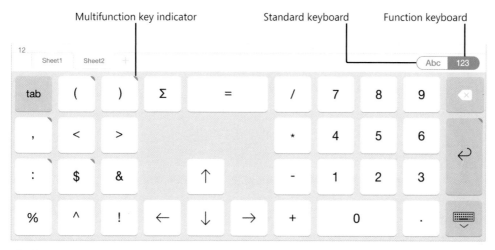

*The function keyboard*

You can begin the entry of a formula in a cell or directly in the Formula Bar. Either way, the formula appears in the Formula Bar. When you complete the formula, Excel validates it to ensure that it meets the syntactic requirements.

*The Formula Bar*

Formulas can reference cells in other worksheets within the workbook and in other workbooks. The syntax for these references is as follows:

- References to cells on other worksheets are preceded by the worksheet name (the name on the worksheet tab) and an exclamation mark. For example, the formula *=December!A2* displays the content of cell A2 of the December worksheet.

- References to other workbooks are preceded by the workbook file name, the worksheet name, and an exclamation point. The workbook name is enclosed in square brackets; that phrase and the worksheet name are enclosed in single quotes. For example, the formula *='[Sales.xlsx]December'!A2* displays the content of cell A2 of the December worksheet of the Sales workbook.

You can include the values of external cells in formulas that perform calculations, or you can simply display the values.

# Efficiently reference cells in formulas

Formulas in an Excel worksheet usually involve functions performed on the values contained in other cells on the worksheet (or on another worksheet). A reference that you make in a formula to a worksheet cell is either a relative reference, an absolute reference, or a mixed reference. It is important to understand the difference and know which to use when creating a formula.

A relative reference to a cell takes the form *A1*. When you copy, fill, or move a formula from its original cell to other cells, a relative reference changes to maintain the relationship between the cell containing the formula and the referenced cell. For example, if a formula refers to cell A1, copying the formula one row down changes the A1 reference to A2; copying the formula one column to the right changes the A1 reference to B1.

An absolute reference takes the form *$A$1*; the dollar sign indicates an unchanging reference to the column or row. When you copy, fill, or move a formula from its original cell to other cells, an absolute reference will not change—regardless of the relationship to the referenced cell, the reference stays the same. For example, if a formula refers to cell $A$1 and you fill the formula five cells to the right, the formula in each cell still refers to $A$1.

A mixed reference refers absolutely to either the column or the row and relatively to the other. The mixed reference *$A1* always refers to column A, and *A$1* always refers to row 1.

If you want help entering absolute and mixed cell references or don't want to enter a lot of dollar signs, Excel provides a simple way of changing a reference from one type to another. Follow these steps:

1. Enter any version of a cell reference (relative is easiest) in the formula.

2. Select the cell reference in the Formula Bar, and then tap the selection to display the shortcut bar.

3. On the shortcut bar, tap **Reference Types** to display a menu of reference options.

4. On the **Cell Reference Types** menu, tap any reference to replace the original reference in the Formula Bar.

It is common to use a version of one formula in multiple cells. For example, if you enter a formula in cell C2 that adds the values in cells A2 and B2, you might want to perform the same operation in row 3 and the remaining rows of the table. You can copy a formula to other cells or fill adjacent cells with the formula. When you use either method, Excel adjusts any relative references in the formula to maintain the relative relationship to the cell that contains the formula.

$fx$ =AVERAGE(B3:D3)

| | A | B | C | D | E |
|---|---|---|---|---|---|
| 1 | | | **1st Quarter** | | |
| 2 | **Name** | **Jan** | **Feb** | **Mar** | **Average** |
| 3 | Allen | $ 7,222 | $ 3,878 | $ 5,369 | $   5,490 |
| 4 | Brock | $ 3,008 | $ 5,203 | $ 7,854 | $   5,355 |
| 5 | Linda | $ 5,311 | $ 7,380 | $ 1,897 | $   4,863 |
| 6 | Max | $ 1,082 | $ 4,404 | $ 5,274 | $   3,587 |
| 7 | Nancy | $ 5,261 | $ 4,742 | $ 7,706 | $   5,903 |
| 8 | Charles | $ 4,280 | $ 7,501 | $ 3,951 | $   5,244 |
| 9 | David | $ 5,098 | $ 4,745 | $ 1,438 | |

A formula filled into adjacent cells to provide averages for each row

## To enter numbers and special symbols from the on-screen keyboard

1. To display numbers and basic symbols, tap the **Number** key (labeled **.?123**) on the left or right side of the standard on-screen keyboard.

2. On the number keyboard, tap the key corresponding to the number or symbol you want to enter.

   *Or*

   To display additional symbols, tap the **Symbol** key (labeled **#+=**) on the left or right side of the number keyboard.

## To display and use the function keyboard and use the multifunction keys

1. Switch to Edit mode to display the on-screen keyboard.

2. At the right end of the status bar, tap the **Function** button (labeled **123**).

3. Enter the visible numbers and symbols by tapping the keys.

   *Or*

To display additional symbols, tap and hold any key that has a green upper-right corner. Slide to the symbol you want to enter, and lift your finger from the screen to enter the selected symbol.

**To switch from the function keyboard to the standard keyboard**

1. At the right end of the status bar, tap the **Alphanumeric** button (labeled **Abc**).

**To enter an equation in a cell**

1. To enter the formula directly in the cell, double-tap the cell to activate it for editing and display the on-screen keyboard, and then enter an equal sign (=) to begin the formula.

   *Or*

   To enter the formula in the Formula Bar, tap the cell to select it, and then tap the **Insert Function** button at the left end of the Formula Bar to enter an equal sign (=).

   The Functions menu opens.

2. If you want to close the **Functions** menu, tap the Formula Bar or worksheet.

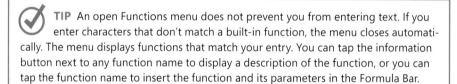

> **TIP** An open Functions menu does not prevent you from entering text. If you enter characters that don't match a built-in function, the menu closes automatically. The menu displays functions that match your entry. You can tap the information button next to any function name to display a description of the function, or you can tap the function name to insert the function and its parameters in the Formula Bar.

3. Enter the following formula elements:

   a. The first operand (a number, cell reference, or cell range)

   b. The operator

   c. The second operand

**To reference a cell or cell range in a formula**

1. To reference a single cell, do one of the following:

   • Tap the cell in the worksheet.

   • Enter the cell reference from the keyboard.

**TIP** You can enter the letter of a cell reference in uppercase or lowercase text. Excel converts it to uppercase when you complete the formula.

2. To reference a range of cells, do one of the following:

   - Tap the cell at either end of the cell range, and then drag the selection handles to select the range.

   - Enter the cell range from the keyboard.

3. After entering the cell or cell range, enter an operator or complete the formula.

### To create an absolute or mixed reference

1. Enter a dollar sign before each column letter or row number that you want to reference absolutely.

*Or*

1. In the Formula Bar, tap the reference you want to change.

2. Tap the selected reference again and then, on the shortcut bar that appears, tap **Reference Types**.

3. On the **Cell Reference Types** menu, tap the absolute or mixed reference you want to use.

 **TIP** When you're working with a cell on a worksheet, Excel is in either Ready mode, in which the cell is selected and not active for editing, or Edit mode, in which the cell is active for editing. For information about entering, working in, and exiting Ready mode and Edit mode, see "Enter and edit data on worksheets" in Chapter 7, "Store and retrieve data."

### To complete the entry of a formula

1. Use one of the following methods:

   - To complete the formula and move to the next cell, tap **Return** on the on-screen keyboard.

   - To complete the formula and select the active cell, tap the **Finish** button (labeled with a check mark) at the right end of the Formula Bar.

   - To cancel the creation of the formula and select the active cell, tap the **Cancel** button (labeled with an X) at the right end of the Formula Bar.

**To copy a formula to adjacent cells**

1. Tap the cell that contains the formula you want to copy.

>  **IMPORTANT** Ensure that the cell references in the formula are correctly entered as relative, absolute, or mixed cell references before copying the formula.

2. Tap the selected cell, and then on the shortcut menu that appears, tap **Fill**.

   Arrows appear on the bottom and right borders of the active cell.

3. Drag the bottom border of the active cell down to fill the formula to the adjacent rows or to the right to fill the formula to the adjacent columns.

>  **TIP** You can't fill formulas up or to the left in Excel for iPad as you can in the desktop versions of Excel.

## Insert formula constructs

The simplest way to familiarize yourself with the use of functions is by inserting an AutoSum formula in a data range or Excel table and then studying the results. The following functions are available as AutoSum formulas:

■ **SUM** This function returns the sum of the numeric values in the selected range.

■ **AVERAGE** This function returns the average of the numeric values in the selected range.

■ **COUNT** When invoked as an AutoSum operation, this function returns the number of cells in the selected range that contain numbers.

>  **TIP** When invoked from the Total row of an Excel table, the COUNT function returns the number of nonblank cells in the range.

■ **MAX** This function returns the largest numeric value in the selected range, ignoring logical values and text.

■ **MIN** This function returns the smallest numeric value in the selected range, ignoring logical values and text.

When you insert an AutoSum formula in a cell, Excel evaluates the surrounding data and selects the most likely data for the specified operation.

Automatically enter formulas

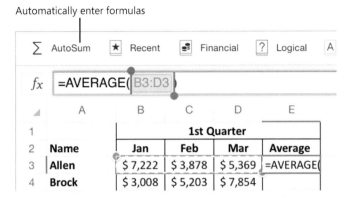

*Excel selects consecutive cells that contain numeric values as likely function arguments*

You can change the data selection to any consecutive range of cells by dragging the selection handles rather than directly editing the formula. You can include nonconsecutive cells by selecting each cell or cell range, inserting a comma after the cell reference in the Formula Bar, and then selecting the next. When you confirm the selection, Excel builds the formula for you.

**To insert an AutoSum formula**

1. Select the cell you want to display the result in.

2. On the **Formulas** tool tab, tap the **AutoSum** button, and then tap the function you want to use.

 **TIP** To use the SUM function, you can tap the Formula Bar to display the keyboard, and then tap the **AutoSum** key on the function keyboard.

3. Verify that the automatically selected range (indicated by an animated dashed outline) contains all the cells you want to include as arguments for the function. If it doesn't, do one of the following:

   - To modify the cell range from the existing selection, drag the selection handles to encompass the cells you want to include.

   - To select a different cell range, select a cell within the range you want to include and then drag the selection handles to encompass the cells.

   - To select nonconsecutive cells, select the first cell or cell range, tap the Formula Bar, insert a comma, select the next cell or cell range, and so on.

4. Complete the formula entry.

## Quickly display statistics

Selecting multiple cells displays a statistic about the selected cells at the right end of the status bar. The default statistic for numeric values is the sum, and for text values it is the number of nonblank cells within the selection.

Tapping the statistic on the status bar displays the average, count, numerical count, maximum, minimum, and sum of the selected cells.

| $3,794.00 | | |
|---|---|---|
| $1,58 | Average | 4216.650485 |
| $3,36 | | |
| $4,10 | Count | 207 |
| $88 | | |
| $2,33 | Numerical Count | 206 |
| $3,05 | Maximum | 9992 |
| $3,25 | | |
| $5,68 | Minimum | 449 |
| $1,47 | ✓ Sum | 868630 |
| $1,36 | | |

Sum : **868630**

*Status bar statistics for a table column that contains numeric values*

The status bar displays the statistic that you tap on the menu and makes it the default statistic for future selections in the same computing session.

## Build complex formulas

Functions evaluate specific arguments (values defined by parameters) and return the results of that evaluation. This sounds difficult, but Excel simplifies it by leading you through the process, providing AutoComplete suggestions for function names and specifying the required and optional parameters for a function.

 **TIP** Parameters define the required and optional data that will be evaluated by a function; arguments are the actual values that are passed for the parameters.

The functions available in Excel for iPad are divided into 10 categories: Financial, Logical, Text, Date & Time, Lookup & Reference, Math & Trig, Statistical, Engineering, Info, and Database. The categories are available from the Formulas tab or from the list that appears when you tap the More Functions button near the right end of that tab.

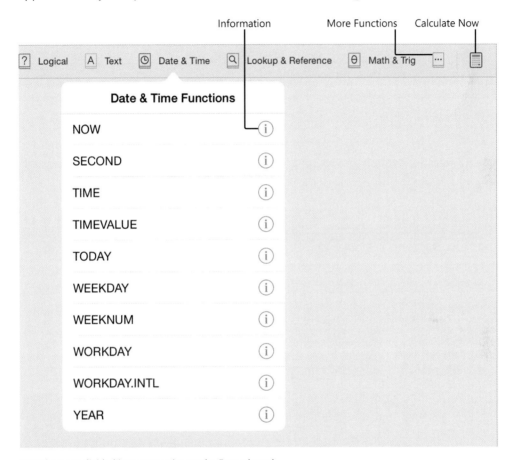

*Functions are divided into categories on the Formulas tab*

When perusing the categories of functions, you'll notice that they evaluate parameters including numbers, dates, text values, system information, and conditions. In all, more than 200 functions are available that evaluate a wide variety of parameters and return values based on the arguments provided for those parameters.

An alphabetical list of functions appears when you begin entering a function into the Formula Bar. Tapping the information icon next to a function on a category menu or function list displays the syntax for and definition of the function.

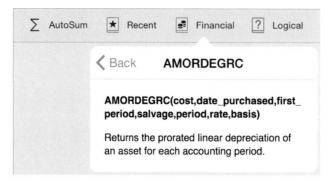

*Excel provides the syntax and description of every function to help you manually enter functions*

Tapping any function enters the function and its parameters in the Formula Bar. All you have to do is supply the arguments for the parameters. Optional parameters are in a lighter shade of gray with a dashed outline.

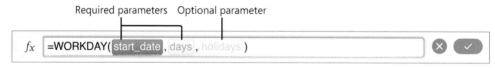

*Excel guides you through the required syntax for a formula based on the function*

### To enter a function and its parameters in the Formula Bar

1. Select the cell you want to display the result in.

2. To enter the function, do one of the following:

   - On the **Formulas** tab, tap the function category you want to display. Then flick through the category menu and tap the function you want to use.

   - Tap the **Insert Function** button, enter the first few letters of the function name, and then in the list of matching functions, tap the function you want to use.

   - To enter a function that you recently used, tap the **Recent** button on the **Formulas** tab. Then on the **Recently Used Functions** menu, tap the function you want to use.

> **TIP** You can create nested functions—functions within other functions—by enclosing the inside functions in parentheses. Use nested functions to calculate a value and pass the calculated value to another function.

## Refresh calculations manually

When using a desktop version of Excel, workbook authors can put a workbook into manual calculation mode. This mode is useful when a workbook contains either a large number of complex calculations that might slow down the program if they are automatically recalculated when data changes, or calculations that reference external sources that are unavailable or take a long time to connect to.

Excel for iPad doesn't support switching between manual calculation mode and automatic calculation mode. If you are working in a workbook that has been set to manual calculation mode, you can update the calculations within the workbook by tapping the Calculate Now button at the right end of the Formulas tab.

**8**

# Display data in charts

Charts are visual representations of data that are created by plotting data points onto a two-dimensional or three-dimensional coordinate system. Charts can be a very useful data analysis tool because they identify trends and relationships that might not be obvious from reviewing the raw data.

*A chart displaying sales by person by month and total sales for the quarter*

A single chart can reference up to 255 data series. Different types of charts are best suited for different types of data. Excel for iPad supports the creation of the following chart types:

- **Area** Displays multiple data series as cumulative layers showing change over time.

- **Bar** Displays variations in value over time or the comparative values of several items at a single point in time.

- **Column** Displays variations in value over time, or comparisons.

- **Line** Displays multiple data trends over evenly spaced intervals.

- **Pie** Displays percentages assigned to different components of a single item as wedges of a circle or doughnut. (Values must be nonnegative and nonzero, and there may be no more than seven values.)

- **Radar** Displays percentages assigned to different components of an item, radiating from a center point.

- **Stock** Displays stock market or similar activity.

- **Surface** Displays trends in values across two different dimensions in a continuous curve, such as a topographic map.

- **X Y (Scatter)** Displays correlations between independent items.

Each chart type has multiple layouts. A layout specifies which elements the chart displays and how they are arranged. Chart elements include the chart title, data labels, data table, and legend.

 **TIP** Some types of charts that plot data points onto standard XY axes are also commonly referred to as *graphs*.

# Create charts

To create a chart, all you have to do is identify the data you want to plot and specify the chart type.

If you want to create a specific type of chart, make sure that your data is correctly set up for that chart type before you start. For example, a pie chart can display only one data series, whereas a bar or column chart can display multiple data series. When you are creating a chart in Excel for iPad, the data you plot must be in a contiguous range of columns or rows. If it isn't already contiguous, you can move or hide columns and rows until it is.

If you want to plot only a subset of the data that is stored in a data range or table, you have three options: you can create a chart based on all the data and then reduce the amount of data that is included in the chart by selecting less of the data table, you can hide the data you don't want to plot and then create the chart, or you can select only the data you want to plot and then create the chart.

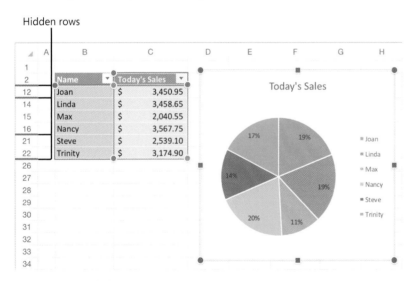

*Excel doesn't plot hidden data*

When you're ready to create the chart, you can choose a chart that Excel recommends based on an analysis of the data pattern, or you can select a chart type on your own. The thumbnails on the Recommended menu display a preview of the actual data you've selected for the chart.

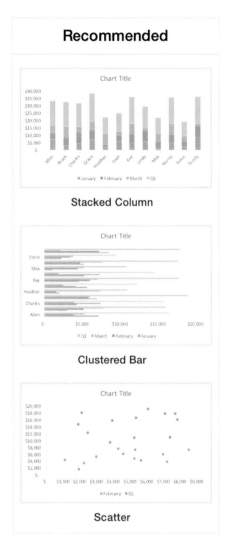

*Excel recommends charts based on your specific data*

 **TIP** The charts that Excel recommends might include combination charts that you couldn't otherwise create in Excel for iPad.

The Charts menu displays generic representations of each chart type.

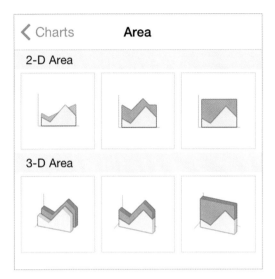

*Simple previews are available for all chart types*

**8**

**To begin plotting an entire data range or table as a chart**

1.  Locate the data range or table that contains the data you want to plot.

2.  Tap any cell in the data range or table. When you create the chart, Excel will plot all the data contained therein.

**To select part of a data range or table to plot as a chart**

1.  Locate the data range or table that contains the data you want to plot.

2.  If the data you want to plot is not in a contiguous range, organize the data by doing any of the following:

    -   Move columns or rows so the data values are adjacent to each other and to the axis values.

    -   Hide columns or rows that you don't want to plot.

3.  When the data you want to plot is arranged in a contiguous range, tap any cell in the data set.

4.  Drag the selection handles to select the data set.

**To create a chart**

1.  Select the data you want to plot.

2.  On the **Insert** tab, tap **Recommended**.

3.  Review the appearance of the selected data in the thumbnails, and then tap the specific chart configuration you want to create.

*Or*

1.  Select the data you want to plot.

2.  On the **Insert** tab, tap **Charts**.

3.  On the **Charts** menu, tap the type of chart you want to create.

4.  On the submenu, review the available versions of the selected chart type.

5.  Tap the specific chart configuration you want to create.

## Modify chart structure

The area within which the chart (and only the chart) is drawn is the *plot area*. The larger area that encompasses the plot area and any accompanying chart elements (such as the title, legend, and axis labels) is the *chart area*. The chart and chart elements change size to fit the chart area. You change the size of a chart by changing the size of the chart area. It might be necessary to specifically change the width or height to make the chart the size you want.

 **SEE ALSO** For information about displaying chart elements, see "Format charts" later in this topic.

Excel creates each chart on the same worksheet as its source data. You can move the chart to a different location on the worksheet or you can move it to its own worksheet. If you plan to present a chart, you can move it to its own worksheet, resize the chart to fill the screen, and then hide the gridlines and headings on the worksheet to focus viewers' attention on the chart.

A chart is linked to its worksheet data, so any changes you make to the plotted data are immediately reflected in the chart.

If you want to add or remove values from a chart, you simply increase or decrease the range of the plotted data in the worksheet.

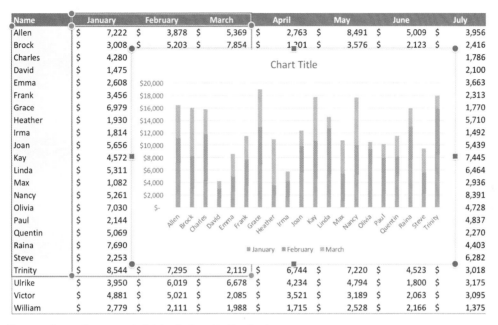

| Name | January | February | March | April | May | June | July |
|------|---------|----------|-------|-------|-----|------|------|
| Allen | $ 7,222 | $ 3,878 | $ 5,369 | $ 2,763 | $ 8,491 | $ 5,009 | $ 3,956 |
| Brock | $ 3,008 | $ 5,203 | $ 7,854 | $ 1,701 | $ 3,576 | $ 2,123 | $ 2,416 |
| Charles | $ 4,280 | | | | | | 1,786 |
| David | $ 1,475 | | | | | | 2,100 |
| Emma | $ 2,608 | | | | | | 3,663 |
| Frank | $ 3,456 | | | | | | 2,313 |
| Grace | $ 6,979 | | | | | | 1,770 |
| Heather | $ 1,930 | | | | | | 5,710 |
| Irma | $ 1,814 | | | | | | 1,492 |
| Joan | $ 5,656 | | | | | | 5,439 |
| Kay | $ 4,572 | | | | | | 7,445 |
| Linda | $ 5,311 | | | | | | 6,464 |
| Max | $ 1,082 | | | | | | 2,936 |
| Nancy | $ 5,261 | | | | | | 8,391 |
| Olivia | $ 7,030 | | | | | | 4,728 |
| Paul | $ 2,144 | | | | | | 4,837 |
| Quentin | $ 5,069 | | | | | | 2,270 |
| Raina | $ 7,690 | | | | | | 4,403 |
| Steve | $ 2,253 | | | | | | 6,282 |
| Trinity | $ 8,544 | $ 7,295 | $ 2,119 | $ 6,744 | $ 7,220 | $ 4,523 | 3,018 |
| Ulrike | $ 3,950 | $ 6,019 | $ 6,678 | $ 4,234 | $ 4,794 | $ 1,800 | 3,175 |
| Victor | $ 4,881 | $ 5,021 | $ 2,085 | $ 3,521 | $ 3,189 | $ 2,063 | 3,095 |
| William | $ 2,779 | $ 2,111 | $ 1,988 | $ 1,715 | $ 2,528 | $ 2,166 | 1,375 |

*You can change the amount of data displayed in the chart*

Charts plot data in the order that it appears in the data source. To change the order of the data in the chart, you must change it in the data source. Excel automatically updates the chart to reflect your changes.

Sometimes a chart does not illustrate the results you expect because the data series are plotted against the wrong axes; that is, Excel is plotting the data by row when it should be plotting by column, or vice versa. You can quickly switch the columns and rows to determine whether that produces the effect you want.

 **TIP** For more precise control of chart content and configuration, edit the chart in a desktop version of Excel.

### To select a chart

1. Tap the chart to select it.

    Excel displays the chart sizing handles around the chart area, and the Chart tool tab appears on the ribbon.

8

**To move a chart on its current worksheet**

1. Select the chart you want to move.

2. To roughly position the chart, drag it to its new location.

   *Or*

   To exactly position the chart, follow these steps:

   a. On the shortcut bar that appears, tap **Cut**.

   b. Tap the cell in which you want to position the upper-left corner of the chart.

   c. Tap the cell a second time to display the shortcut bar, and then tap **Paste** on the shortcut bar.

> **TIP** Tapping a chart selects the chart and its data source for editing, and displays the tools you can use to manage the chart: the Chart tool tab, the shortcut bar, and sizing handles. In the data source, shading identifies the plotted chart data and handles appear in the upper-left and lower-right corners of each data element.

**To move a chart to another worksheet**

1. If necessary, create the worksheet you want to move the chart to.

2. Select the chart you want to move.

3. On the shortcut bar that appears, tap **Cut**.

4. Switch to the worksheet you're moving the chart to.

5. Tap the cell in which you want to position the upper-left corner of the chart. Then tap the cell a second time to display the shortcut bar.

6. On the shortcut bar, tap **Paste**.

**To resize a chart**

1. Select the chart you want to resize.

2. Drag the chart sizing handles to change the height or width of the chart area.

   Excel automatically rearranges the active chart elements to fit the chart.

> **TIP** The corner sizing handles don't maintain the aspect ratio of an Excel chart as they do when you are resizing pictures and shapes. For information about resizing graphic elements, see "Insert and format pictures" in Chapter 5, "Add visual elements to documents."

**To change the order of data on a chart**

1. Display the source data.

2. Cut and paste columns or rows to put the data in the order you want to present it.

3. Tap the chart to identify the plotted chart data in the data source. If necessary, drag the handles to encompass all the data you want to plot in the chart.

**To swap chart data over the axis**

1. Select the chart you want to modify.

2. On the **Chart** tool tab, tap **Switch**.

**To change the data plotted in a chart**

1. Select the chart you want to modify.

2. In the data source, drag the selection handles to encompass only the data you want to plot in the chart.

**To replot chart data as a different type of chart**

1. Select the chart you want to modify.

2. On the **Chart** tool tab, tap the **Types** button, tap the chart type you want to create, and then tap the specific chart configuration you want.

   *Or*

   On the **Chart** tool tab, tap the **Recommended** button, and then tap the specific chart configuration you want.

**To finish editing a chart**

1. Tap anywhere on the worksheet other than the chart and its data source.

**To delete a chart**

1. Select the chart you want to delete.

2. On the shortcut menu that appears, tap **Delete**.

8

## Format charts

When you select a chart type, Excel inserts a generic version of that chart with the default colors and chart elements. You can apply predefined chart styles and color schemes, and you can modify the layout of the chart elements to convey the impression you want.

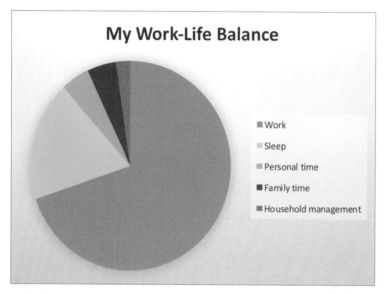

*A pie chart with a title and legend*

Chart styles configure a variety of display attributes such as the color of the chart area and data labels, the font of the chart title, the layout of chart elements, and other visual effects such as shadows that give the appearance of depth.

A chart includes many elements, some required and some optional. Each data series is represented in the chart by a unique color. You can add or modify these elements to help people understand the chart:

- A chart title can identify the chart content.

- A legend can identify the data series by color.

- Data labels next to or on the chart or a data table below the chart can identify data point values.

- Axis titles can identify the axes the data is plotted against.

- Gridlines can more precisely indicate data point values.

Other optional elements include trend and variance indicators such as trendlines, up/down bars, and error bars.

 **TIP** Data labels can clutter up all but the simplest charts. If you need to show the data for a chart on a separate chart sheet, consider using a data table instead.

Most chart elements can be displayed in multiple locations within the chart area or plot area (the area defined by the axes). You can remove any or all of the identification elements.

You can configure the display of chart elements in several ways:

- By selecting individual chart element settings from the Elements menu
- By applying a chart layout that defines the presence and position of multiple chart elements
- By applying a chart style that incorporates a chart layout

You must set the element display location in one of these ways; you can't manually position or format any of the chart elements in Excel for iPad.

**8**

### To change the style of a chart

1. Tap the chart you want to modify.
2. On the **Chart** tool tab, tap the **Styles** button.
3. On the **Styles** menu, review the available styles, noting the chart area color, the presence and position of chart elements, and any visual effects.
4. Tap the style you want to apply to your chart.

### To change the color scheme of the data series

1. Tap the chart you want to modify.
2. On the **Chart** tool tab, tap the **Colors** button.
3. On the **Colors** menu, review the available Colorful and Monochromatic color schemes.
4. Tap the color scheme you want to apply to your chart.

**To apply a preconfigured layout of chart elements**

1. Tap the chart you want to modify.

2. On the **Chart** tool tab, tap the **Layouts** button.

3. On the **Layouts** menu, review the thumbnails of the chart elements.

4. Tap the layout you want to apply.

**To configure the display of individual chart elements**

1. Tap the chart you want to modify.

2. On the **Chart** tool tab, tap the **Elements** button.

3. On the **Elements** menu, review the available chart elements.

4. Tap an available chart element that you want to configure, and then on the submenu, tap the specific location or setting you want.

 **TIP** Only the chart elements that are valid for the current chart type are available on the Elements menu. Unavailable chart elements are dimmed.

**To remove individual chart elements**

1. Tap the chart you want to modify.

2. On the **Chart** tool tab, tap the **Elements** button.

3. On the **Elements** menu, tap the chart element you want to remove, and then tap **None**.

# Display data from PivotTables

PivotTables are excellent tools for displaying views of multidimensional data. In other words, by using PivotTables you can look at a lot of data in a lot of different ways. More importantly, PivotTables make it easy to display many combinations of data fields and help you turn data into information.

You might think of a PivotTable as a kind of Rubik's Cube, with each colored side representing a data field. In the same way that you can turn each section of the Rubik's Cube to display different combinations of colors on the faces of the cube, you can group, filter, and sequence data in a PivotTable.

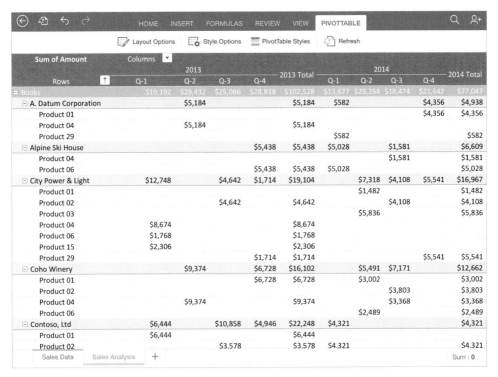

| Sum of Amount | Columns | | | | | | | | | | |
|---|---|---|---|---|---|---|---|---|---|---|---|
| | | 2013 | | | | 2013 Total | 2014 | | | | 2014 Total |
| Rows | | Q-1 | Q-2 | Q-3 | Q-4 | | Q-1 | Q-2 | Q-3 | Q-4 | |
| ⊟ Books | | $19,192 | $29,432 | $25,086 | $28,818 | $102,528 | $13,677 | $23,254 | $18,474 | $21,642 | $77,047 |
| ⊟ A. Datum Corporation | | | $5,184 | | | $5,184 | $582 | | | $4,356 | $4,938 |
| Product 01 | | | | | | | | | | $4,356 | $4,356 |
| Product 04 | | | $5,184 | | | $5,184 | | | | | |
| Product 29 | | | | | | | $582 | | | | $582 |
| ⊟ Alpine Ski House | | | | | $5,438 | $5,438 | $5,028 | | $1,581 | | $6,609 |
| Product 04 | | | | | | | | | $1,581 | | $1,581 |
| Product 06 | | | | | $5,438 | $5,438 | $5,028 | | | | $5,028 |
| ⊟ City Power & Light | | $12,748 | | $4,642 | $1,714 | $19,104 | | $7,318 | $4,108 | $5,541 | $16,967 |
| Product 01 | | | | | | | | $1,482 | | | $1,482 |
| Product 02 | | | | $4,642 | | $4,642 | | | $4,108 | | $4,108 |
| Product 03 | | | | | | | | $5,836 | | | $5,836 |
| Product 04 | | $8,674 | | | | $8,674 | | | | | |
| Product 06 | | $1,768 | | | | $1,768 | | | | | |
| Product 15 | | $2,306 | | | | $2,306 | | | | | |
| Product 29 | | | | | $1,714 | $1,714 | | | | $5,541 | $5,541 |
| ⊟ Coho Winery | | | $9,374 | | $6,728 | $16,102 | | $5,491 | $7,171 | | $12,662 |
| Product 01 | | | | | $6,728 | $6,728 | | $3,002 | | | $3,002 |
| Product 02 | | | | | | | | | $3,803 | | $3,803 |
| Product 04 | | | $9,374 | | | $9,374 | | | $3,368 | | $3,368 |
| Product 06 | | | | | | | | $2,489 | | | $2,489 |
| ⊟ Contoso, Ltd | | $6,444 | | $10,858 | $4,946 | $22,248 | $4,321 | | | | $4,321 |
| Product 01 | | $6,444 | | | | $6,444 | | | | | |
| Product 02 | | | | $3.578 | | $3.578 | $4.321 | | | | $4.321 |

Sales Data  Sales Analysis  +  Sum : 0

*A PivotTable displaying sales of products to customers, grouped by category*

---

 **SEE ALSO** For information about the history of the Rubik's Cube (and how to solve one), visit Rubik's official website at *www.rubiks.com.*

---

For example, an online retailer might store the following data about inventory items in Excel:

- Product information such as name, category, supplier, wholesale price, retail price, shipping weight, material, size, color, pattern, height, width, depth, and whether the item is breakable

- Target market information such as gender, age, and location

- Performance information such as sales volume, sales location, return percentage, and reason for return

If the retailer's marketing manager can extract useful information from that data, the marketing team can plan targeted campaigns that build on historical purchasing trends. It would be a lot of work to plan and assemble all the reports that might be pertinent to this effort. This is where PivotTables are valuable. By using a PivotTable, the retailer can quickly and easily identify useful information such as:

- Items sold in the month of January of any year, grouped by state

- Sales volume of books purchased by men in the Southwest region of the United States

- All items that have a return rate of more than 25 percent, grouped by supplier

- Clothing items for women that have sold more than 1,000 units per year with a return rate of less than 5 percent

- Gift items that weigh less than 2 pounds and have a profit margin of more than 30 percent

The key to a useful PivotTable is the data storage structure. PivotTables can reference data stored in the workbook or in an external database. The data that is referenced in the PivotTable must be stored in a simple, logical structure to return clean results.

You can't create a PivotTable in Excel for iPad, but you can work with a PivotTable that was created in a desktop version of Excel. You can expand and collapse groups, filter the data to display specific fields, sort the data in groups by field, and drill down from the PivotTable to the details of specific data points. You can modify the structure of the PivotTable to display data differently, and you can change the color scheme applied to the table. If the PivotTable is based on external data, you can refresh the connection to update the results.

> ⚠ **IMPORTANT** At the time of this writing, you can't add fields to a PivotTable or pivot the data in Excel for iPad. To optimize a PivotTable for display on an iPad, the PivotTable creator should include all fields that people are likely to want to use as filter or sort criteria.

PivotTables can be structured in many ways. All PivotTables consist of at least two fields of information, but most include groups and subgroups. You can expand the groups and subgroups to display more detailed information, or you can collapse them to display only summary information.

Depending on the design of a PivotTable, a button called a Pivot Filter might be located in the top row, the first column, or both locations. Pivot Filters are similar in appearance and functionality to the Sort & Filter buttons in Excel table column headers.

| Sum of Amount | Columns ▼ | | |
|---|---|---|---|
| Rows ↑ | 2013 | 2014 | Grand Total |
| ⊞ Books | $102,528 | $77,047 | $179,575 |
| ⊞ Computer Peripherals | $35,564 | $32,536 | $68,100 |
| ⊞ Computer Software | $85,654 | $55,074 | $140,728 |
| ⊞ Data Storage Media | $32,322 | $35,105 | $67,427 |
| ⊞ Food & Beverages | $53,122 | $39,606 | $92,728 |
| ⊞ Furniture | $57,908 | $44,715 | $102,623 |
| ⊞ Printing Supplies | $56,168 | $30,466 | $86,634 |
| ⊞ Small Appliances | $56,778 | $74,037 | $130,815 |
| **Grand Total** | **$480,044** | **$388,586** | **$868,630** |

*The PivotTable collapsed to show only the primary groups and grand totals*

Some PivotTables include one or more Report Filters above the column headers. Report Filters display lists of the entries in a specific field. You can filter the displayed content by selecting fields from either of these tools. Using filters limits the data displayed to only those cells that meet selected criteria.

A filter symbol on a Pivot Filter button indicates that the column or row is filtered.

*You can sort and filter at the selected level*

You can modify five different aspects of the structure of a PivotTable:

- The display of subtotals for groups

- The display of grand totals for columns and rows

- The form of the PivotTable: compact, outline, or tabular

- The frequency of item labels

- The display of blank rows after items

*A PivotTable in tabular form with blank rows between items and without grand totals*

You can apply the same styles to PivotTables as you can to Word tables and Excel tables. You can choose to emphasize the row headers, emphasize the column headers, band the rows, and band the columns.

> **TIP** The style options available for Excel PivotTables are very similar to those for Excel and Word tables. For information about applying table styles and selecting style options, see "Present content in tables" in Chapter 5, "Add visual elements to documents," and "Create and manage Excel tables," earlier in this chapter.

### To display more or less detail in a PivotTable

1. In the row headers or column headers, tap any header at the level you want to modify.

2. Do either of the following:

   - To display the next level of detail for all groups at the selected level, tap **Expand** on the shortcut menu.

   - To hide the next level of detail for all groups at the selected level, tap **Collapse** on the shortcut menu.

### To display more or less detail for a specific group in a PivotTable

1. To expand a collapsed group, tap the plus sign (+) on the group's header.

2. To collapse an expanded group, tap the minus sign (–) on the group's header.

### To display only specific fields in a PivotTable

1. In the row headers or column headers, tap any entry at the level you want to filter.

2. In the first column or row of the table, tap the **Pivot Filter** button.

 **TIP** If necessary, tap the ribbon to hide the shortcut menu without selecting a different cell.

3. On the **Pivot Filter** menu, do any of the following:

   - Tap **(Select All)** to display or hide all entries.

 **TIP** A green check mark indicates that a field is selected.

   - Tap a specific field to display or hide that field.

### To display all fields in a PivotTable

1. Tap any **Pivot Filter** button that displays a filter icon.

2. On the **Pivot Filter** menu, tap **Clear Filter**.

3. Repeat steps 1 and 2 to clear any additional filters.

**To change the layout of a PivotTable**

1. On the **PivotTable** tool tab, tap the **Layout Options** button.

2. On the **Layout Options** menu, do any of the following:

   - Tap **Grand Totals**, and then tap either **Off for Rows and Columns**, **On for Rows and Columns**, **On for Rows Only**, or **On for Columns Only**.

   - Tap **Subtotals**, and then tap either **Do Not Show Subtotals**, **Show all Subtotals at Bottom of Group**, or **Show all Subtotals at Top of Group**.

   - Tap **Report Layout**. In the top section of the menu, tap either **Show in Compact Form**, **Show in Outline Form**, or **Show in Tabular Form**. In the bottom section of the menu, tap either **Repeat All Item Labels** or **Do Not Repeat Item Labels**.

   - Tap **Blank Rows**, and then tap either **Insert Blank Line after Each Item** or **Remove Blank Line after Each Item**.

> **TIP** If the PivotTable you're working with is connected to an external data source, you can update the PivotTable to reflect changes to the source data by refreshing the connection. To refresh the connection, tap Refresh on the PivotTable tool tab, or tap any cell and then tap Refresh on the shortcut menu.

# Collaborate on workbook content

Excel for iPad doesn't have the robust coauthoring features of Word for iPad—only one person can actively edit a workbook at a time. However, multiple people can display and move around in a locked copy of the workbook. When a second person opens a workbook from a shared storage location, a message box provides the information that the file is locked, and displays these options for working in the locked file:

- **Read-Only** This option opens the file as read-only. You can display the file content and move around in the file. You can also make changes in the file—you simply can't save those changes in the locked workbook. Instead, you can save a separate copy of the modified file with another name or in another location.

- **Duplicate** Save a duplicate copy of the file that you can work in.

Recent desktop versions of Excel include a change-tracking function that highlights changes as users make them. Excel for iPad doesn't support this feature. When you open a workbook that contains tracked changes, Excel opens a read-only copy and displays an information bar to inform you that the file contains content that isn't supported by Excel for iPad. You can close the information bar and work in a read-only copy of the workbook, or you can save a copy of the workbook that doesn't include the tracked changes, and edit the copy.

Workbooks that were created or edited in a desktop version of Excel might contain comments attached to specific worksheet cells. Hidden comments are indicated by a red triangle in the upper-right corner of a cell, and by a comment icon when the cell is selected.

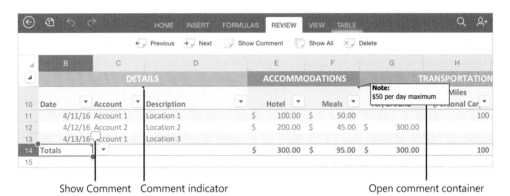

You can review and delete comments created in other versions of Excel

You can't create or edit comments on a worksheet in Excel for iPad, but you can display, review, and delete them by using the commands on the Review tab of the ribbon.

 **SEE ALSO** For more information about comments, see "Collaborate on document content" in Chapter 6, "Enhance document content."

### To move among comments in a workbook

1. On the **Review** tab, tap **Previous** or **Next**.

 **TIP** Tapping the Previous or Next button moves among all the comments on all the worksheets in the workbook.

**To display or hide a comment**

1. Tap the cell the comment is attached to.

2. Tap the comment icon that appears outside the upper-right corner of the cell.

   *Or*

   On the **Review** tab, tap **Show Comment**.

**To display all comments in the workbook**

1. On the **Review** tab, tap **Show All**.

**To delete a comment**

1. Tap the cell the comment is attached to.

   *Or*

   Tap the open comment container.

2. On the **Review** tab, tap **Delete**.

> **TIP** Tapping an active comment container displays gray handles on the sides and in the corners. The handles are inactive in Excel for iPad. You can modify the comment containers by using these handles in other versions of Excel.

# Skills review

In this chapter, you learned how to:

- Create and manage Excel tables
- Perform data-processing operations
- Display data in charts
- Display data from PivotTables
- Collaborate on workbook content

# Practice tasks

The practice files for these tasks are located in the iPadOfficeSBS\Ch08 folder.

## Create and manage Excel tables

Start Excel, open the CreateTables workbook, and then perform the following tasks:

1. Format the range A2:M23 as a table with headers. Notice the default table style.

2. Apply a table style from the **Dark** category.

3. Add a Total row to the table. Notice that Excel inserts the sum of the December sales at the bottom of the *Dec* column.

4. Select the **Average** statistic in cell M24 to display the average sales per person in December. Review the formula in the Formula Bar.

5. In the Total row, insert a calculation from the list for each column. Include at least one instance of each of the eight options.

6. Delete row 22 from the table, and note the changes to the Total row values.

7. Convert the table to a data range.

8. Create a blank table in cells O2:Q10. Apply a table style from the **Light** category.

9. Extend the blank table by adding two columns to the right edge, and then insert a blank row anywhere inside the table.

## Perform data-processing operations

Open the ProcessData workbook, and then perform the following tasks:

1. Review the *Schedule* worksheet, which provides a structure for scheduling the creation of three products that go through eight process phases. Specifically notice the following:

   - Cell B3 contains the project start date.

   - Column C is empty.

   - E3:L3 contain the phase numbers.

   - E4:L4 contain the corresponding process names.

   - E5:L5 contain the number of days required to complete each process.

2.  If cell E6 displays ###, AutoFit column E to display the date in the cell.

3.  Select cell E6 and review the formula in the Formula Bar. Notice that it calculates the Phase 1 (Design) completion date for Product 1 (Widgets) based on the project start date and the number of days allocated to the Design phase.

4.  Copy the formula from cell E6 to E7 and then evaluate the formula. Notice that the relative reference tries to calculate the date based on the empty cell B4 and the date in E6.

> 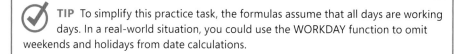 **TIP** To simplify this practice task, the formulas assume that all days are working days. In a real-world situation, you could use the WORKDAY function to omit weekends and holidays from date calculations.

5.  Edit the formula in cell E6 to absolutely reference the project start date ($B$3).

6.  Edit the formula in cell E7 to =E6+E5. This indicates that the Design team will complete work on Product 1 and then start work on Product 2.

7.  Fill the formula from cell E7 to E8 and then evaluate the formula. Notice that the relative formula tries to add E7 to E6.

8.  Edit the formula in cell E7 to absolutely reference cell E5 ($E$5) so that it always adds the number of days specified in cell E5 to the completion date of the previous product. Then fill the formula from cell E7 to E8 and verify that the date returned is *12-Feb* (February 12).

>  **TIP** AutoFit columns after copying or filling formulas if necessary to display the formula results.

9.  Fill only the formula (but not the formatting) from cell E6 to cell F6, and then evaluate it. Notice that it calculates the Phase 2 (Review) completion date based on the project start date instead of the Phase 1 completion date.

10. Edit the formula in cell F6 to =E6+$F$5 so that it adds the specified number of Review days to the previous phase completion date.

11. Copy the formula from F6 to F7 and F8 and verify the calculated dates.

12. Copy the formulas from cells F6:F8 to cells G6:G8, and then evaluate them. Notice that they add four days instead of three.

13. In cell F6, change $F$5 to a mixed reference that always references row 5 of the current column. Then repeat steps 11 and 12 and notice the change in the Document phase dates.

14. Copy the formula from G6:G8 through the remaining project phases and verify that the Delivery date for Product 3, in cell L8, is March 11. Notice that the formula is =K8+L$5.

15. Select column C and delete it. Notice that the formula in cell K8 automatically changes to =J8+K$5 to account for the deleted column.

16. If you want to, update the schedule to use the WORKDAY function, which takes the form **=WORKDAY(*start_date*, *number_of_days*)**. The final completion date should be April 8.

17. Experiment with changing the start date in cell B3 and the number of days for each process.

## Display data in charts

Open the CreateCharts workbook, and then perform the following tasks:

1. Create a bar chart of your choice based on the entire table. Then move the bar chart to the right of the table.

2. Correct the order of the data in the bar chart by moving the September data in column D to follow the August data in column J.

3. Swap the bar chart data over the axis. Notice that both versions of the bar chart are difficult to read due to the number of data points on each axis.

4. Change the bar chart to a clustered column chart layout that displays the salespeople's names on the x-axis.

5. Change the clustered column chart to a stacked column chart, and notice the immensely improved readability of the chart.

6. Modify the column chart to include only data from January through June.

7. Apply some of the available chart styles to the column chart. Finish by applying the style that you like best.

8. Apply any monochromatic color set to the column chart. Consider the effect this has on the information presented by the chart.

9. Apply any layout that includes a chart title and a data table. Review the information in the data table, and then remove it from the chart area.

10. Create a line chart of your choice based only on the data in columns A and B of the table.

11. Move the line chart to the *January Sales Chart* worksheet and resize it to about 25 percent larger. Notice that the chart still references the Sales data in the table on the *Sales* worksheet.

12. Apply various chart types to the line chart and consider the benefits of each chart type. Finish by applying the chart type and style you like the best.

## Display data from PivotTables

Open the PivotData workbook, and then perform the following tasks:

1. Review the table on the *Sales Data* worksheet, and then review the information in the PivotTable on the *Sales Analysis* worksheet. Consider the relationship between the table and the PivotTable.

2. On the *Sales Analysis* worksheet, collapse the Books category.

3. In the Computer Peripherals group, expand the customer records to display the specific products sold to each customer.

4. Use the Columns Pivot Filter to display only data from 2014.

5. Collapse the columns to display only the full year and not the quarters. Then collapse the rows to display only the product categories. Notice that the overview of information is clear and concise, and consider the detail you can drill down to.

6. Change the layout of the PivotTable to display grand totals for rows but not for columns.

## Collaborate on workbook content

Open the ReviewComments workbook, and then perform the following tasks:

1. Move among the comments in the workbook. Notice that hidden comments appear only while they are active for review.

2. Hide the *$50 per day maximum* comment. Then display all the comments in the workbook.

3. Delete any one of the comments.

# Part 4

# Microsoft PowerPoint for iPad

# Create compelling presentations

PowerPoint presentations are no longer used solely by business executives to present information at board meetings. They're commonly used in business and educational settings to share information, not only in group presentations, but also in electronic communications and online settings. Because of the way that elements on a PowerPoint slide float independently, PowerPoint presentations offer simpler options for creatively presenting information than Word documents and have become an alternative delivery format for reports. Even primary school students are assigned PowerPoint presentations as homework projects.

There are many methods by which you can convey information on PowerPoint slides. Gone are the days of presenters reading a list of bullet points to the audience—now you can use images, diagrams, animations, charts, tables, and other visual elements. Presenters can concentrate on delivering the details, which can be conveniently documented in the speaker notes attached to the slides.

This chapter guides you through procedures related to creating presentations and slides; presenting information on slides by using text, tables, and animated graphics; inserting video content on slides; and managing the playback of audio and video recordings.

## In this chapter

- Create presentations
- Create and manage slides
- Add text to slides
- Add visual elements to slides

## Practice files

For this chapter, use the practice files from the iPadOfficeSBS\Ch09 folder. For practice file download instructions, see the Introduction.

# The PowerPoint feature set

Microsoft has created multiple versions of PowerPoint that are optimized for various computer, mobile device, and online platforms. The functionality available in each version varies—the version of PowerPoint designed for computers running Windows has the full feature set, and the versions designed for other platforms have less functionality. You can display presentations in all versions, but the extent of the elements that you can create and fully utilize varies. Here is a brief comparison of the features of the versions of PowerPoint you're likely to have access to if you're reading this book.

## PowerPoint for iPad features

After you sign in to the Office apps by using a Microsoft account, you can do the following:

- Create presentations from built-in templates.

- Save presentations on your iPad or on your OneDrive, OneDrive for Business, SharePoint, or Dropbox site.

- Edit presentations in Normal view (only), and display presentations in Slide Show view.

- Add slides to a presentation, rearrange slides, and remove slides from a presentation.

- Apply built-in themes and slide background colors, and display slide background images.

- Insert, modify, and format tables, text boxes, and shapes.

- Align slide elements by using Smart Guides that indicate the position of an element relative to other elements and to the page.

- Enter, edit, and format text.

- Insert, modify, and format pictures that are available on your iPad.

- Add, change, and remove slide transitions.

- Play slide animations.

- Insert video recordings that are available on your iPad, resize and move video images on slides, and play videos on slides or in full-screen view while presenting.

- Play audio recordings on slides while presenting, and control the volume of audio and video recordings during playback.

- Remove audio and video recordings from slides.

- Display and move among comments.

- Document speaker notes for each slide.

- Personalize presentations by hiding slides and changing the slide aspect ratio.

- Use presenter tools to annotate or pause a presentation.

- Print slides and presentations to AirPrint printers.

- Email copies of presentations in PowerPoint or PDF file format.

The following premium features require that you sign in by using an account that is associated with a qualified Office 365 subscription:

- Display presentations, upcoming slide thumbnails, and speaker notes in Presenter View.

- Format shapes by applying custom line and fill colors.

- Insert and edit WordArt.

- Add shadows and reflection styles to pictures.

- Apply shading to individual table cells.

- Add and modify chart elements.

9

## PowerPoint Online features

In addition to the features that are available in PowerPoint for iPad, you can use PowerPoint Online to do the following:

- Create presentations from online templates and download copies of presentations to your computer.

- Change the slide layout of a slide and apply slide background images.

- Modify color schemes by applying theme variants.

- Insert common symbols, local images, and online images.

- Create SmartArt graphics and reorder animation effects.

- Insert and reply to comments on slides, and review presentations in Reading view.

- Embed a presentation in a blog or on a webpage.

PowerPoint Online has fewer slide transitions and animation effects than the PowerPoint for iPad app. For more information, visit *technet.microsoft.com/en-us/library/PowerPoint-online-service-description.aspx*. To start using any of the Office Online apps, go to *www.office.com/start*.

## PowerPoint desktop version features

The desktop versions of PowerPoint—PowerPoint 2011 on a Mac computer and PowerPoint 2013 on a computer running Windows—have the most functionality. You can use PowerPoint 2013 to do the following:

- Create presentations from a greater variety of online templates or by importing content from a Word document, save presentations in a wide variety of formats and locations, and export presentations as videos, handouts, or packaged for delivery on a CD.

- Configure options for the appearance and functionality of the PowerPoint working environment.

- Display and manage slide elements in the Selection pane, and align slide elements with gridlines.

- Create and edit slide masters and slide layouts, handout masters, and notes masters.

- Organize slides in sections, manage slides in Slide Sorter view, review content in Outline view, and work on a presentation in multiple windows.

- Find and replace content within a presentation.

- Insert tables of a specific size, draw tables, and create tables from data stored on Excel worksheets.

- Capture and insert screen shots and screen clippings; insert equations, a wide variety of symbols, Flash animations, the date and time, the slide number, or the contents of an external file.

- Apply gradient, texture, and pattern slide backgrounds.

- Create and edit charts based on data that PowerPoint saves with the presentation.

- Assign actions that occur when the presenter points to or clicks a slide element.

- Manage the sound, duration, and trigger action for slide transitions and slide element animations, and manage animations in the Animation pane.

- Create headers and footers for slides, notes, and handouts.

- Insert audio and video recordings from online sources, record audio directly in a presentation, and edit audio and video recordings.

- Record, edit, and run macros.

- Create custom slide shows, configure slide show settings for different methods of presentation, rehearse slide timings and record your presentation of a slide show, including audio narrations and gestures.

- Compare a presentation with previous versions.

- Create a grayscale version of a presentation to optimize it for print.

- Create notes in a OneNote notebook that link to specific slide content.

9

# Create presentations

When creating a new presentation, you can create a blank presentation or create a presentation that is based on a template. Unlike the templates provided for Word and Excel, PowerPoint templates are most commonly design templates that control thematic elements (colors, fonts, and graphic effects) and slide layouts rather than content templates designed to give you a head start when creating purpose-specific documents or workbooks. Each template has a corresponding theme, so you can create a presentation based on one template but then entirely change its appearance by applying a different theme.

> **TIP** If you're using an external keyboard with your iPad, you can perform many operations by using keyboard shortcuts. For a complete list of keyboard shortcuts, see the Appendix, "Touchscreen and keyboard shortcuts."

An important thing to be aware of when you create a presentation in PowerPoint is that you have the choice of two slide aspect ratios, which are referred to (slightly inaccurately) as *slide sizes*. The default slide size is Widescreen (16:9), which is optimized for narrow rectangular displays such as those found on many laptop screens and desktop monitors these days.

*Widescreen slides are shorter than Standard slides*

The alternative slide size is Standard (4:3), which is optimized for wide rectangular screens such as that of the iPad.

> ⚠️ **IMPORTANT** You perform many tasks in Word for iPad, Excel for iPad, and PowerPoint for iPad by using the same processes. Common processes include those for giving commands in the Office user interface and for opening, saving, searching, and distributing files. For more information, see Chapter 3, "Create and manage files."

**Standard slide size**

- ▶ 4:3 aspect ratio
- ▶ Matches screen resolutions such as:
    - ▶ 800 x 600
    - ▶ 1024 x 768 (1st/2nd generation iPad)
    - ▶ 1152 x 864
    - ▶ 1600 x 1200
    - ▶ 2048 x 1536 (3rd generation iPad)
    - ▶ 2560 x 1920
- ▶ Matches the aspect ratio of the iPad screen
- ▶ Exactly fills the screen in the Slide pane and when presented on an iPad

*Standard slides fit the iPad screen*

When you display the built-in templates on the New page of the Backstage view, the Slide Size setting appears in the upper-right corner of the page. You can change the setting to display the template thumbnails at each slide size.

It's advisable to select the slide size before you tap a template thumbnail, because tapping the thumbnail creates the slide deck. You can change the slide size after you create the slide deck, but doing so might cause graphic elements (especially those on master slides) to look different, and text and other slide elements to not fit on slides as intended. In other words, if you're going to change the slide size of a presentation, it's best to do it before you create the content.

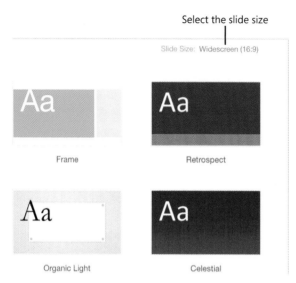

*Tap the slide size to display the alternative option*

If you find it necessary to change the slide size of a presentation to best fit the display you're presenting it on, you can easily do so. Remember, though, that you'll need to carefully review the slides to ensure that your original content still fits. The desktop versions of PowerPoint give you the option of scaling slide content to fit the new slide size; PowerPoint for iPad doesn't currently provide this option.

> **IMPORTANT** Images that are part of the slide layout rather than the content sitting on top of the layout will be squeezed (when changing from Widescreen slide size to Standard) or stretched (when changing from Standard slide size to Widescreen) when the slide size changes. You can correct the problem by changing the Scale Width setting for affected pictures on the slide masters, which you can edit in the desktop versions of PowerPoint. The Scale Width setting is available from the Size & Position task pane for the picture.

The 19 templates that are built in to PowerPoint for iPad have unique color schemes, font sets, and graphic elements. None of the built-in templates include text or any content other than the placeholders and graphic elements on the slide layouts. You can get a good idea of the thematic elements from the thumbnails displayed on the New page of the Backstage view.

The thumbnails depict the title slide layout, graphic elements, and the theme fonts—the uppercase letter represents the Headings font (the default font for headings) and the lowercase letter represents the Body font (the default font for regular text). The other slide layouts generally use similar but sleeker versions of the title slide graphics.

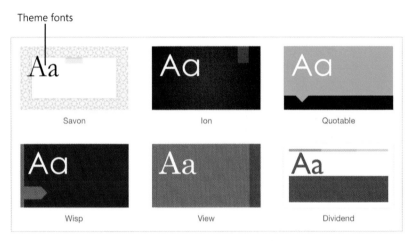

*The basic thematic elements of the built-in templates are featured on the title slide thumbnails*

Notice that PowerPoint for iPad doesn't have a Blank template option like that available in Word and Excel. There is no Blank template because every template includes predefined slide layouts in addition to the color and font settings. The Office Light template is the closest match to a blank presentation; it has black text on white slides, uses the default Office fonts—Calibri Light for headings and Calibri for body content—and has no colors or graphic elements integrated with the slide layouts. The Office Dark template is identical to Office Light, other than that it has white text on black slides. If you're planning to design your own unique template, one of these would be a good place to start.

> **✓ TIP** A few additional design templates are available for PowerPoint Online, and more than 300 templates are available for PowerPoint for Windows. Some of the PowerPoint 2013 templates include both content and design specifications. For information about creating files from the online and desktop versions of the Office apps, see "Create documents from templates" in Chapter 4, "Create professional documents."

When you create a presentation from a design template, the only slide that is immediately available is the title slide. This slide is visible in the Thumbnails pane on the left side of the app window and in the Slide pane that takes up most of the window.

*A title slide in the PowerPoint for iPad app window*

The width of the Thumbnails pane is fixed in PowerPoint for iPad. You can't change the relationship between the Thumbnails pane and the Slide pane by dragging the divider.

> **TIP** The Notes pane is below the Slide pane but is collapsed by default. For information about working in the Notes pane, see "Add notes to slides" in Chapter 10, "Prepare and deliver slide shows."

> **SEE ALSO** For information about saving and duplicating Office files, see "Create, open, and save files" in Chapter 3, "Create and manage files."

**To create a new presentation**

1. On the **New** page of the Backstage view, on the **File** bar, tap **New**.

2. In the upper-right corner of the window, tap **Slide Size**, and then tap either **Widescreen (16:9)** or **Standard (4:3)** depending on your intended presentation method. If in doubt, tap **Standard** because it creates a narrower slide; if you later need to change the slide size, the slide content is likely to fit on a widescreen slide.

3. Locate and then tap the thumbnail of the presentation template you want to use.

**To change the slide size of a presentation**

1. On the **Design** tab, tap the **Slide Size** button, and then tap **Standard (4:3)** or **Widescreen (16:9)**.

2. Review your slides for any content that might have shifted due to the change in aspect ratio.

# Create and manage slides

9

If you're accustomed to using a desktop version of PowerPoint, one of the first differences you might notice in the PowerPoint for iPad environment is that you can develop and manage slides in Normal view only. This view displays thumbnails of the existing slides in the Thumbnails pane on the left side of the window and a larger version of the currently selected slide in the Slide pane. You insert, cut, copy, paste, duplicate, and delete slides in the Thumbnails pane, and create slide content in the Slide pane.

The appearance and structure of slides is defined by the slide layouts associated with the design template. Slide layouts define the elements on specific types of slides, such as:

- Slide backgrounds and incorporated graphics.

- Text box locations, sizes, and formats.

- Default paragraph and character formats for each text box location.

- Standard headers or footers.

> **TIP** Text boxes can contain static content that can't be changed by the presentation author (for example, a company logo) or serve as placeholders that define the default formatting of content entered within the text box.

A template could have only one slide layout, but most have unique slide layouts for slides that display the presentation title, section titles, and various combinations of slide titles and content, and a blank slide with only the background. Each slide layout is named; the name suggests the primary application of the slide layout, but you aren't limited to that suggestion; you can enter any type of content in any slide layout and modify the layout of any slide. The slide layouts that are available in a presentation are displayed on the New Slide menu.

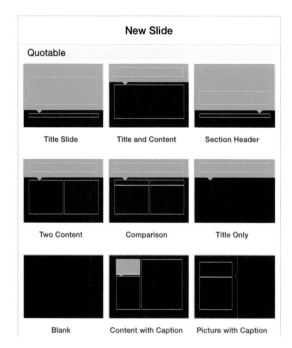

*The structure and design of each slide layout is visible on its thumbnail*

In the desktop versions of PowerPoint, you can modify the built-in slide layouts, create your own slide layouts, or create entirely new sets of slide layouts called slide masters, and you can reset slides to match their slide layouts, or apply different slide layouts to existing slides.

You can't edit or create slide layouts in PowerPoint for iPad, but you can arrange and format text, placeholders, and graphic elements on a slide and then duplicate that slide for each similar slide you want to create.

You add a slide to a presentation by selecting the layout of the slide you want to create. The new slide is inserted after the current slide; if necessary, you can move it to a different location within the presentation.

If you create a slide and then later realize that you don't need it, you can delete it. If you don't need the slide for a presentation to a specific audience but might need it later, you can hide the slide instead. Hidden slides aren't presented in slide shows. They remain available from the Thumbnails pane, but their thumbnails are dimmed and marked with a prohibition sign (⊘), which is also referred to as the *universal no symbol*.

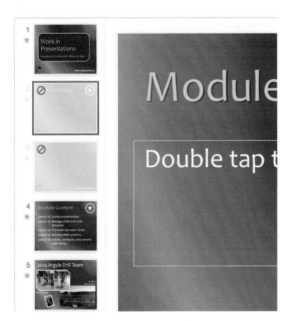

*Hidden slide content is active and editable*

When you select a hidden slide, the Hide Slide button on the Slide Show tab is shaded to indicate that the command is in effect. You can edit a hidden slide in the Slide pane just as you can any other, so you might use this feature to keep a slide that you're still working on hidden until it's final. You can unhide a slide to include it in the slide show.

**To add a slide to a presentation**

1. In the **Thumbnails** pane, tap the slide that you want to insert the new slide after.

2. On the **Home** tab or the **Insert** tab, tap **New Slide**.

3. On the **New Slide** menu, tap the thumbnail of the slide layout you want to insert. (Flick the menu up and down if necessary to display all the slide layouts.)

**To select and display a slide**

1. In the **Thumbnails** pane, tap the slide to select it for modification and display it in the **Slide** pane.

**To move a slide within a presentation**

1. In the **Thumbnails** pane, tap and hold the slide that you want to move, until the thumbnail increases slightly in size.

2. Drag the thumbnail to its new position in the **Thumbnails** pane.

*Or*

1. Select the slide that you want to move.

2. In the **Thumbnails** pane, tap the selected slide to display the shortcut bar.

3. On the shortcut bar, tap **Cut**.

4. In the **Thumbnails** pane, select the slide that you want to move the cut slide after.

5. Tap the selected slide and then, on the shortcut bar, tap **Paste**.

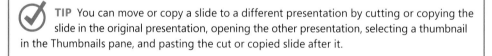 **TIP** You can move or copy a slide to a different presentation by cutting or copying the slide in the original presentation, opening the other presentation, selecting a thumbnail in the Thumbnails pane, and pasting the cut or copied slide after it.

**To insert a copy of a slide immediately following the original slide**

1. Select the slide that you want to copy.

2. In the **Thumbnails** pane, tap the selected slide and then, on the shortcut bar, tap **Duplicate**.

**To insert a copy of a slide elsewhere in the presentation**

1.  Select the slide that you want to copy.

2.  In the **Thumbnails** pane, tap the selected slide and then, on the shortcut bar, tap **Copy**.

3.  In the **Thumbnails** pane, select the slide that you want to place the copied slide after.

4.  Tap the selected slide and then, on the shortcut bar, tap **Paste**.

>  **TIP** Repeat steps 3 and 4 to paste additional copies of the slide into the presentation.

**To delete a slide**

1.  Select the slide that you want to delete.

2.  In the **Thumbnails** pane, tap the selected slide and then, on the shortcut bar, tap **Delete**.

**To hide a slide**

1.  Select the slide that you want to hide.

2.  In the **Thumbnails** pane, tap the selected slide and then, on the shortcut bar, tap **Hide**.

    *Or*

    On the **Slide Show** tab, tap the **Hide Slide** button.

**To unhide a slide**

1.  Select the slide that you want to unhide.

2.  In the **Thumbnails** pane, tap the selected slide and then, on the shortcut bar, tap **Unhide**.

    *Or*

    On the **Slide Show** tab, tap the **Unhide Slide** button.

9

# Add text to slides

PowerPoint presentations originally consisted primarily of bulleted lists of speaking points. Text is still common on slides, but presenters are incorporating fewer bullet points and more images and animations. Even with all the imagery, a typical presentation uses text on the title slide, in the slide titles, and in the slide content.

## Manage text containers

Most slide layouts associated with presentation templates include various configurations of content containers that hold slide titles and slide content. A notable difference between PowerPoint for iPad and the desktop versions of PowerPoint is that PowerPoint for iPad supports only simple text boxes that define the font characteristics of their content, whereas the desktop versions support rich content containers from which you can choose to insert a table, chart, SmartArt graphic, picture, or video.

 **TIP** When you open a presentation that was created in a desktop version of PowerPoint, any rich content containers that were in the original file appear as simple text boxes.

If the text boxes that are part of a slide layout don't meet your needs, you can modify the existing text boxes or create your own. It is safest to create your own, because modifications to the slide layout elements can be reset in other versions of PowerPoint by reapplying the slide layout. (You can't reapply a slide layout in PowerPoint for iPad.)

When you insert a text box on a slide, PowerPoint creates the text box at a default size and location. You can then move and resize the text box, and this is when you'll discover another of the great features of PowerPoint for iPad—Smart Guides. Smart Guides appear when an edge of the object you're moving or resizing aligns with another object or creates a symmetrical relationship with other objects. Smart Guides make it easy to position slide content in a perfectly balanced layout.

 **TIP** You manage and format text boxes on slides by using the same techniques as you do in Word documents. For more information, see "Draw and format text boxes" in Chapter 6, "Enhance document content."

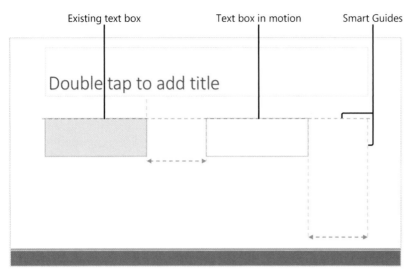

*Red guides indicate alignment, and gray guides indicate relationships*

You can specify formatting options for a text box and the content that will be entered into it. You can format the text box by applying shape styles, fill colors, and outline colors. You can format the text box content by specifying the font name, size, characteristics, and color; specifying the paragraph alignment, indent, list formatting, and text direction; and applying WordArt styles.

**To insert a text box on a slide**

1. In the **Thumbnails** pane, select the slide you want to insert the text box on.

2. On the **Insert** tab, tap the **Text Box** button to insert the default text box in the center of the slide.

**To select a text box for structural modification**

1. Tap the text box once.

**To move a text box on a slide**

1. Select the text box that you want to move.

2. Drag the text box to the new location.

**To move a text box to another slide**

1. Select the text box that you want to move.

2. On the shortcut bar, tap **Cut**.

3. Display the slide that you want to move the text box to.

4. In the **Slide** pane, tap anywhere on the slide to activate it. Then tap the slide to position the cursor at the approximate location where you want to insert the text box.

5. On the shortcut bar, tap **Paste**.

**To align a text box with other slide elements**

1. Drag the text box on the slide until Smart Guides indicate that at least one edge of the text box aligns with another object on the slide.

2. If necessary, drag the sizing handles to align other edges of the text box with objects on the slide.

**To remove a text box from a slide**

1. Select the text box that you want to remove.

2. Tap anywhere in the selected text box and then, on the shortcut bar, tap **Delete**.

## Insert and manage text

The words you choose to display on the slides of a PowerPoint presentation are important; you need them to convey enough information to be useful without providing so much information that you, the presenter, become unnecessary.

You can enter text directly into any text box on a slide, and then format either the text box (to affect all its contents) or individual text elements. If the text you want to display already exists elsewhere—for example, in a Word document—you can paste the text onto a slide either inside or outside the confines of a text box.

When you paste text outside of a text box, PowerPoint creates a text box that surrounds the text; you can format the text box as you would any other, move the text box where you want it, or move the text into another text box.

*You can paste text outside of existing text boxes*

When you're moving and editing text on an iPad screen, it can be difficult to position the cursor precisely within existing text. A nice feature of PowerPoint for iPad and Word for iPad is that you can magnify a circle of text on the slide or document to help you place the cursor in a specific position.

**9**

*Positioning the cursor precisely is easier with magnification*

> **TIP** You can insert a tab character or new line character (soft return) in text within a text box by displaying the shortcut bar at the cursor and then tapping the character you want to insert. You can't insert a hyperlink in PowerPoint for iPad, but you can edit hyperlinks that were created on a slide in another version of PowerPoint.

If a word on a slide doesn't appear in the dictionary that the Office for iPad apps reference, a wavy red underline indicates a possible spelling mistake. From the shortcut bar that appears when you select the word, you can choose the correct spelling from a list of suggestions, or you can add the word to the dictionary.

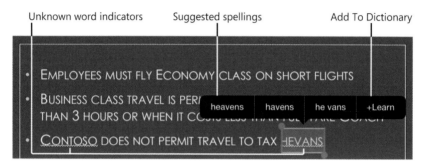

*PowerPoint offers corrections for unknown words*

### To activate a text box

1. Double-tap anywhere in the text box.

*Or*

1. Select the text box.

2. Tap the selected text box and then, on the shortcut bar, tap **Edit Text**.

### To enter text on a slide

1. Display the slide on which you want to add text.

2. Activate the text box, and then enter the text from the on-screen keyboard or a connected external keyboard.

### To insert text from a Word document on a slide

1. Start Word, open the document, and locate the text.

2. Select the text that you want to move and then, on the shortcut bar, tap **Copy**.

3. Switch to PowerPoint and display the slide that you want to insert the text on.

4.  In the **Slide** pane, tap anywhere on the slide to activate it.

5.  Do either of the following:

    - To insert the copied text in an existing text box, activate the text box, tap to position the cursor, and then, on the shortcut bar, tap **Paste**.

    - To insert the copied text in its own text box, tap a location on the slide that is outside of any existing text box to position the cursor, and then, on the shortcut bar, tap **Paste**.

    >  **TIP** PowerPoint centers the pasted text on the point that you tapped.

**To select text in a text box**

1.  Use any of these methods:

    - To select a word, double-tap anywhere in the word.

    - To select a paragraph, triple-tap anywhere in the paragraph.

    - To select the contents of a text box, tap anywhere in the text box and then, on the shortcut bar, tap **Select All**.

**To magnify text in a text box**

1.  Tap and hold until the magnifying circle appears.

2.  Without lifting your finger, drag to move the magnifying circle.

**To correct spelling errors in slide text**

1.  Select the word that is marked with a red wavy underline.

2.  On the shortcut bar, tap **Suggest**.

3.  On the shortcut bar, tap a suggested spelling of the word to replace it on the slide, or tap **+Learn** to add the word to the dictionary.

9

**To move text within a text box or to a different text box**

1. Select the text that you want to move.

2. On the shortcut bar, tap **Cut**.

3. If you're moving the text to a different text box, activate the text box that you're moving the text to.

4. Tap to position the cursor where you want to insert the text.

5. On the shortcut bar, tap **Paste**.

> **SEE ALSO** For information about entering text, applying styles and formatting, aligning text, changing text direction, converting text to columns, and deleting text, see Chapter 4, "Create professional documents." For information about formatting text in lists, see "Present content in lists" in Chapter 5, "Add visual elements to documents."

## Present information in tables

Tables provide a tidy structure for the presentation of text on a PowerPoint slide. When you create a table directly on a slide, PowerPoint for iPad inserts a table that has three rows and three columns and matches the color scheme of the presentation theme. The first row is formatted as a header row, and the following rows are banded. You can modify the structure and appearance of the table by using the same techniques that you do when working with tables in Word for iPad.

> **SEE ALSO** For information about inserting, deleting, formatting, and moving tables and table elements, see "Present content in tables" in Chapter 5, "Add visual elements to documents."

If the information you want to present is already in a tabular format in a Word document or Excel workbook, you can copy the existing table to your slide and then modify it as necessary to fit your presentation.

**To insert a standard blank table on a slide**

1. Display the slide that you want to insert the table on.

2. On the **Insert** tab, tap the **Table** button to insert a starter table near the center of the slide.

**To insert a table from a Word document on a slide**

1. Start Word, open the document, and locate the table that you want to copy to the slide.

2. Tap the table selector (outside the upper-left corner of the table) and then, on the shortcut bar, tap **Copy**.

3. Switch to PowerPoint and display the slide that you want to insert the table on.

4. In the **Slide** pane, tap anywhere on the slide to activate it. Then tap the slide in the approximate location where you want to insert the table.

5. On the shortcut bar, tap **Paste**.

**To insert a table from an Excel worksheet on a slide**

1. Start Excel, open the workbook, and locate the table or data range that you want to copy to the slide.

2. If the information is in an Excel table, tap anywhere in the table, and then tap the table selector.

    *Or*

    If the information is in a data range, select the data range, and then tap the selection.

3. On the shortcut bar, tap **Copy**.

4. Switch to PowerPoint and display the slide that you want to insert the table on.

5. In the **Slide** pane, tap anywhere on the slide to activate it. Then tap the slide in the approximate location where you want to insert the table.

6. On the shortcut bar, tap **Paste**.

9

# Review comments

If you're working with other people to develop a presentation, or if you simply want to leave yourself reminder notes when working on a presentation in a desktop version of PowerPoint, you can enter comments on the slides. You can display and move among existing comments in a PowerPoint presentation when using PowerPoint for iPad, but you can't create or manage comments.

You can turn on the display of comments on the Review tab. If the Previous Comment or Next Comment button is active, the presentation contains comments and you can move between them by tapping the buttons.

*Commands on the Review tab*

Comments on slides are indicated by transparent comment icons. Moving to a comment by tapping the Previous Comment or Next Comment button displays the comment text; you can also display the text by tapping a comment icon. The active comment opens in a rounded rectangular callout next to the comment icon.

*Each comment includes information about the person who entered the comment and the time it was entered*

**SEE ALSO** For more information about comments, see "Collaborate on document content" in Chapter 6, "Enhance document content."

# Add visual elements to slides

You can incorporate images into slide content to illustrate a concept, to draw attention to something, or just for decoration.

## Insert pictures

In PowerPoint for iPad, you can insert pictures that are available on your iPad (such as those in your Camera Roll or Photo Stream album) or shapes. If you want to use an image that is already present in another Office file—for example, a SmartArt graphic embedded in a Word document—you can copy the image from the source file and paste it onto the slide. PowerPoint inserts pictures in the center of the slide, and then you can move them where you want them. When you copy a formatted picture from a document to a slide, it retains the formatting. You can reset it and format it in PowerPoint if you want to.

You insert and format pictures on a slide the same way you do on a document page. The Picture tool tab offers the same options for applying fancy styles, shadows, and reflections, cropping and resetting the picture, and stacking pictures.

9

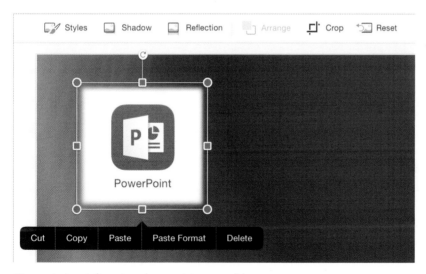

*It's easy to insert, format, and move pictures on slides*

 **SEE ALSO** For information about inserting, formatting, and reordering pictures, see "Insert and format pictures" in Chapter 5, "Add visual elements to documents."

It's easier to manipulate pictures on a slide than it is in a document, because you don't have to concern yourself with the way that text wraps around the picture—pictures and text are entirely separate elements. The only modification you might need to make is in the order of pictures, text, and other elements that overlap on a slide.

### To insert a picture from your Camera Roll or Photo Stream on a slide

1. Display the slide that you want to insert the picture on.

2. On the **Insert** tab, tap the **Pictures** button.

3. On the **Photos** menu, browse to the picture you want to insert, and then tap the picture to insert it.

### To insert a picture from a Word document on a slide

1. Start Word, open the document, and locate the picture that you want to copy to the slide.

2. Tap the picture and then, on the shortcut bar, tap **Copy**.

3. Switch to PowerPoint and display the slide that you want to insert the picture on.

4. In the **Slide** pane, tap anywhere on the slide to activate it. Then tap the slide in the approximate location where you want to insert the picture.

5. On the shortcut bar, tap **Paste**.

### To select a picture

1. Tap the picture once.

### To remove formatting from a picture

1. Select the picture.

2. On the **Picture** tool tab, tap the **Reset** button, and then tap **Reset Picture**.

### To move a picture on a slide

1. Select the picture that you want to move.

2. Drag the picture to the new location.

**To move a picture to a different slide**

1. Select the picture that you want to move.

2. On the shortcut bar, tap **Cut**.

3. Display the slide that you want to move the picture to.

4. In the **Slide** pane, tap the slide to activate it. Then tap it again to display the shortcut bar.

5. On the shortcut bar, tap **Paste**.

# Insert shapes

An extensive library of shapes is available in the Office for iPad apps. You can use these shapes to illustrate a concept on a slide, or you can animate the shapes to convey actions or draw attention to specific elements.

---

 **SEE ALSO** For information about animating shapes and text on slides, see "Animate slide elements" later in this topic.

---

Shapes can be simple, such as lines, circles, or squares; or more complex, such as stars, hearts, and arrows. Some shapes are three-dimensional (although most are two-dimensional).

*After you insert a shape, you can change its dimensions*

Some of the shapes have innate meanings or intentions, and others are simply shapes.

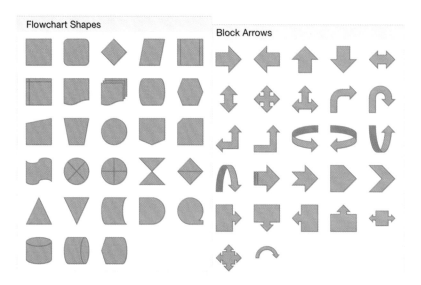

*Specialized flowchart shapes represent specific actions or objects*

PowerPoint inserts shapes in the center of the slide, and then you can move them where you want them. You can apply different colors to the outline and inside (fill) of a shape. When working with text in shapes, you can apply colors, or you can apply preset text effects (also referred to as *WordArt*) from the Formatting menu on the Home tab or from the WordArt Styles menu on the Shape tab, whichever is more convenient at the time, in the same way that you do to regular text.

> **SEE ALSO** For information about font formatting and text effects, see "Change the appearance of text" in Chapter 4, "Create professional documents." For information about shapes, see "Insert and format shapes" in Chapter 5, "Add visual elements to documents."

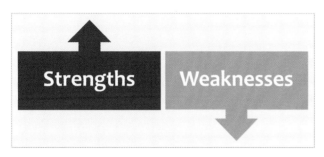

*Shapes can help to visually reinforce a concept*

**To insert a shape on a slide**

1. Display the slide that you want to insert the shape on.

2. On the **Insert** tab, tap the **Shapes** button.

3. On the **Shapes** menu, locate the shape you want to insert, and then tap the shape to insert it.

**To select a shape**

1. Tap the shape once.

**To move a shape on a slide**

1. Select the shape that you want to move.

2. Drag the shape to the new location.

**To move a shape to a different slide**

1. Select the shape that you want to move.

2. On the shortcut bar, tap **Cut**.

3. Display the slide that you want to move the shape to.

4. In the **Slide** pane, tap the slide to activate it. Then tap it again to display the shortcut bar.

5. On the shortcut bar, tap **Paste**.

**To add text to a shape**

1.  Select the shape that you want to add text to.

2.  On the shortcut bar that appears, tap **Add Text** to activate the cursor within the shape.

3.  Enter the text you want to display on the shape.

**To format text on a shape**

1.  Select the shape, and then triple-tap the shape text to select it.

2.  On the **Shape** tool tab, tap **WordArt Styles**. Then on the **WordArt Styles** menu, tap the style you want to apply.

    *Or*

    On the **Home** tab, use the font formatting commands to change the font, size, color, or formatting of the text.

## Animate slide elements

When used appropriately, animated slide elements can both capture the audience's attention and effectively convey information. You can animate any individual element on a slide, including each individual text container. You can't animate the elements on the slide background, other than during the initial transition to the slide.

---

 **SEE ALSO**  For information about slide transitions, see "Animate slide transitions" in Chapter 10, "Prepare and deliver slide shows."

---

Animations can be very informative, particularly for audience members who are more receptive to visual input than to auditory input. Animations have the added benefit of being available to provide a very specific, consistent message in a presentation with or without a presenter to discuss or externally illustrate a process.

You can configure animation effects for three processes. The available effects for each process are categorized as Basic, Subtle, Moderate, and Exciting (although you might have a different concept of exciting than the PowerPoint developer who categorized the effects). More animation effects are available for text than for other elements. The three types of effects are:

- **Entrance effects**  If an object has an entrance effect, the object is not visible on the slide when the slide is first shown. (It is visible during the development process, but not when you present the slide show.) It then appears on the slide in the manner specified by the entrance effect.

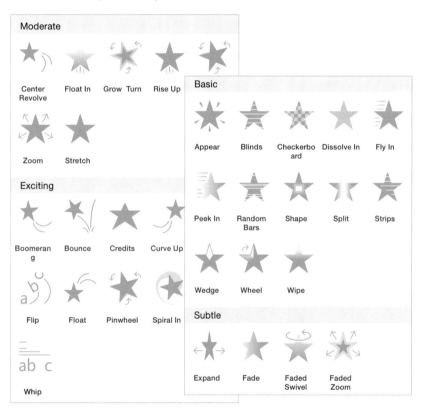

*The entrance animation effects available for text and images*

- **Emphasis effects** These effects animate an object that is already visible on the slide to draw attention to it, usually by moving it or changing the color.

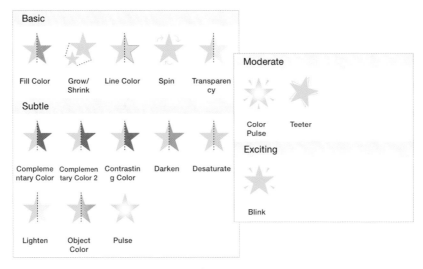

*The emphasis animation effects available for images*

- **Exit effects** These effects take an existing object through a process that results in the object no longer being visible on the slide.

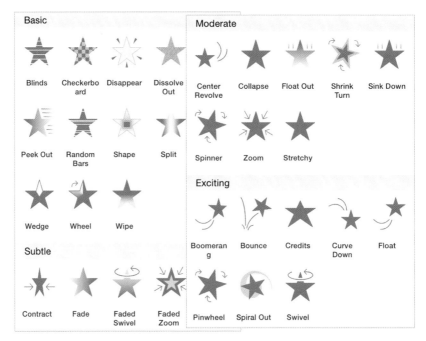

*The exit animation effects available for images*

Entrance and exit effects cause slide elements to appear and disappear when you're previewing or presenting a slide. However, all the elements are visible while you're working in the Slide pane. As you prepare a slide that will contain animated objects, position the objects for animation as follows:

- **Entrance effects**  Position the object where you want it to end up after it enters the slide.

- **Emphasis effects**  Position the object where it will be before and after the effect.

- **Exit effects**  Position the object where it will be before it leaves the slide.

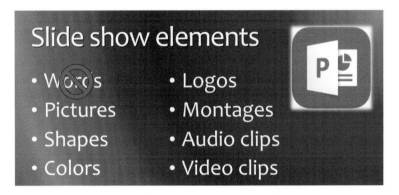

*Preparing the slide elements before applying animation effects*

You can apply multiple animation effects (for example, an entrance effect and an emphasis effect) to a slide element.

After all the elements are in place, animate them in the order you want the animations to occur. It's helpful to map out the process before starting. For example, when presenting information about the elements that a slide show can include, you might want to do the following:

1. Start with only the slide title and list items visible.

2. Pulse the list items one by one to draw attention to them.

3. Forcefully display the prohibition sign on top of *Words*.

4. Subtly remove the prohibition sign.

5. Swoop the PowerPoint icon in like a superhero.

As you animate slide objects, numbers appear on the objects to specify the order of the animation effects. To implement your plan, you could use the animation effects shown in the following table.

| Element | Effect type | Category | Name | Option |
|---|---|---|---|---|
| Slide content | Emphasis | Subtle | Pulse | By Paragraph |
| Prohibition sign | Entrance | Moderate | Zoom | Out |
| Prohibition sign | Exit | Basic | Dissolve Out | n/a |
| PowerPoint icon | Entrance | Exciting | Curve Up | n/a |

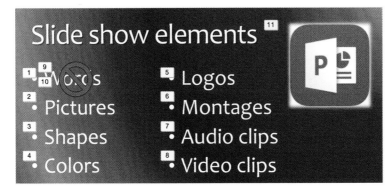

*The animated slide elements*

After you apply an animation, the selected effect icon appears on the Animations tab, on the button for that effect type, when you select the animated slide element.

**To apply an animation effect to a slide element**

1. Select the slide element that you want to animate.

2. On the **Animations** tab, tap the **Entrance Effect**, **Emphasis Effect**, or **Exit Effect** button to indicate the type of effect that you want to apply.

3. On the **Effect** menu, tap the effect that you want to apply.

4. If the **Effect Options** button is active, tap it to display the options for the selected effect. Then, on the **Effect Options** menu, tap the direction or other effect option that you want to apply.

5. If the **Effect Color** button is active, tap it to display the color charts. Then, on the **Effect Color** menu, tap the color you want to use in the animation effect.

**To select an applied animation effect**

1. In the **Slide** pane, on the slide, tap the number corresponding to the animation effect.

   A red outline appears around the number of the currently selected animation.

**To choose or change an effect option**

1. Select the animation effect that you want to configure.

2. On the **Animations** tab, tap the **Effect Options** button if it is available.

3. On the **Effect Options** menu, select the direction or other option that you want.

**To choose or change an effect color**

1. Select the animation effect that you want to configure.

2. On the **Animations** tab, tap the **Effect Color** button if it is available.

3. On the **Effect Color** menu, tap the color that you want to use in the animation effect.

**To apply more than one effect to a slide element**

1. Select the slide element.

2. Apply the first animation effect.

3. Choose the effect option and color, if available.

4. Apply any other animation effects that precede the second effect on the element you animated in step 2.

5. Select the slide element (not the animation number) of the element that you want to apply a second animation effect to.

6. Apply the second animation effect and choose the effect option and color, if appropriate.

 **IMPORTANT** You can't change the order of animation effects in PowerPoint for iPad. If you need to do so, edit the presentation in a desktop version of PowerPoint.

9

**To remove an animation effect from a slide element**

1.  Select the animation number of the effect that you want to remove.

 **IMPORTANT** Be sure to select the animation, not the slide element.

2.  On the shortcut bar, tap **Delete**.

## Skills review

In this chapter, you learned how to:

- Create presentations
- Create and manage slides
- Add text to slides
- Add visual elements to slides

# Practice tasks

The practice files for these tasks are located in the iPadOfficeSBS\Ch09 folder.

## Create presentations

Start PowerPoint, and then perform the following tasks:

1. Create a new presentation by first specifying a **Standard (4:3)** slide size, and then selecting the **Wisp** template.

2. Save the presentation on your iPad as My Presentation.

3. Open the **ChangeSize** presentation. This presentation has a Standard slide size.

4. Review the slides and notice the location of the check marks on the Quiz slides.

5. Change the slide size to **Widescreen (16:9)**. Review the slides again, and notice the change in location of the check marks.

## Create and manage slides

Open the ManageSlides presentation, and then perform the following tasks:

1. Insert a blank slide after slide 1.

2. Select slide 7, and then insert a copy of it directly after the slide.

3. Select slide 2, and then insert a copy of it after slide 10.

4. Move slide 3 so that it becomes slide 4.

5. Delete slide 7.

6. Hide slide 2, and then unhide slides 8 and 9.

7. Ensure that the slides are in the following order:

   a. Work in Presentations

   b. &lt;blank slide&gt;

   c. Quiz Question (You import an outline...)

   d. Quiz Question (You need to ensure...)

   e. Quiz Question (How many transitions...)

   f. Quiz Question (Which of the following is a...)

   g. Quiz Question (Which of the following keyboard...)

   h. Quiz Review

   i. Quiz Review (continued)

   j. &lt;blank slide&gt;

## Add text to slides

Open the AddText1 presentation, and then perform the following tasks:

1. Select slide 2, and then insert a text box.

2. Select the text box, and then move it so that it's centered below the graphic that's at the top of the slide.

3. In the selected text box, enter Copyright 2015.

4. Open the **AddText2** document in Word for iPad, and then copy the text from the document to the text box on slide 3 of the presentation.

5. In the text box, select the first paragraph (*Lesson 11:...*), and delete it. Then delete the blank paragraph mark at the bottom of the text box.

6. Magnify any text on the slide, and then drag your finger to move the magnifying circle to other parts of the slide.

7. On slide 40, locate the word *silde*, which has a wavy underline, and then correct the spelling.

8. Review the comments in the presentation.

9. Open the **AddText3** workbook. Copy the table from the workbook to the text box on slide 42 of the presentation.

## Add visual elements to slides

Open the AddGraphics1 presentation, and then perform the following tasks:

1. On slide 18, insert a picture from your Camera Roll. Then center the picture above the *Thank You!* text.

2. Open the **AddGraphics2** document. Copy the image in the document to slide 18 of the presentation. Then center the image below the *Thank You!* text.

3. Move one image from slide 18 to the upper-right corner of slide 1 and resize it so it doesn't cover any of the slide text.

4. On slide 18, insert a dodecagon shape (a 12-sided polygon) from the **Basic Shapes** section of the **Shapes** menu. Then move the shape to the lower-right corner of the slide.

5. In the banner shape, enter Congratulations! You completed the module. Then resize the shape so it's about the same width as the *Thank You!* text.

6. Format the text in the shape by using any WordArt style.

7. Select the shape. Apply the **Fill Color** effect from the **Basic** section of the **Emphasis Effect** menu to the shape. Then change the effect color to a different shade of purple.

8. Select the text box below the shape, change the effect option, and add any other effect to the element.

9. Remove your least favorite animation effect from the slide.

# Prepare and deliver slide shows

After you create the most important content of your PowerPoint presentation—the slides—there are other modifications that you can make in preparation for actually presenting the slide show to an audience. Among these are the addition of notes, slide transitions, and embedded media.

Notes are a valuable feature of PowerPoint slide shows. You can add notes to each individual slide; for example, as development notes, speaking points, or supporting information for handouts.

Animated slide transitions can liven up a presentation and help to keep the audience's attention. You can assign a variety of animations to accompany the change from one slide to the next.

If the information you're presenting in your slide show is supported by video content—for example, statements by experts that support the concepts you discuss—you can streamline the presentation process (and also ensure that the information is always available with the slide show) by embedding the video on a slide.

This chapter guides you through procedures related to adding notes to slides, animating the transitions between slides, embedding and managing media recordings, and presenting slide shows.

## In this chapter

- Add notes to slides
- Animate slide transitions
- Incorporate external media content
- Manage and present slide shows

## Practice files

For this chapter, use the practice files from the iPadOfficeSBS\Ch10 folder. For practice file download instructions, see the Introduction.

# Add notes to slides

A PowerPoint slide show can include many types of information; the information on the slides is intended for the audience, and the information stored in the notes attached to the slides is usually intended for the presenter. You can also provide the slide content and notes to attendees by printing Notes pages from a desktop version of PowerPoint.

> **TIP** PowerPoint for iPad currently prints only full-page slides. You can use the desktop versions of PowerPoint to print various permutations of slides, notes, and note-taking areas.

You can enter ancillary information in the Notes pane while you're developing a slide show in Normal view, or when you preview or present a slide show in Presenter view.

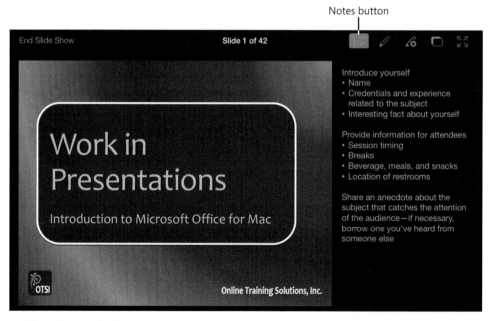

*A slide and its associated notes in Presenter view*

In Normal view, you open the Notes pane by tapping the Notes button in the lower-right corner of the Slide pane. This moves the Notes header up to the top of the pane above the note content area. When a slide has associated notes, a red-outlined note icon appears to the left of the word *Notes* in the header to alert you to that fact.

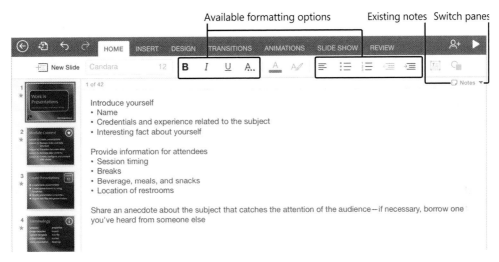

*The Notes page of a slide in Normal view*

You can't display both the Slide pane and the Notes pane at the same time, but the Thumbnails pane remains available and the current slide is indicated therein by a thick red outline. You can switch to the Notes pane for a specific slide without closing the Notes pane by tapping the thumbnail of the slide you want to switch to.

Regardless of the font that is assigned to the headings and body text of the slides in your presentation, the content of the Notes pane is always 12-point Calibri. Note content can include standard paragraphs, bulleted lists, and numbered lists. In PowerPoint for iPad, you can apply basic character formatting options—bold, italic, underline, and strikethrough—and basic paragraph formatting options—alignment, indent level—to the notes when you're working in the Notes pane. Other formatting options are unavailable. If you need to apply fancier formatting to your notes, edit them in a desktop version of PowerPoint.

**TIP** You can't apply formatting to notes in Presenter view. To format note text, display the Notes pane in Normal view and then apply formatting from the ribbon.

10

**To display the Notes pane**

1. In Normal view, tap the **Notes** button in the lower-right corner of the **Slide** pane to display the **Notes** pane.

*Or*

1. In Presenter view, tap the **Notes** button on the **Presenter** toolbar to display the **Notes** pane if necessary.

**To add notes to a slide**

1. In Normal view or Presenter view, display the **Notes** pane.

2. Double-tap the **Notes** pane to activate it for editing, and then enter the note text.

**To apply character formatting to text**

1. In Normal view, display the **Notes** pane and activate it for editing.

2. Select the text you want to format.

3. On the **Home** tab, do either or both of the following:

   • To apply font attributes, tap the **Bold**, **Italic**, or **Underline** button.

   • To strike through the selected text, tap the **Formatting** button (labeled **A...**) and then, on the **Formatting** menu, tap **Strikethrough**.

**To clear character formatting from text**

1. Select the text you want to clear the formatting from.

2. On the **Home** tab, tap the **Formatting** button, and then tap **Clear Formatting**.

**To apply paragraph formatting to text**

1. In Normal view, display the **Notes** pane and activate it for editing.

2. Tap anywhere in the paragraph you want to format.

>  **TIP** To format multiple paragraphs at one time, select all the paragraphs that you want to apply the same formatting to.

3. On the **Home** tab, do any of the following:

- To change the paragraph alignment, tap the **Alignment** button and then, on the **Alignment** menu, tap **Left**, **Center**, **Right**, or **Justify**.

- To format the paragraph as a bulleted list, tap the **Bullets** button and then, on the **Bullets** menu, tap the bullet symbol you want to use.

- To format the paragraph as a numbered list, tap the **Numbering** button and then, on the **Numbering** menu, tap the numbering format you want to use.

- To change the paragraph indent, tap the **Increase Indent** or **Decrease Indent** button.

**To hide the Notes pane**

1. In Normal view, tap the **Notes** button in the upper-right corner of the **Notes** pane to redisplay the **Slide** pane.

*Or*

1. In Presenter view, tap the **Notes** button on the Presenter toolbar to hide the **Notes** pane.

10

# Animate slide transitions

The action that occurs between the display of one slide and the display of the next slide is the slide transition. By default, when you are presenting a slide show by using PowerPoint for iPad, there is no visible transition; the content of one slide is simply replaced with the content of the next slide.

To help keep the audience's attention, you can add an interesting animation effect that occurs as the slide show transitions from one slide to the next. In PowerPoint for iPad, you can choose from the same 46 slide transitions that are available in the desktop versions of PowerPoint.

The slide transitions are divided into three categories:

- **Subtle transitions** These transition effects provide a reasonably clean and simple movement between slides.

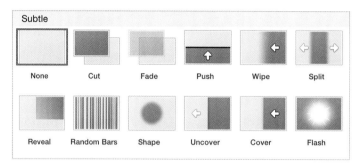

*The Subtle category of transition effects*

- **Exciting transitions** These include many three-dimensional effects that are a lot of fun—but be cautious, because it's easy to overuse these effects.

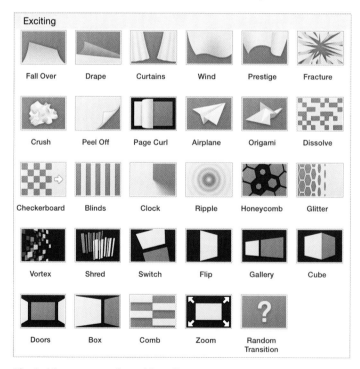

*The Exciting category of transition effects*

■ **Dynamic Content transitions** These effects animate the slide content only, and not the slide background. This creates a unique effect that can be both more dramatic and more subtle than the full-slide effects.

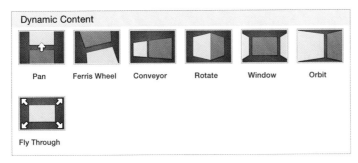

*The Dynamic Content category of transition effects*

The Exciting category includes the Random Transition option. It might be tempting to apply this to every slide in your presentation, but think carefully before doing so about whether random transitions will catch the attention of your audience or distract them from the slide show subject.

For almost every transition effect, you can choose from options to configure the specific behavior of the transition. Most frequently, you can choose the starting location or the direction in which the transition moves. Sometimes you can specify the shape of the effect as it occurs. Transition aspects that you can't specify in PowerPoint for iPad (but can in the desktop versions of PowerPoint) are the trigger of the transition, the duration of the transition effect (the length of time from the beginning to the end of the transition), and the sound that plays during the transition.

You apply slide transition effects to the incoming slide—in other words, to affect the transition from slide 2 to slide 3, you apply the effect to slide 3. If you apply a transition effect to slide 1, it plays when you start the slide show.

In the Thumbnails pane and Presenter view, a shooting star adjacent to the slide number indicates that a slide transition is applied to the slide.

*You can tell at a glance which slides have animated transitions*

For the most professional and least frazzling audience experience, choose one slide transition effect for all the slides in your presentation or, if the presentation includes specific types of slides (for example, slides that display the overview, objectives, teaching points, or lab description for each section of the presentation), you can provide consistent visual cues for the audience by assigning a specific transition effect to all slides of a specific type.

### To animate the transition to a slide

1. Select the slide to which you want to apply the transition.

2. On the **Transitions** tab, tap the **Transition Effect** button.

3. On the **Transition To This Slide** menu, tap the transition effect you want to apply.

### To configure options for a transition effect

1. Apply the transition effect to the slide.

2. On the **Transitions** tab, tap the **Effect Options** button.

3. On the **Effect Options** menu, tap the option you want to apply to the selected transition effect on the currently selected slide.

### To apply one transition effect to all slides

1. Apply the transition effect to one slide and configure the effect options for the transition.

2. On the **Transitions** tab, tap the **Apply To All** button.

### To remove the transition effect from a slide

1. Select the slide that you want to remove the transition effect from.

2. On the **Transitions** tab, tap the **Transition Effect** button.

3. On the **Transition To This Slide** menu, in the **Subtle** section, tap the **None** thumbnail.

# Incorporate external media content

In PowerPoint for iPad, you can insert a video recording from your iPad directly onto a slide, and then play the video while presenting the slide show. If you're accustomed to switching between a presentation and video clips, this is a much smoother way of presenting information from multiple sources.

When you're selecting a video to embed, you can preview videos at their regular speed with the soundtrack or slide forward or backward through the video content. When you select the video you want to use, PowerPoint for iPad compresses it and embeds it on the slide. You can insert multiple videos on one slide. The video images stack in order of insertion.

*Video preview controls*

A video that is embedded on a slide is represented by an image of the first frame of the video. There is no special tool tab for working with embedded videos, but you can use the sizing handles to resize the video on the slide, and the commands on the shortcut bar to cut, copy, paste, or delete it.

> **TIP** In PowerPoint for iPad, you can't modify aspects of an embedded video, such as its length. If you want to modify a video, you can edit it in another program before you insert it, or insert it and then edit it by using the tools in a desktop version of PowerPoint.

**10**

# Format embedded video images

There are no formatting options for videos, but you can work around that by copying formatting from another object or positioning a shape behind a video image to give the appearance of a frame. An easy way to apply a professional style to the embedded video and its representative image is to copy the formatting from another object.

For example, you can insert any picture on any slide (it can even be a blank slide that you use specifically as a staging location for this sort of thing), apply a picture style to the picture, copy the picture, and then paste only the formatting onto the video image.

*Paste the format of a reference image onto a video preview image*

**SEE ALSO** For information about inserting and formatting pictures on slides, see "Add visual elements to slides" in Chapter 9, "Create compelling presentations."

You can play audio and video content on a slide only while you're presenting the slide show. The easiest way to preview embedded audio and video recordings is to start the slide show from the current slide, either in regular presentation mode or in Presenter view. PowerPoint for iPad has a conveniently placed button at the right end of the ribbon that you can tap to start the slide show from the current slide.

When you're presenting a slide show, you can play (and pause) embedded audio or video, move around within the recording, and control the volume by using the controls that appear when the audio icon or video placeholder image is active. When playing back a video, you can display it at the embedded size or full screen.

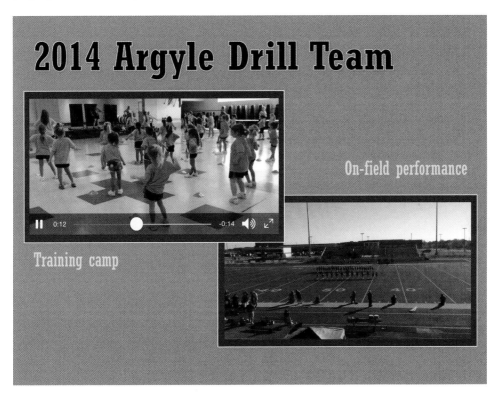

*Playing an embedded video*

> ✓ **TIP** A method you can use to provide a framelike effect is to insert and format a shape that is slightly larger than the video image. Position the shape on top of the image, and then on the Shape tool tab, tap the Send Backward command on the Arrange menu.

10

PowerPoint for iPad doesn't officially allow you to insert audio recordings on slides, although it does support the playback of audio recordings that have been inserted in presentations by using a desktop version of PowerPoint. By default, audio recordings are represented by a discreet speaker icon on the slide. With the exception of the Full Screen option, the playback controls that are available for audio recordings are the same as those for video recordings.

*Playing back an embedded audio recording*

However, because PowerPoint for iPad supports the insertion of video and video soundtracks, you can get around the limitations of the app in this regard by saving the audio as a video soundtrack (with a simple video image such as a speaker icon or a video that has some significance), and then embedding that video.

> **TIP** From a desktop version of PowerPoint, you can insert audio clips onto slides and configure them to play for a specific period of time, while a specific slide is displayed, or through the end of the slide show.

### To embed a video on a slide

1. On the **Insert** tab, tap the **Videos** button.

2. Flick through the **Videos** library menu to locate the library that contains the video you want to use, and then tap the library to display its contents.

3. Flick through the library to locate the video you want to insert. Preview the video in any of these ways:

   - To display the video thumbnail at menu width, tap the thumbnail.

   - To preview a video, tap its thumbnail and then tap the **Play** button.

   - To move through a video preview, drag the slider at the top of the **Videos** menu.

4. To insert a video from the **Videos** menu preview, tap **Use**.

   *Or*

   To return to the **Videos** library, tap **Videos**.

**To select an embedded video**

1. On the slide, tap the video preview image.

**To change the dimensions of an embedded video**

1. Select the video image.

2. Drag the sizing handles to resize the video image in any of the following ways:

   - To resize the shape and maintain its aspect ratio, drag any round corner handle.

   - To change only the height, drag the square handle on the top or bottom of the shape.

   - To change only the width, drag the square handle on the left or right side of the shape.

**To rotate an embedded video**

1. Select the video image.

2. Drag the **Rotate** handle in a clockwise or counterclockwise direction until the shape is at the angle of rotation you want.

**To move an embedded video**

1. Select the video image.

2. To move the video to another location on the slide, drag the video to the location where you want it.

3. To move the video to a different slide, follow these steps:

   a. On the shortcut bar, tap **Cut**.

   b. In the **Thumbnails** pane, tap the slide you want to move the video to.

   c. Tap the approximate location at which you want to insert the video.

   d. On the shortcut bar, tap **Paste**.

**To delete an embedded video**

1. Select the video image.

2. On the shortcut bar, tap **Delete**.

**10**

**To change the stacking order of videos on a slide**

1. If there are two videos on the slide, follow these steps:

   a. Select the video you want to be on top.

   b. On the shortcut bar, tap **Cut**.

   c. Tap an empty area of the slide to display the shortcut bar.

   d. On the shortcut bar, tap **Paste**.

2. If there are more than two videos on the slide, follow step 1 for each video, starting with the video you want to have second from the back and continuing in order to the video you want to have in front.

 **TIP** PowerPoint for iPad always displays videos on the slide in the order of insertion.

**To preview video content**

1. At the right end of the ribbon, tap the **Play** button.

   *Or*

   On the **Slide Show** tab, tap the **From Current** button.

1. On the slide, tap the video you want to play.

2. In the player controls that appear, tap the **Play** button.

*Video player controls*

3. When you finish previewing the video, tap the top of the screen to display the presenter tools, and then tap **End Slide Show**.

**To manage the playback of a video**

1. On the slide, tap the video preview image.

2. In the player controls that appear, tap the **Play** button.

3. To manage the video playback, do any of the following:

   - To pause the video, tap the **Pause** button.

   - To move to a different location in the video, drag the progress slider.

   - To adjust the audio volume, tap the **Volume** button, and then drag the volume slider.

   - To display the video at its maximum size, tap the **Full Screen** button.

   - To return to the original video size, tap the **Exit Full Screen** button.

 **TIP** If the player controls disappear, tap the video to redisplay them.

**To manage the playback of an audio recording**

1. On the slide, tap the audio icon.

2. In the player controls that appear, tap the **Play** button.

3. To manage the audio playback, do any of the following:

   - To pause the audio playback, tap the **Pause** button.

   - To move to a different location in the audio recording, drag the progress slider.

   - To adjust the audio volume, tap the **Volume** button, and then drag the volume slider.

10

# Manage and present slide shows

All the work you've done to create and finalize your presentation is about to pay off—you'll deliver your presentation, the audience will go wild, and you'll get a raise, a book contract, or international speaking engagements. Possibly. The important thing is that you will have effectively communicated information to your audience.

If you're going to present the slide show from your iPad, you can choose from two presentation interfaces:

- **Standard view**  This method runs the slide show on your iPad and shows the same view of the slides on any other screen you're connected to (such as a conference room or auditorium display screen).

- **Presenter view**  This method displays a multipanel view of the slide show on your iPad and the Standard view of the slide show on the other screen. So while the remote display shows only the current slide, your iPad shows the current slide, its associated notes, and thumbnails of all the slides in the show.

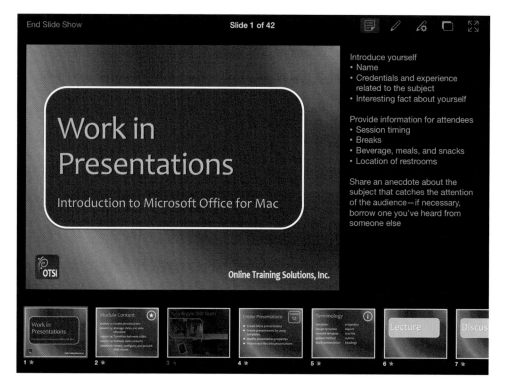

*Presenter view gives you access to all aspects of a slide show*

Presenter view is one of the greatest cures for stage fright that's come along in years (a close second to picturing your audience in their underwear), because you can reference the current slide without turning your back on the audience, you can refer to the notes you've included to support the slide content, you know what slide is coming up next, and, if you need to, you can easily skip a slide or display a specific slide from elsewhere in the presentation.

You can run Presenter view on one monitor for the purpose of rehearsing the delivery of information and adding speaker notes. Actually delivering a presentation in Presenter view requires two monitors: one displays Presenter view for your use, and the other displays the Standard slide show view for the audience.

In either view, you have access to a set of presenter tools—displayed all the time in Presenter view and on request in Standard view.

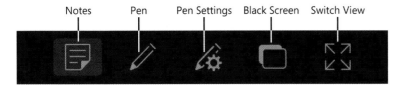

You can mark up a slide and control the display of slides by using the presenter tools

The presenter tools include a pen with multiple settings to mark up slides as you present them, and commands you can use to display a black screen when you pause a presentation and to switch to the Standard view of the presentation.

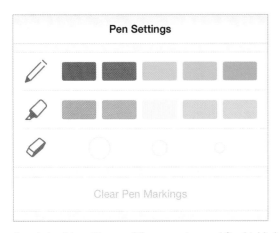

Annotate slides with any of five pen colors and five highlighter colors

**To start a slide show from the current slide in Presenter view**

1.  On the **Slide Show** tab, tap **Presenter View**.

*Or*

1.  While displaying a slide show in Standard view, display the Presenter toolbar, and then tap the **Switch View** button.

**To start a slide show from the beginning in Standard view**

1.  On the **Slide Show** tab, tap **From Start**.

**To start a slide show from the current slide in Standard view**

1.  On the **Slide Show** tab, tap **From Current**.

*Or*

1.  At the right end of the ribbon, tap the **Play** button.

*Or*

1.  While displaying a slide show in Presenter view, on the Presenter toolbar, tap the **Switch View** button.

**To display the presenter tools in Standard view**

1.  Swipe down from the top of the screen to display the **End Slide Show** button and the Presenter toolbar.

**To move among slides**

1.  To move forward in a presentation, flick from right to left.

2.  To move backward, flick from left to right.

**To pause and restart a slide show**

1.  To pause the slide show, on the Presenter toolbar, tap the **Black Screen** button.

2.  To restart the slide show, tap the **Black Screen** button again.

**To skip a slide**

1.  In Presenter view, in the thumbnail pane, tap the slide you want to display next.

**TIP** To skip one or more slides in a slide show, hide them before presenting the slide show. For more information, see "Create and manage slides" in Chapter 9, "Create compelling presentations."

**To end a slide show**

1. On the Presenter toolbar, tap the **End Slide Show** button.

**To display or hide speaker notes in Presenter view**

1. On the Presenter toolbar, tap the **Notes** button.

**To annotate a slide in Presenter view**

1. On the Presenter toolbar, tap the **Pen** button.

2. To mark up the slide, drag your finger.

3. To change the pen color or pen type, tap the **Pen Settings** button, and then tap the pen or highlighter color you want to change to.

4. To delete annotations, tap the **Pen Settings** button, and tap the eraser size you want to use. Then drag your finger to delete annotations.

 **TIP** The eraser won't delete slide content other than your annotations.

*Or*

On the **Pen Settings** menu, tap **Clear All**.

# Skills review

In this chapter, you learned how to:

- Add notes to slides

- Animate slide transitions

- Incorporate external media content

- Manage and present slide shows

# Practice tasks

The practice files for these tasks are located in the iPadOfficeSBS\Ch10 folder.

## Add notes to slides

Start PowerPoint, open the EnterNotes presentation, and then perform the following tasks:

1.  Display slide 2 and open the **Notes** pane. Then enter Bunnies can have babies every 30 days. If you do not plan to breed your bunnies, be sure to have them spayed or neutered.

2.  Select the text *30 days*, and then apply bold formatting to it.

3.  Make the second sentence a separate paragraph, and then center both paragraphs.

4.  Hide the **Notes** pane.

## Animate slide transitions

Open the AnimateTransitions presentation, and then perform the following tasks:

1.  Apply a transition effect of your choice to slide 1.

2.  Configure the effect options for the transition, if it has any. Then apply the slide 1 transition to all the slides.

3.  Clear the transition effect from all the slides.

4.  Apply the following types of transition effects:

    *   **Slide 1**  Any **Exciting** transition

    *   **Slides 2 through 12**  Any one **Subtle** transition (apply the same transition to all 11 slides)

    *   **Slide 13**  Any **Dynamic Content** transition

## Incorporate external media content

Open the ManageRecordings presentation, and then perform the following tasks:

1. On slide 9, insert a video recording from your Camera Roll. Resize the video preview image to about one-fourth the size of the slide.

2. On slide 9, insert a picture from your Camera Roll. Resize the picture so that it is slightly smaller than the video image.

3. Apply a fancy picture effect to the picture. Then copy the picture effect to the video image.

4. Position the picture so that it overlaps the video preview image. Then change the stacking order so the video image is on the top.

5. Preview slide 9 and play the video recording, first at the embedded size and then at full screen size.

6. Move the embedded audio recording from slide 1 to slide 8, and position it to the right of the list of tips.

7. Resize the picture that the audio clip is attached to so it fits in the right margin of the slide. Maintain the original aspect ratio of the picture.

8. Preview slide 8 and play the audio clip.

## Manage and present slide shows

Open the PresentShow presentation, and then perform the following tasks:

1. Display slide 2. Start the slide show from slide 2 in Standard view.

2. Switch to Presenter view, and move forward through the next three slides.

3. Use the pen tool to circle the picture of the bunny you like best with a green pen. Then circle the other picture with a red pen.

4. Pause the slide show, return to slide 1, and restart the slide show.

5. Hide the **Notes** pane, and then switch to Standard view.

6. Wait for the presenter tools to disappear, then redisplay them and choose any color of highlighter.

7. Use the highlighter to add an annotation to any slide in the presentation.

# Part 5

# Microsoft OneNote for iPad

# Store information in digital notebooks

OneNote is a very useful program that you can use to store many types of information and then access that information from any device. OneNote is equally useful for home and business purposes and is available for a wide variety of computer, tablet, and smartphone systems.

After you spend a short time using OneNote for iPad, you'll undoubtedly find it a convenient way to store many types of information, such as task lists, itineraries, frequent flyer accounts, supplier contact information, meeting notes, research findings, technical data, and printouts of contracts, receipts, and other documents you want to archive for future reference.

This chapter guides you through procedures related to creating and opening notebooks, adding sections to notebooks, adding pages to sections, adding content to pages, managing notebook content, and closing notebooks.

## In this chapter

- Create, open, and close notebooks
- Configure notebook storage structure
- Add information to notebooks
- Manage pages and sections

## Practice files

For this chapter, use the practice files from the iPadOfficeSBS\Ch11 folder. For practice file download instructions, see the Introduction.

# The OneNote feature set

OneNote is available for use on many platforms, including Windows, Windows Phone, Mac, iPad, iPhone, Android, and Internet browsers. The Windows version of OneNote has significantly more features than any of the others.

Here is a brief comparison of the features you can use in the iPad, Office Online, and Windows versions of OneNote. More information about all the current versions is available at *www.onenote.com*.

## OneNote for iPad features

When using OneNote for iPad, you can perform the following tasks:

- Create notebooks in cloud storage locations.

- Create, rename, and delete sections.

- Change the background colors of individual pages.

- Embed files, PDF printouts, local or photo stream images, Office Lens images, and links in notes.

- Format paragraphs and characters, and apply basic styles.

- Classify notes by applying predefined tags.

- Manage the password protection of notebook sections.

- Move and reorder sections, pages, and subpages.

OneNote for iPad doesn't have any premium features that require an Office 365 subscription.

## OneNote Online features

You can use OneNote Online to do the following:

- Move and resize note containers.

- Delete individual sections or entire notebooks.

- Locate edits made by other authors in a shared notebook.

- Display content created or modified by specific authors.

- Change the color of a section, which affects the section tab and page navigator background.

- Play audio and video recordings that were embedded in notes by using a desktop version of OneNote.

For more information about OneNote Online, visit *technet.microsoft.com /en-us/library/onenote-online-service-description.aspx*.

## OneNote for Windows features

The Windows version of OneNote has the most functionality. You can use OneNote 2013 on a computer running Windows to do the following:

- Change the color of a notebook, which affects the notebook cover.

- Change the display name of the notebook. This doesn't change the name of the folder that contains the notebook content.

- Create and delete section groups.

- Create pages based on content-driven or artistic templates.

- Merge note containers, and select full notebook pages.

- Edit embedded files from within OneNote.

- Integrate tagged tasks with your Outlook task list, and send content from Outlook to OneNote.

- Record and embed audio and video recordings directly on a page, and coordinate the playback of recordings with your written notes.

- Capture and insert screen clips from within OneNote.

- Search notes by tag, by author, or by date, and search the content of audio recordings and the text in images.

- Generate a summary of tagged notes by storage location or date.

- Insert mathematical equations into notes.

- Draw or handwrite notes (by using your finger or a stylus).

11

# Create, open, and close notebooks

OneNote stores information in files that are referred to as *notebooks*. You can store all your information in one notebook or create multiple notebooks for different purposes. For example, you could store general business information in one notebook, sensitive business information in a second notebook, and personal information in a third notebook.

In some versions of OneNote, you can create and work with notebooks that are stored locally on your computer or remotely in a connected storage location such as a OneDrive site or SharePoint site. In OneNote for iPad, you can work only with notebooks that are stored remotely.

## Create notebooks

When creating a notebook in OneNote for iPad, you must create it on a OneDrive site or SharePoint site. A benefit of creating a notebook in one of these remote storage locations is that you can get to the information from any location or device. If you want to share some or all of the information in your notebook with other people, you can do that, too.

**To create a notebook**

1. Start OneNote and display the Backstage view.

2. On the **File** bar, tap **Notebooks**.

3. On the **Notebooks** page of the Backstage view, tap **Create Notebook**.

4. In the **Create Notebook** box, enter a name for the new notebook in the **Name** box.

5. If the **Location** box doesn't display the storage location you want to use, tap the box. Then on the **Location** page that appears, tap the storage location you want.

6. In the **Create Notebook** box, tap the **Create** button to create and open a notebook that has the basic storage structure as a starting point.

---

 **SEE ALSO** For information about creating and configuring structural elements of a notebook, see "Configure notebook storage structure" later in this chapter.

---

# OneNote gets you started

The first time you start OneNote for iPad, the app creates a notebook for you on the OneDrive site that is associated with your user account. This notebook includes a built-in section named *Quick Notes* that contains a bit of information about how and why to use OneNote and some sample content.

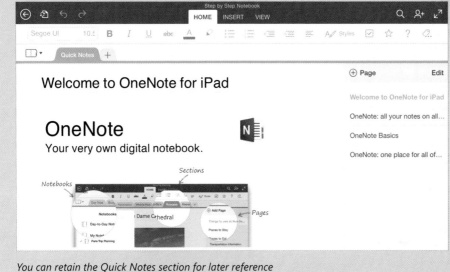

*You can retain the Quick Notes section for later reference*

Some of the information in the Quick Notes section applies to versions of OneNote other than OneNote for iPad. You can add, remove, and update information in the Quick Notes section if you want to.

## Open and switch among notebooks

The first time you open an existing notebook in OneNote for iPad, you must open it from its source location, which can be any storage location you're connected to. When you open a notebook from a remote storage location, OneNote creates a copy on the device you're working on, and synchronizes the local copy with the server copy. Because of this feature, you can access information that is stored in a notebook even when you're offline, from any device on which you've previously opened the notebook.

11

If you store or reference information in multiple notebooks, OneNote can maintain active connections to all of them when it's running. You can display the content of only one notebook in the main app window at a time, but all the connected notebooks are "open" and synchronizing content, and you can easily switch among them. The currently open notebooks are shown on the Notebooks page of the Backstage view and the Notebooks menu in the OneNote app window.

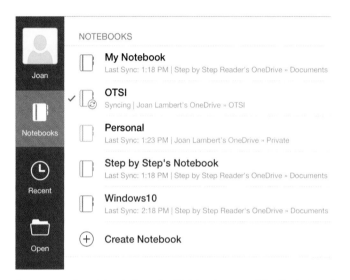

*Open or create notebooks from the Notebooks page of the Backstage view*

### To open an existing notebook for the first time

1. Start OneNote and display the Backstage view.

2. On the **File** bar, tap **Open** to display the storage locations you're connected to.

3. If the storage location the notebook is stored in doesn't already appear in your Places list, connect to it.

>  **SEE ALSO** For information about connecting to storage locations, see "Connect to additional storage locations" in Chapter 2, "Get connected."

4. Tap the storage location. If necessary, tap through the folder structure until you reach the notebook. Then tap the notebook.

5. If OneNote prompts you to enter user credentials, enter the account name and password for the account that has permission to access the notebook.

**To switch to a different open notebook**

1. Start OneNote and display the Backstage view.

2. On the **File** bar, tap **Notebooks**.

3. In the list of open notebooks on the **Notebooks** page of the Backstage view, tap the notebook you want to display.

*Or*

1. With any notebook displayed in OneNote for iPad, tap the **Notebooks** button at the left end of the notebook header to display the currently open notebooks.

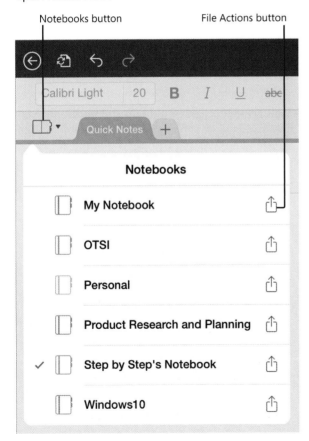

*You can manage currently open notebooks from the Notebooks menu*

2. On the **Notebooks** menu, tap the notebook you want to display.

## Close and reopen notebooks

It isn't necessary to close a notebook before exiting OneNote. It's simplest to leave all the notebooks that you use open all the time so that you can easily search their content. The notebooks will continue to synchronize in the background and you'll have access to current content when you need it. If you no longer need access to the information that is stored in a notebook—for example, if its content pertains only to a completed project—you can close it to keep the Notebooks menu and the Notebooks page of the Backstage view tidy.

After you close a notebook, it remains available to reopen from the Recent page of the Backstage view, or from its original storage location. If you want to ensure that you can quickly access a closed notebook at a later time, you can pin it to the Recent page and it will always be available from the Pinned section at the top of the page.

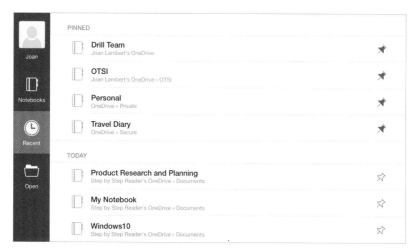

*Pinned notebooks are convenient to access*

### To close a notebook

1. On the **Notebooks** page of the Backstage view, tap the **File Actions** button for the notebook you want to close.

2. On the **Notebook Options** menu, tap **Close Notebook**.

*Or*

1. At the left end of the notebook header, tap the **Notebooks** button.

2. On the **Notebooks** menu, tap the **File Actions** button for the notebook you want to close.

3. On the notebook-specific menu, tap **Close Notebook**.

**To reopen a notebook**

1. On the **Recent** page of the Backstage view, tap the notebook you want to open.

> **SEE ALSO** For information about sharing notebooks and synchronizing notebook content, see "Protect and share information" and "Synchronize notebook content" in Chapter 12, "Locate and share notebook content."

# Configure notebook storage structure

The notebook storage structure in OneNote reflects that of a physical tabbed notebook such as those used by students. You can divide notebooks into one or more sections. Each section contains one or more pages. You store information on individual pages.

A new notebook contains one section and one page. You can add sections and pages to provide a structure for the content you intend to store in the notebook.

11

Section tab    New Section button    Notebook header        Page navigator    Add Page button

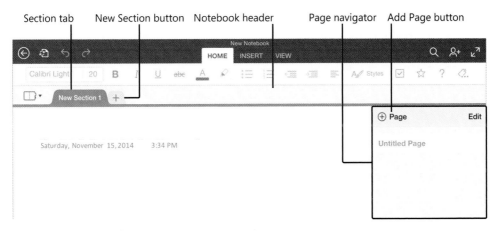

The OneNote user interface elements

As you add sections, you can name them in a way that is appropriate for the content. Be sure to give each section a meaningful name so you can easily identify it when you're sending content to OneNote from another program.

>  **TIP** In some versions of OneNote, you can optionally group sections into elements called *section groups*, which provide another layer of organizational structure. You can't create section groups in OneNote for iPad, but you can navigate through section groups that already exist in notebooks created in other versions of OneNote.

When you're adding content to a notebook, you can create blank pages or pages that already contain content. If you have a clear idea of the kind of information you're going to store in a notebook, you might find it simplest to build the notebook structure and then add content within that structure. But it isn't necessary to build the structure first—if you prefer, you can send content to your notebook and then organize pages and sections by moving or copying them. Whatever works best for you will work with OneNote.

**To create a section**

1. In the notebook header, tap the **New Section** button.

**To rename a section**

1. In the notebook header, double-tap the tab of the section you want to rename.

   *Or*

   Tap the section tab, and then tap **Rename** to activate the title for editing.

*The shortcut bar displays options for working with the selected title*

2. Enter the new section name, and then tap the **Done** key on the on-screen keyboard.

>  **TIP** If you're working with an external keyboard connected to your iPad, you can press the Enter key to perform the action of the Done key in any procedure.

**To create a page**

1. Display the section in which you want to create the page.

2. At the top of the page navigator, tap the **Add Page** button.

**To change a page to a subpage**

1. At the top of the page navigator, tap the **Edit** button.

2. Tap the selector to the left of the page name.

3. On the action bar at the top of the page navigator, tap the **Demote** button.

>  **TIP** To change a subpage to a standard page, follow the same process but tap the Promote button.

**To name or rename a page or subpage**

1. In the page navigator, tap the page or subpage.

2. In the title area at the top of the page, replace the page title.

# Add information to notebooks

You can use OneNote for iPad to create and gather notes in a variety of ways.

## Enter and format text

To enter text on a page, you can tap the on-screen keyboard or type on an external keyboard. You can use the dictation functionality of the iPad to dictate notes verbally, which can be a great time-saver after you become accustomed to the process. These processes are the same as those that you use to enter content in a document when using Word for iPad, so you're probably already familiar with them from the Word coverage earlier in this book.

> **SEE ALSO** For information about keyboard and dictation text-entry methods, including keyboard shortcuts and dictation commands, see "Enter text in documents" in Chapter 4, "Create professional documents."

**11**

If you want to keep track of the dates on which you enter specific notes, you can quickly insert the current date on your notebook page in *mm/dd/yy* format by tapping the Date button on the Insert tab. You can reference information that exists on a website rather than recording separate notes about it by linking from a placeholder on the notebook page to the webpage on the Internet.

>  **SEE ALSO** For information about inserting hyperlinks to a webpage, see "Reference additional information" in Chapter 6, "Enhance document content."

Formatting options for notebook page content include only the basics:

- You can apply a limited number of purpose-specific styles, including styles for a page title, six heading levels, normal paragraphs (the default), citations, quotes, and code.

- You can format characters by applying bold, italic, underline, and strikethrough font styles, changing the font color, and highlighting content.

- You can format paragraphs in these ways:

  - Change the paragraph indent in half-inch increments.

  - Create bulleted lists that use the default bullet characters.

  - Create numbered lists that use the default numbering formats.

The style and formatting options are available from the Home tab of the ribbon. You use the same methods to apply the available styles and formatting to page content in OneNote for iPad that you use in Word for iPad.

>  **SEE ALSO** For more information, including step-by-step procedures for applying styles and formatting, see "Align, space, and indent paragraphs" and "Change the appearance of text" in Chapter 4, "Create professional documents," and "Present content in lists" in Chapter 5, "Add visual elements to documents."

## Work with notebook containers

When you enter information onto a notebook page, the information is stored inside a note container rather than directly on the page. A page can contain multiple note containers; tapping an empty area of the page that is not in or near an existing note container creates a new one.

Two note containers on a page

In OneNote for iPad, it's generally simplest to keep all your page content in one note container because you can't manipulate the containers as you can in OneNote for Windows. Double-tapping the header of a note container selects it and displays a shortcut bar of commands for manipulating the content.

Options for working with a selected note container

> ⚠ **IMPORTANT** When you select a note container it might appear as though you actually selected the content. You can easily differentiate between the selection of a note container and its content: selecting only the content displays handles, whereas selecting the container does not.

In the Windows version of OneNote, you can move and merge note containers by dragging them on the page. This functionality is not currently available in OneNote for iPad; however, you can move a note container by moving its content.

**11**

Like the other Office for iPad apps, OneNote automatically saves the changes you make to a notebook. You can undo all the changes you've made to a Word document, Excel workbook, or PowerPoint presentation in the current app session by restoring the file to its most recently opened state. However, due to the way that OneNote stores information, you can't restore OneNote notebooks. This can be both good and bad—you can enter notes and then exit the notebook without losing them, but you must take care when modifying content that you don't delete information you might need later.

## Organize notes in tables

Certain types of information that you store in a notebook will be easier to track if you organize it in tables. OneNote for iPad includes limited table functionality, but it does provide the option of inserting and then populating a table. The initial table created by OneNote for iPad when you insert a blank table is two columns wide by two columns high. You can insert additional rows or columns as necessary. OneNote for iPad doesn't include any special formatting options for tables.

**To insert a blank 2-by-2 table**

1. On the **Insert** tab, tap the **Table** button.

**To add rows or columns to a table**

1. To insert a single row or column, tap to position the cursor in a table cell adjacent to where you want to insert the row or column.

   *Or*

   To insert multiple rows or columns, select the number of existing rows or columns you want to insert adjacent to where you want to insert the new rows or columns.

2. On the **Table** tool tab, tap the **Insert** button.

3. On the **Insert** menu, tap **Rows Above**, **Rows Below**, **Columns Left**, or **Columns Right**.

**To remove rows or columns from a table**

1. To remove a single row or column, tap to position the cursor anywhere in that row or column.

   *Or*

   To remove multiple rows or columns, select cells in the rows or columns you want to remove.

2. On the **Table** tool tab, tap the **Delete** button.

3. On the **Delete** menu, tap **Rows** or **Columns**.

**To delete a table**

1. Tap to position the cursor anywhere in the table.

2. On the **Table** tool tab, tap the **Delete** button.

3. On the **Delete** menu, tap **Table**.

> **TIP** If you are working with an external keyboard connected to your iPad, you can create a table while inserting information. To do so, enter content and then press the Tab key to move to or create the next cell in the row, and the Return key in the last cell of the table to create a new row.

# Insert images

**11**

One of the great things about OneNote is that you can store not only your own notes, but also many other types of information. Pictures, of course, are worth a million words—and when you're using OneNote for iPad, you have the advantage of working on a device that you can use to easily capture images at the same time you're taking notes.

You can insert photos that you've already taken with your iPad or another device and stored on your iPad or in your photo stream, or you can capture and insert photos from within OneNote. This simplifies the process of documenting something because you can intersperse pictures among your written notes as appropriate.

Your iPad has its own camera app, but OneNote for iPad also comes with its own picture-management app, Office Lens. Office Lens has been specially engineered to enhance images of text, but you can use it to work with any photo.

*A photo captured from within OneNote and displayed in Office Lens*

When you capture images of whiteboards, printed documents, sticky notes, or other items that display text, Office Lens can enhance the image to make the text content easier to read. You can crop and straighten the image, and when you're happy with the result, Office Lens inserts the enhanced image into your notebook.

 **TIP** If you prefer to use the standard iPad camera app rather than Office Lens, you can turn off Office Lens from the iPad settings for OneNote.

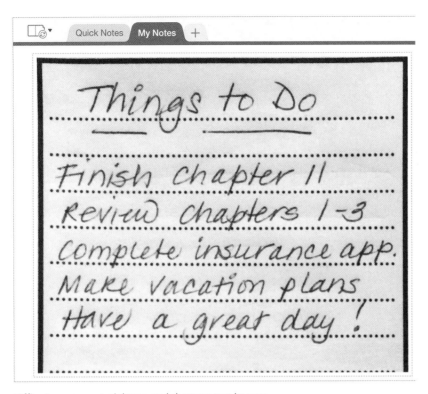

*Office Lens crops, straightens, and sharpens text images*

The Office Lens app is simple to use—it includes only four controls.

- The Back button returns to the active notebook page without inserting the photo.

- The Whiteboard, Photo, and Document modes analyze the photo and crop, straighten, and sharpen it to different standards.

- The Crop button displays handles that you can drag to designate the area of the photo you want to keep.

- The Finish button accepts the current settings and inserts the photo on the notebook page.

**11**

### To select or insert an existing photo from your iPad or photo stream

1. Tap to position the cursor where you want to insert the photo on the page.

2. On the **Insert** tab, tap the **Pictures** button.

3. On the **Photos** menu, tap the storage area that contains the photo you want to insert.

4. Locate the photo and tap it.

   If you're using the default OneNote for iPad camera setting, the photo opens in Office Lens and you can enhance it before you insert it on the page. If you've turned off the option to use Office Lens, the photo appears on the page.

> ⚠ **IMPORTANT** OneNote for iPad doesn't include picture configuration options such as those that are available in Word and PowerPoint. You can reposition a photo by dragging it but you can't specify the text wrapping or format the photo.

### To capture a picture or text image from within OneNote

1. Tap to position the cursor where you want to insert the photo on the page.

2. On the **Insert** tab, tap the **Camera** button.

3. Position the iPad so the image you want to capture is in focus on the screen.

4. Tap the **Capture** button (the circle).

   If you're using the default OneNote for iPad camera setting, the photo opens in Office Lens; otherwise it appears on the page.

### To enhance and insert a photo from Office Lens

1. If you want Office Lens to automatically enhance the image content, tap the **Whiteboard** and **Document** buttons to preview the results, and then tap the mode that best fits your needs.

2. If you want to crop or straighten the photo, tap the **Crop** button to display the original image with crop handles positioned where Office Lens senses that the image corners should be.

3. Drag the handles to define the area of the final image and its bottom edge, from which Office Lens calculates the alignment of the image.

4. Tap the **Finish** button to insert the photo.

**To turn off Office Lens**

1. Start the Settings app.

2. Near the bottom of the **Settings** list, tap **OneNote**.

3. On the **OneNote** page, in the **Photos & Camera section**, tap **Camera Setting**.

4. On the **Camera Setting** page, tap the **Use Office Lens** slider to change its background to white.

## Insert files from cloud storage locations

In OneNote for iPad, you can insert files from a cloud storage location into your notes. Different types of files create different results. For example:

- Inserting a Word document displays a labeled document icon on the page. You can display the file content and then open the file for editing.

- Inserting a graphic file displays the graphic on the page.

- Inserting a video file displays a labeled generic icon. You can play the video recording.

You can change the icon label from the file name to something more descriptive, but note that the labels wrap after approximately 13 characters.

 **IMPORTANT** At the time of this writing, OneNote for iPad supports inserting files only from iCloud and Dropbox storage locations.

11

You can search your cloud storage location for files that contain specific terms. To simplify the process of locating a file in your iCloud storage, you can sort the search results by Date, Name, or Tags.

*The sorting options for search results*

**To insert a file from iCloud or Dropbox storage**

1. Tap to position the cursor where you want to insert the file content on the page.

2. On the **Insert** tab, tap **File**.

   A window displays your iCloud storage.

3. If you're inserting a file from iCloud, you can do the following:

   - To switch between the file thumbnail and file list views of your iCloud storage, tap the button that represents the view you want.

   - To search for a specific file, tap the **Search** box and enter the search parameter.

   - To change the sort order of files, tap **Date**, **Name**, or **Tags**.

4. If you want to insert a file from Dropbox, you can do the following:

   - To display your Dropbox storage, tap **Locations** in the upper-left corner of the window, and then tap **Dropbox**.

   - To search for a specific file in the Dropbox window, tap the **Search** box and enter the search parameter.

5. Locate and then tap the file you want to insert.

**To change a file icon label**

1. Tap the icon, and then on the shortcut bar, tap **Rename**.

2. In the **Rename** box, enter the label you want, and then tap **Save**.

**To preview a file from an embedded icon**

1. Double-tap the icon.

   *Or*

   Tap the icon, and then on the shortcut bar, tap **Open**.

2. Flick to scroll through the file.

3. To close the preview, tap **Done** in the upper-left corner of the window.

## Send, print, and link content to notes

When you are using the Windows version of OneNote in conjunction with other programs in the Office suite, there are many additional ways you can store information in OneNote for safekeeping. For example, you can:

- Send email messages directly from Outlook to a OneNote notebook.

- Link tagged tasks in a notebook to your Outlook task list.

- Take meeting notes in personal or shared notebooks.

- Create notes that are linked directly to specific locations in a Word document or PowerPoint presentation.

- Print any Office file to a OneNote notebook.

Although you can't perform these same actions in OneNote for iPad, you can work with the content of notebooks that are stored in shared locations in the iPad and Windows versions of OneNote.

### To open a file for editing from a preview window

1. In the upper-right corner of the preview window, tap the **File Actions** button.

2. In the window that opens, tap the icon of the app you want to open the file in.

### To manage cloud storage providers

1. On the **Insert** tab, tap the **File** button.

2. In the upper-left corner of the window, tap **Locations**. Then on the **Locations** menu, tap **More**.

3. In the **Manage Storage Providers** window, do either of the following:

   - To make your storage location with a cloud storage provider available, tap the provider's slider to change its background color to green.

   - To remove a cloud storage provider from the **Locations** menu, tap the provider's slider to change its background color to white.

4. In the upper-right corner of the **Manage Storage Providers** window, tap **Done**.

**11**

# Manage pages and sections

From time to time you might find it necessary to modify the storage structure of a notebook or move content around within the notebook. Fortunately, it's much easier to move information around in an electronic notebook than it is in a physical notebook.

You can rearrange notebook elements in the following ways:

■ Move pages within a section, to another section in the same notebook, or to a section in any open notebook.

■ Move sections within a notebook or to any other notebook that you have open. When you move a section to a different notebook, it is inserted as the last section in the notebook, and the section tab appears to the right of the other section tabs in the notebook header.

You can also assign background colors to notebook pages to provide a visual indicator of the purpose or status of a page—for example, a green background to indicate that the page content is final or an orange background to indicate that a page contains confidential information.

 **TIP** Changing the page background color in OneNote for iPad doesn't affect the color of the page tab in the page navigator.

You control the movement of pages by activating the edit functions in the page navigator.

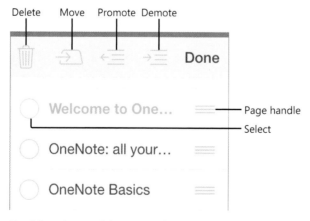

*Tap Edit at the top of the page navigator to activate the edit functions*

After you finish organizing your notebook content, you might find that you have extra or empty notebook elements. You can delete any notebook element other than a section group and the notebook itself from within OneNote for iPad.

 **TIP** You can delete notebooks and section groups when working with a notebook in the Windows version of OneNote.

**To change the color of the active page or subpage**

1. On the **View** tab, tap the **Page Color** button.

2. On the **Page Color** menu, tap the color swatch you want to apply to the page.

   *Or*

   On the **Page Color** menu, tap the **No color** button to remove the page background color.

**To move a page within a section**

1. At the top of the page navigator, tap **Edit**.

2. In the page navigator, tap and hold the handle of the page you want to move, and then drag it vertically to the new location.

**To move one or more pages to a different section or notebook**

1. At the top of the page navigator, tap **Edit**.

2. In the page navigator, select the pages you want to move.

    **TIP** To select a page, tap the empty circle that precedes the page name. A check mark appears when the page is selected.

3. On the action bar at the top of the page navigator, tap the **Move** button to display a window showing the sections and section groups available in the current notebook.

**11**

Move this page to a new section.

**<** Notebooks                     **OTSI**                     Cancel

**Remote servers**
1 page

Team Admin-Tools

Project Management

Content and Editing

Indexing

How-to

Layout

Troubleshooting

Resources

Specific Projects                                              **>**

*You might need to swipe the list to display all the sections and section groups in the notebook*

4.   To move the selected pages to a different section of the current notebook, tap
     the section you want to move them to.

     *Or*

     To move the pages to a different notebook, tap **Notebooks** to display a
     window showing the currently open notebooks; tap the notebook, the section
     group if appropriate, and then the section you want to move the pages to.

> **TIP** When you move a page to a different section, it is inserted as the last page in the
> section, at the bottom of the page navigator for that section. When you move a
> section to a different notebook, it is inserted as the last section in the notebook, to the right
> of the existing section tabs in the notebook header.

**To move a section within a notebook**

1. In the notebook header, tap and hold the tab of the section you want to move, until the tab changes to a lighter color.

2. Drag the section tab laterally to the location you want it in relation to the other section tabs.

**To move a section to a different notebook**

1. Display the section you want to move.

2. Tap the section tab once.

3. On the shortcut bar, tap **Move** to display a window showing the currently open notebooks and any section groups they contain.

Move this section to a new notebook.

**Notebooks**                    Cancel

**Toy Ideas**
1 section

Step by Step's Notebook

Windows10

My Notebook

Personal

OTSI

Specific Projects

Product Research and Planning

*The section you're moving is identified above the notebook list*

4. In the **Notebooks** window, tap the notebook you want to move the section to.

**11**

### To delete a page

1. Display the section that contains the page you want to delete.

2. In the page navigator, swipe left or right on the tab of the page you want to delete, and then tap **Delete**.

 **IMPORTANT** OneNote stores your deleted pages in the Recycle Bin of the OneDrive site or SharePoint site the notebook is stored on. You can restore deleted pages from that Recycle Bin until they are permanently deleted (usually after 60 days).

### To delete a section

1. Display the section you want to delete.

2. In the notebook header, tap the active section tab.

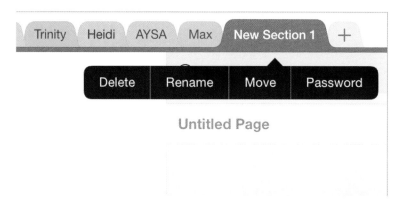

*When you tap the tab once, the shortcut bar displays options relevant to the section*

 **IMPORTANT** Tap a section tab once to display the shortcut bar, or twice to activate the section tab for editing.

3. On the shortcut bar, tap **Delete**.

# Skills review

In this chapter, you learned how to:

- Create, open, and close notebooks
- Configure notebook storage structure
- Add information to notebooks
- Manage pages and sections

**11**

# Practice tasks

The practice files for these tasks are located in the iPadOfficeSBS\Ch11 folder.

## Create, open, and close notebooks and configure storage structure

Start OneNote, and then perform the following tasks:

1. Create a new notebook in your OneDrive storage location and name it My Notes.

2. Without closing your new notebook, open the **StoreNotes** notebook from the practice file folder.

3. Close the **StoreNotes** notebook, and then reopen it from the list of recent notebooks.

4. Switch to the **My Notes** notebook.

5. Rename the *Welcome* section as Practice One, and create a new section named Practice Two. Move the *Practice Two* section so it immediately follows the *Practice One* section.

6. In the *Practice Two* section, rename the untitled page as Page 1 and create a new page named Page 2.

7. Make *Page 2* a subpage of *Page 1*, and rename it as Subpage One.

8. Exit OneNote without closing the open notebooks.

## Add information to notebooks

Open the StoreNotes notebook if it isn't already open, and then perform the following tasks:

1. In the *Add Content* section, on the *Text Practice* page, enter the following text just below the page title: Taking notes on the iPad is easy. Keep track of important information, and access it from anywhere.

2. Tap halfway down the page to create a second note container. In the new note container, insert a 2-by-2 table.

3. In the first column of the table, enter January in the first row and February in the second row. In the second column, enter Garnet in the first row and Amethyst in the second row.

4. Add a third row to the end of the table. In the new row, enter March in the first column and Aquamarine in the second column.

5. Insert a row at the top of the table. In the new row, enter Month in the first column and Birthstone in the second column. Select the two cells, and then apply bold formatting to the words so they look like column headings.

6. Switch to the *Image Practice* page. From within OneNote, use your iPad and the Office Lens utility to capture an image of something (such as a notepad, whiteboard, or sticky note) that has handwritten text on it.

7. Enhance and crop the image by using Office Lens. Insert the modified image below the title of the *Image Practice* page.

8. Exit OneNote without closing the open notebooks.

## Manage pages and sections

Open the StoreNotes notebook if it isn't already open, and open the MoveNotes notebook. Then perform the following tasks:

1. Display the **StoreNotes** notebook.

2. In the *My Pages* section of the notebook, change the color of *Page A* to any shade of blue. Then change the color of *Page B* to any shade of green.

3. Move *Page C* above *Page A*.

4. Move *Page A* and *Page B* to the *Practice Pages* section of the notebook.

5. Move the *Practice Pages* section so that it precedes the *My Pages* section.

6. Move the *Practice Pages* section to the **MoveNotes** notebook. Then create a copy of the *Practice Pages* section in the **StoreNotes** notebook.

7. In the **StoreNotes** notebook, delete the *My Pages* section. Then in the *Practice Pages* section, delete *Page B*.

8. Exit OneNote without closing the open notebooks.

# Locate and share notebook content

The primary point of recording information in a OneNote notebook (or recording it anywhere, for that matter) is so you can release it from your active memory (to make room for more information) but retain it for later reference. In other words, if you write it down, you can forget it—all you have to remember is where you wrote it down.

One of the great things about OneNote is that no matter how neatly or messily you store information, it's still easy to find what you're looking for when you need it. It's also easy to share that information with other people or invite them to contribute information to your notebook. You can provide different people with differing levels of access to notebook content.

This chapter guides you through procedures related to displaying different views of notebook content, searching for information in notebooks, password-protecting notebook sections, sharing notebooks and notebook pages, and synchronizing local notebooks with server versions.

## In this chapter

- Display notes in different ways
- Find information in notebooks
- Protect and share information
- Synchronize notebook content

## Practice files

For this chapter, use the practice files from the iPadOfficeSBS\Ch12 folder. For practice file download instructions, see the Introduction.

# Display notes in different ways

Sometimes it is more convenient to have the entire section and page structure of a notebook visible. At other times, you might prefer to display only the content of a specific page, or to display the note content in a larger format.

## Switch notebook views

OneNote for iPad provides two preconfigured views of notebook content—Normal view and Full Page view—that make it easy to switch quickly between viewing all the notebook elements and viewing only the page content.

Normal view displays the active ribbon tab and the notebook section tabs above the page, and the page navigator to the right of the page. When you're in Normal view, the button at the right end of the ribbon displays two outward pointing arrows, and tapping the button switches to Full Page view.

Full Page View button

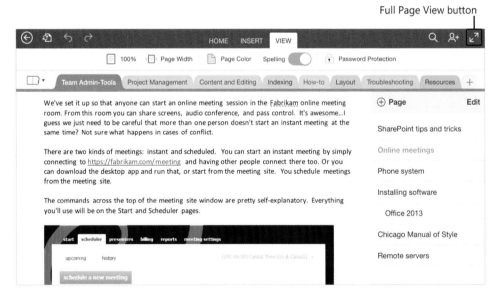

*A notebook page in Normal view*

Full Page view hides the ribbon, the section tabs, and the page navigator so you can focus on the content of the current page. When you're in Full Page view, the button at the right end of the ribbon displays two inward-pointing arrows, and tapping the button switches to Normal view.

Normal View button

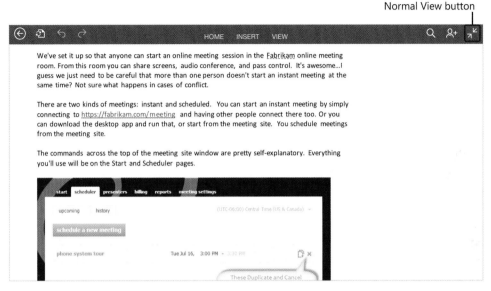

A notebook page in Full Page view

When working in Full Page view, you have direct access only to the menus and commands that are available from the ribbon header. You can display individual menus and tabs in Full Page view without switching to Normal view.

 **TIP** OneNote maintains the most recently selected view when you switch between notebooks.

### To change the notebook view

1. To switch from Normal view to Full Page view, tap the **Full Page View** button at the right end of the ribbon.

2. To switch from Full Page view to Normal view, tap the **Normal View** button at the right end of the ribbon.

### To work with content in Full Page view

1. Perform any of these actions as you would in Normal view:

   - Tap to position the cursor to enter content.

   - Double-tap to select content and display shortcut bars.

   - Tap the commands that are available on the shortcut bars.

12

2. Use any of these features as you would in Normal view:

- File menu commands
- Search functionality
- Share functionality

3. To access a command on the ribbon without displaying other hidden notebook elements:

   a. Tap any tab title on the ribbon header to display the tab.

   b. Tap the command and complete the associated operation.

   c. Tap the title of the displayed tab to hide the tab.

## Fit content to the page

In addition to changing the structure within which the content of a page is displayed, you can adjust the magnification level to display the content at its actual size or to fit the width of the page, whether the notebook is in Normal view or Full Page view.

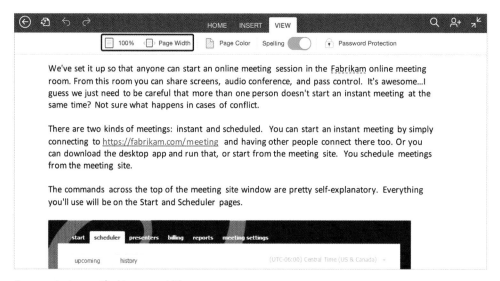

*Page content magnified to page width*

## Zoom by touch

In OneNote for iPad, you can manually change the magnification level of the page content by pinching or spreading your fingers on the iPad screen. When you use this method to zoom in on or out from the content, a marker appears between your fingers and displays the current magnification level (ranging from Minimum to Maximum with specific percentages in between).

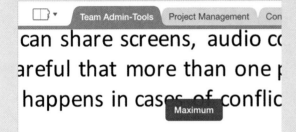

*The magnification level appears when you pinch or stretch the page*

OneNote for iPad is programmed to change the magnification of only the page content, not the entire app window, when you use manual zoom techniques.

# Find information in notebooks

The purpose of storing information in a OneNote notebook is not only so that you no longer have to remember it but also so that you can easily retrieve the information later, from any computer or device that is running OneNote. You can easily search for keywords or specific information stored in any of your OneNote notebooks and narrow down the results by location. You can also attach tags (icons that have specific meanings) to content to help you locate information about the related topic on a page.

**12**

# Tag information for reference and retrieval

You can tag individual paragraphs to provide a visual indicator of some sort of information about the content of the paragraph. For example, you might want to tag information that you need to follow up on, that is linked to a specific project, or that is a high priority. You can apply multiple tags to a paragraph; the tags appear within the note container to the left of the first line of the paragraph.

Tags

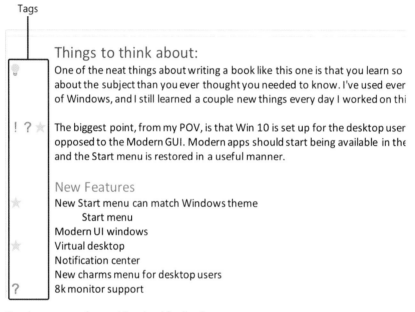

*Tagging paragraphs provides visual feedback*

In OneNote for iPad you can apply any of 27 standard tags. Three common tags are available directly from the Home tab of the ribbon, and all the tags are available on the menu that expands when you tap the adjacent Tag button.

> **IMPORTANT** Tags provide only a visual cue in OneNote for iPad, but they are extremely useful in OneNote for Windows, because you can generate summaries of tagged content by storage location or time period. You can also link To Do tags to your Outlook task list and update the task status from either location.

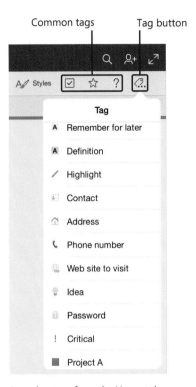

*Inserting tags from the Home tab*

## To tag a paragraph

1. Tap anywhere in the paragraph.

2. On the **Home** tab, tap the **To Do**, **Important**, or **Question** button.

   *Or*

   On the **Home** tab, tap the **Tag** button. Then on the **Tag** menu, tap the tag you want.

## To remove a tag from a paragraph

1. Tap anywhere in the paragraph.

2. On the **Home** tab or **Tag** menu, tap the tag you want to remove.

**12**

# Search for text

In OneNote for iPad, you can search for text that was entered directly on a page or that appears in files that were printed to OneNote.

 **TIP** In OneNote 2013, you can search for spoken words in audio and video recordings and for printed words in images.

The default search settings locate information stored in any open notebook. This is very convenient because you don't have to remember where you stored the information or navigate through a series of notebooks, sections, and pages to get to it.

As you enter text in the search box, OneNote highlights matches on all pages within the search scope, displays the total number of pages that contain the search term at the right end of the search box, and displays links to those pages in the Search Results pane. The Search Results pane displays the results in two groups: pages that have the search result in the title and pages that have the search result only on the page (but not in the title).

 **TIP** A search result group header is shown only if the search returns pages in that group. A page will appear in only one group.

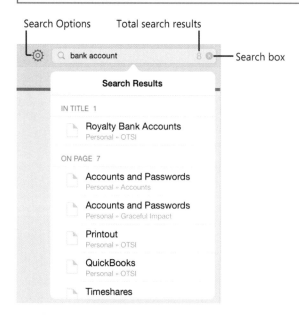

*Search results appear alphabetically in groups*

Search results are listed within each group in alphabetical order by page title. The specific location of the page (notebook and section) is shown below the page title. This can be helpful in determining the relevance of the search results on that page, so you can quickly find the page that contains the information you're looking for.

By default, OneNote locates all pages that contain the words entered in the search box in any order, in all open notebooks. You can get more-focused results by adding search terms, specifying that you want to match only exact phrases, or narrowing the scope of the search to only the current notebook, section, or section group.

 **TIP** The current search scope appears in the search box until you enter the first character of the search term.

### To search within the default or most recent scope

1. On the ribbon header, tap the **Search** button to activate the search box.

2. Enter the word or words you want to find.

### To narrow or expand the search parameters

1. If you want to expand the search to return more results, do any of the following:

   - Remove words from the search term.

   - Remove word endings (such as *ed*, *ing*, or *s*).

   - Search all notebooks.

2. If you want to narrow the search to return fewer results, do any of the following:

   - Add words to make the search term more specific.

   - Add a space after a root word that you want to match exactly.

   - Enclose phrases that should be exact matches in quotation marks.

   - Search only the current notebook or section.

### To modify the search scope

1. Tap the **Search Options** button.

2. On the **Options** menu, below **Search In**, tap **This Section**, **This Section Group**, **This Notebook**, or **All Notebooks**.

**12**

**TIP** OneNote retains the search term in the search box until you clear it and retains the selected search scope until you change it. These remain stored even when you switch notebooks or exit OneNote.

**To clear the search term**

1. Tap the **Search** button, and then tap in the search box.

2. Tap the **Delete** button that appears at the right end of the search box.

# Protect and share information

OneNote can provide an excellent platform for the collaborative collection of information. People can access the information in a OneNote notebook from many different computer systems and devices and can store or link to almost any type of information.

When you create a OneNote notebook in a remote storage location, that notebook is accessible only to people who have specific user credentials with permission to access that location. When you create a notebook by using OneNote for iPad, you might do so in a shared storage location that other people already have access to, such as a SharePoint document library, or you might create it in a more private location that is accessible only to you, such as your personal OneDrive site. If you want to share information that is stored in a notebook, you can grant permission for people to view or edit the notebook.

## Protect notebook sections

Before you share a notebook with other people, consider whether any sections of the notebook contain information that you want to keep private or provide to only specific people. If so, it isn't necessary to move those sections out of the notebook; you can hide the content of any section by assigning a password to the section and then locking it. You can password-protect only sections, not individual pages.

You can assign the same password to multiple sections or assign unique passwords to different sections. You must lock all password-protected sections of a notebook at the same time. You can unlock sections individually.

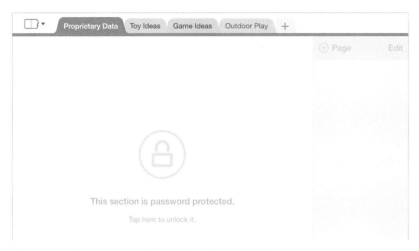

*The pages and page content of a locked section are hidden*

If you want to allow other people to access a password-protected section, you can share the password with those people. The password protection becomes effective for all users (including you) after the notebook synchronizes with the server. The section can be unlocked only by entering the correct password.

 **SEE ALSO** For information about synchronization, see "Synchronize notebook content" later in this chapter.

**To password-protect a notebook section**

1. Display the section you want to protect.

2. On the **View** tab, tap **Password Protection**. Then, on the **Password Protection** menu, tap **Protect This Section**.

   *Or*

   Tap the section tab, tap **Password** on the shortcut bar, and then tap **Protect**.

3. In the **Password Protection** box, enter and reenter a password for the section, and then tap **Done**.

 **IMPORTANT** Take any necessary precautions to ensure that you can remember or locate the password, because you will not be able to unlock the section without it.

**12**

**To lock all protected sections in a notebook**

1. On the **View** tab, tap **Password Protection**.

2. On the **Password Protection** menu, tap **Lock Protected Sections**.

*Or*

1. Display a protected section.

2. Tap the section tab, tap **Password** on the shortcut bar, and then tap **Lock All**.

**To unlock a protected section**

1. Display the section you want to unlock, and then tap the lock icon in the center of the page.

2. In the **Protected Section** box, enter the password assigned to the section, and then tap **Unlock**.

**To change the password assigned to a protected section**

1. Unlock the section.

2. On the **View** tab, tap **Password Protection**. Then, on the **Password Protection** menu, tap **Change Password**.

   *Or*

   Tap the section tab, tap **Password** on the shortcut bar, and then tap **Change**.

3. In the **Change Password** box, enter the password that is currently assigned to the section, enter and reenter the new password, and then tap **Change**.

**To remove a section password**

1. Unlock the section.

2. On the **View** tab, tap **Password Protection**. Then, on the **Password Protection** menu, tap **Remove Password**.

   *Or*

   Tap the section tab, tap **Password** on the shortcut bar, and then tap **Remove**.

3. In the **Remove Password** box, enter the password assigned to the section, and then tap **Remove**.

# Share notebook content

There are several ways in which you can share the content of a notebook that is stored in a shared location:

- You can send a link to the notebook in an email message, instant message, or other online communication. You have the option of sending a link that permits read-only access or a link that permits read/write access.

  When you send a link, message recipients can open the notebook by clicking or tapping the link. Thereafter, it will appear in their lists of open notebooks.

- You can attach a PDF version of a notebook page to an email message.

  Sending a PDF file is a convenient way to share information with people who don't use OneNote or can't access your storage location.

Multiple people can work in a shared OneNote notebook at the same time.

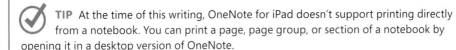

> **TIP** At the time of this writing, OneNote for iPad doesn't support printing directly from a notebook. You can print a page, page group, or section of a notebook by opening it in a desktop version of OneNote.

### To send a PDF file of a notebook page to other people

1. Display the notebook page you want to share.

2. At the right end of the ribbon, tap the **Share** button.

3. On the **Share** menu, tap **Email Page**.

   OneNote creates a PDF file of the active page. The Mail app creates an email message with the PDF file attached and automatically sets the file name and message subject to the page title.

4. In the message window, enter the recipient information, modify the subject if you want to, and enter any additional message content.

5. In the upper-right corner of the message window, tap **Send**.

> **SEE ALSO** For information about creating and sending links to notebooks, see "Distribute files" in Chapter 3, "Create and manage files."

**12**

# Synchronize notebook content

OneNote periodically synchronizes all local copies of a shared notebook with the server copy to distribute content changes to all users. The most recent synchronization date and time for each open notebook are shown on the Notebooks page of the Backstage view.

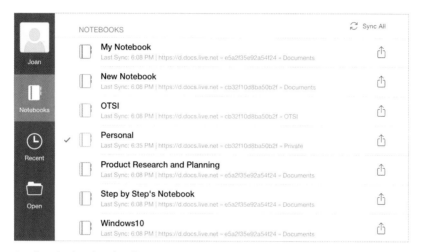

*Synchronization data for all open notebooks*

If you prefer, you can manually synchronize one or all open notebooks any time that your iPad is online. For example, if a colleague mentions that he or she just updated the content of a shared notebook and you want to review the updated content, you can synchronize the notebook and have immediate access to the changes.

**To synchronize the current notebook**

1. On the ribbon, tap the **File** button.

2. On the **File** menu, tap **Sync This Notebook**.

**To synchronize any one open notebook**

1. In the notebook header, tap the **Notebooks** button.

2. On the **Notebooks** menu, tap the **File Actions** button to the right of the notebook you want to synchronize.

3. On the notebook-specific menu, tap **Sync Now**.

*Or*

1. On the **Notebooks** page of the Backstage view, tap the **File Actions** button to the right of the notebook you want to synchronize.

2. On the **Notebook Options** menu, tap **Sync Now**.

**To synchronize all open notebooks**

1. Display the **Notebooks** page of the Backstage view.

2. In the upper-right corner of the page, tap **Sync All**.

# Skills review

In this chapter, you learned how to:

- Display notes in different ways

- Find information in notebooks

- Protect and share information

- Synchronize notebook content

**12**

# Practice tasks

The practice file for these tasks is located in the iPadOfficeSBS\Ch12 folder.

## Display notes in different ways

Start OneNote, open the ShareNotes notebook, and then perform the following tasks:

1. Display the notebook in Normal view and navigate to the *Display Notes* section.

2. Display the *Change Views* page in Full Page view.

3. Use touch to zoom out to the minimum magnification level, so that the text appears smaller. Then zoom in to the maximum magnification level, so that the text appears larger.

4. Display the **View** tab and tap the button to display the text at 100 percent. Then tap the button to fit the page content to the width of the page.

5. Switch back to Normal view.

## Find information in notebooks

Open the ShareNotes notebook if it isn't already open, and then perform the following tasks:

1. In the *Add Tags* section, on the *Tag Practice* page, add an **Important** tag and a **Remember for later** tag to the paragraph.

2. Remove only the **Important** tag from the paragraph.

3. Search the notebook for all instances of the word *tag*. Note the number of search results.

4. Modify the search scope to return only instances of the word that are in the *Find Text* section.

5. Narrow the search results to instances of the exact phrase *tags summary*.

6. Clear the search term.

## Protect and share information

Open the ShareNotes notebook if it isn't already open, and then perform the following tasks:

1. Assign the password **P@ssw0rd** (using the number zero instead of the letter O) to the *Protect Notebooks* section.

2. Assign the password **Top%Secret** to the *Lock Sections* section.

3. Lock both of the protected sections.

4. Unlock the *Protect Notebooks* section, and change its password to **Top%Secret**.

5. Unlock the *Lock Sections* section, and remove its password.

6. Email the *Share Content* page of the *Lock Sections* section to yourself as a PDF.

7. Email a read-only link to the notebook to yourself.

## Synchronize notebook content

Open the ShareNotes notebook if it isn't already open, and then perform the following tasks:

1. Rename the *Welcome* section **Synchronize Notebooks**.

2. On the **Notebooks** page of the Backstage view, note the date and time each open notebook was last synchronized with the server.

3. Synchronize only the **ShareNotes** notebook with the server and note the change on the **Notebooks** page of the Backstage view.

4. Synchronize all open notebooks with the server.

5. If you want to, close all the open notebooks related to the practice tasks for this book.

# Appendix

# Touchscreen and keyboard shortcuts

The standard method of working with content in the Office for iPad apps is to tap the relevant commands. You can perform some tasks faster by using specific gestures or on-screen keyboard shortcuts or, if your iPad is connected to an external keyboard, by pressing specific key combinations.

## Touchscreen gestures

You can use the gestures described in the following table to move around in a file when working in Word for iPad, Excel for iPad, PowerPoint for iPad, or OneNote for iPad.

| Action | Touchscreen gesture |
| --- | --- |
| Scroll | Swipe up, down, left, or right |
| Scroll quickly | Flick up, down, left, or right, then tap to stop scrolling |
| Zoom in | Stretch two fingers apart |
| Zoom out | Pinch two fingers together |

You can use the gestures described in the following table to work with text content on document pages, in text boxes, and on notebook pages in the Office for iPad apps.

| Action | Touchscreen gesture |
| --- | --- |
| Select a word | Double-tap the word |
| Select a paragraph | Triple-tap the paragraph |
| Expand or contract a selection | Drag the selection handles |
| Select all content in a document, worksheet, content container, or notebook page | Tap text and then tap Select All on the shortcut bar |

You can use the gestures described in the following table to work with workbook structural elements and content in Excel for iPad.

| Action | Touchscreen gesture |
| --- | --- |
| Select a cell | Tap the cell once |
| Select multiple cells | Tap any cell and then drag the selection handles |
| Select from the current cell to the next empty cell above or to the left | Flick the upper-left selection handle |
| Select from the current cell to the next empty cell below or to the right | Flick the lower-right selection handle |
| Select a column or row | Tap the column heading or row heading |
| Activate a cell for editing | Double-tap the cell, or tap in the Formula Bar |
| Display the shortcut bar for a cell | Slowly tap the cell twice |
| Move selected cells, columns, or rows | Tap and hold the selection, then when a dotted line appears around the selection, drag it to the new location |
| Resize a column or row | Tap and drag the column heading or row heading |
| Fit a column or row to its contents | Double-tap the column heading or row heading |

# On-screen keyboard tips

The on-screen keyboard appears when you tap an area of a document, worksheet, slide, or notebook page in which you can enter text. This keyboard has several forms.

 **TIP** If your iPad is connected to an external keyboard, the on-screen keyboard doesn't appear.

- The standard on-screen keyboard displays the alphabet in QWERTY keyboard format and the most common punctuation symbols.

  As you tap letters on the keyboard, common words beginning with the letters you've entered are shown above the top row of letters; the most likely match is in the center. You can tap a word to enter it and display the next predicted words. This predictive technology is so good that it will frequently predict all or most of the sentence you're entering.

  Entering a lot of text from the standard on-screen keyboard can be an arduous task. To simplify the process and tap fewer times to achieve the result you want, you can use the shortcuts described in the following table.

| Function | Action |
| --- | --- |
| Enter a period and trailing space | Double-tap the Spacebar twice at the end of a sentence |
| Enter a single quotation mark | Tap and hold the Comma key |
| Enter a quotation mark | Tap and hold the Period key |
| Enter an accented vowel | Tap and hold a vowel, then slide to the accented vowel you want |
| Enter a single uppercase letter | Tap and slide from the Shift key to the letter |
| Turn on or release the Caps Lock function | Double-tap the Shift key |
| Enter a single character from the number keyboard | Tap and slide from the Number key to the number or symbol |

- The number keyboard displays one row of numbers and two rows of common symbols. You switch to the number keyboard by tapping the Number key (labeled .?123) on either side of the standard keyboard or symbol keyboard.

On the number keyboard, use the shortcuts described in the following table to enter special characters.

| Character | Action |
| --- | --- |
| Upside-down exclamation point | Tap and hold the exclamation point key and then slide to the character |
| Upside-down question mark | Tap and hold the question mark key and then slide to the character |
| Opening and closing quotation marks | Tap and hold the quotation mark key, then slide to the opening or closing mark |
| Opening and closing single quotes | Tap and hold the single quotation mark key, then slide to the opening or closing mark |
| Opening and closing chevrons | Tap and hold the quotation mark key, then slide to the opening or closing chevron |
| Grave accent | Tap and hold the single quotation mark key, then slide to the accent |

- The symbol keyboard displays three rows of symbols. You switch to the symbol keyboard by tapping the Symbol key (labeled #+=) on the left or right side of the number keyboard.

- The function keyboard (available only in Excel) displays symbols commonly used in formulas on the left, arrow keys in the center, and a calculator-style number pad on the right. You switch to the function keyboard by tapping the Function button (labeled 123) at the right end of the status bar, which appears above the keyboard in Excel.

**A**

To display additional symbols on the function keyboard, tap and hold any key that has a green upper-right corner. Slide to the symbol you want to enter, and lift your finger from the screen to enter the selected symbol.

>  **TIP** Tap the Alphanumeric button (labeled *Abc*) at the right end of the status bar to switch from the function keyboard to the standard keyboard.

The on-screen keyboard takes up a significant percentage of the iPad screen. You can display more of the file content by splitting the keyboard into two halves.

- To split the keyboard, either drag with two fingers from the center of the keyboard to the sides of the screen, or tap and hold the Keyboard key and then slide to the Split command.

- To rejoin the keyboard halves, either drag the halves with two fingers to the center of the screen, or tap and hold the Keyboard key and then slide to the Dock & Merge command.

To hide the on-screen keyboard, tap the Keyboard key.

# External keyboard shortcuts

The Bluetooth technology built into the iPad makes it easy to wirelessly connect an external keyboard to your iPad. A Bluetooth symbol appears next to the power meter in the upper-right corner of your iPad screen when Bluetooth is turned on. The symbol is gray when the iPad isn't connected to a device, and black when it is.

To access Bluetooth settings, open the Settings app and then tap Bluetooth in the first group of settings. From the Bluetooth page, you can turn on the Bluetooth function, see Bluetooth devices that you've approved for connection, and manage the connections and settings for those devices.

When you turn on Bluetooth, your iPad becomes discoverable. When you subsequently turn on your external Bluetooth keyboard, the two devices should "discover" each other. The keyboard will appear in the device list on the Bluetooth page, and you can tap it to connect to it.

If you're working with an external keyboard connected to your iPad, you might find it much easier to enter text into documents, workbooks, presentations, and notebooks by typing than by tapping. You can also use iPad versions of many of the classic Office keyboard shortcuts, including those described in the following table.

## General Office app keyboard shortcuts

| To do this | Press |
| --- | --- |
| Undo the last action | ⌘+Z |
| Repeat the last action | Shift+⌘+Z |
| Copy the selected content to the Clipboard | ⌘+C |
| Cut the selected content to the Clipboard | ⌘+X |
| Paste the most recent Clipboard content | ⌘+V |
| Select content from the current location | Shift+Arrow |
| Select all content in a document, on a worksheet, in a content container, or on a notebook page | ⌘+A |
| Apply bold formatting to the selected characters | ⌘+B |
| Italicize the selected characters | ⌘+I |
| Underline the selected characters | ⌘+U |
| When searching, move between the Find and Replace boxes | Tab |
| Perform the action of the Done key (on the on-screen keyboard) in any procedure | Enter or Return |

## Word for iPad keyboard shortcuts

In addition to the general Office keyboard shortcuts, you can use the shortcuts described in the following table when working in a document in Word for iPad.

| To do this | Press |
| --- | --- |
| Move cursor to beginning of document | ⌘+Up Arrow |
| Move cursor to end of document | ⌘+Down Arrow |
| Move cursor to beginning of current line | ⌘+Left Arrow |
| Move cursor to end of current line | ⌘+Right Arrow |
| Move cursor up by one paragraph | Option+Up Arrow |
| Move cursor down by one paragraph | Option+Down Arrow |
| Move cursor left by one word | Option+Left Arrow |
| Move cursor right by one word | Option+Right Arrow |
| Select text (up, down, left, and right) | Shift+Arrow |
| Select paragraph above | Shift+Option+Up Arrow |
| Select paragraph below | Shift+Option+Down Arrow |
| Select word to the left | Shift+Option+Left Arrow |
| Select word to the right | Shift+Option+Right Arrow |
| Select from current position to beginning of document | Shift+⌘+Up Arrow |
| Select from current position to end of document | Shift+⌘+Down Arrow |
| Select from current position to beginning of line | Shift+⌘+Left Arrow |
| Select from current position to end of line | Shift+⌘+Right Arrow |

**A**

## Excel for iPad keyboard shortcuts

In addition to the general Office keyboard shortcuts, you can use the shortcuts described in the following table when working in a worksheet in Excel for iPad.

| To do this | Press |
| --- | --- |
| Move one cell to the right | Tab |
| Move one cell up, down, left, or right (in Ready mode) | Arrow keys |
| Move within cell text (in Edit mode) | Arrow keys |
| Select a range of cells | Shift+Left/Right Arrow |
| Insert a line break in a cell | Alt+Return |
| Move cursor to beginning of current cell | ⌘+Up Arrow |
| Move cursor to end of current cell | ⌘+Down Arrow |
| Move cursor to beginning of current line in a cell | ⌘+Left Arrow |
| Move cursor to end of current line in a cell | ⌘+Right Arrow |
| In a cell that contains a line break, move cursor up by one paragraph | Option+Up Arrow |
| In a cell that contains a line break, move cursor down by one paragraph | Option+Down Arrow |
| Move cursor left by one word | Option+Left Arrow |
| Move cursor right by one word | Option+Right Arrow |

## PowerPoint for iPad keyboard shortcuts

In addition to the general Office keyboard shortcuts, you can use the shortcuts described in the following table when working in a text box in PowerPoint for iPad.

| To do this | Press |
| --- | --- |
| Move cursor to beginning of text box | ⌘+Up Arrow |
| Move cursor to end of text box | ⌘+Down Arrow |
| Move cursor to beginning of current line | ⌘+Left Arrow |
| Move cursor to end of current line | ⌘+Right Arrow |
| Move cursor left by one word | Option+Left Arrow |
| Move cursor right by one word | Option+Right Arrow |
| Select character above, below, left, or right | Shift+Arrow |
| Select word to the left | Shift+Option+Left Arrow |
| Select word to the right | Shift+Option+Right Arrow |
| Select from current position to beginning of text box | Shift+⌘+Up Arrow |
| Select from current position to end of text box | Shift+⌘+Down Arrow |
| Select from current position to beginning of line | Shift+⌘+Left Arrow |
| Select from current position to end of line | Shift+⌘+Right Arrow |

# Glossary

**absolute reference**  In a formula, the exact address of a cell, regardless of the position of the cell that contains the formula.

**active cell**  The selected cell in which data is entered when you begin typing. Only one cell is active at a time. The active cell is bounded by a heavy border.

**AirPrint**  A feature that enables Apple operating systems to print over a wireless network without requiring the installation of printer-specific drivers.

**alignment**  The consistent positioning of text, graphics, and other objects.

**anchor**  See *object anchor.*

**animation**  In PowerPoint, an effect that you can apply to text or an object to produce an illusion of movement.

**argument**  A value that a function uses to perform operations or calculations. The type of argument is defined by a parameter of the function. Common arguments include numbers, text, cell references, and names. See also *parameter.*

**aspect ratio**  The ratio of the width of an item (such as a screen, page, or image) to its height.

**attribute**  An individual item of character formatting, such as size or color, that determines how text looks.

**AutoComplete**  A feature that evaluates existing text input and predicts the remainder.

**AutoFill**  A feature that evaluates a cell entry and enters previously provided information into other cells.

**background**  The colors, shading, texture, and graphics that appear behind the text and objects on a document page, a worksheet, or a slide.

**Backstage view**  A full-screen user interface area that exposes file-level functionality in Office applications. This is a companion feature to the Office ribbon and helps users discover and use the features that fall outside of the authoring features on the ribbon.

**balloon**  A container that displays a markup element, such as a comment or revision, in the margin of a document.

**bar chart**  A chart with bars that compares the quantities of two or more items.

**browser**  A software program used to display webpages and to navigate the Internet.

**bullet point** Slang term for a bulleted list item.

**button** An on-screen control that provides input to the operating system, software program, or app when tapped or clicked.

**case** The capitalization (uppercase or lower-case) of a word or phrase. In title case, the first letter of all important words is capitalized. In sentence case, only the first letter of the first word is capitalized.

**category axis** The axis (usually the x-axis) used for plotting categories of data in a chart.

**cell** The data container located at the intersection of a row and column in a worksheet or a table.

**cell padding** The space between the inside edge of a cell and its content.

**cell range** A block of adjacent cells in a worksheet, expressed in the form *A1:D4*.

**cell reference** The location of a cell, expressed as its column letter and row number, as in *A1*.

**character** A symbol, letter, or number

**character formatting** Formatting that affects the appearance of characters but does not affect the structure of the paragraph that contains them.

**character spacing** The distance between characters in a line of text. Can be adjusted by expanding or condensing the space between characters.

**character style** A combination of character formatting options that is identified by a style name.

**chart** A graphic or diagram that displays data or the relationship between sets of data by plotting a series of values from a table or worksheet.

**chart area** A region in a chart that is used to position chart elements, render axes, and plot data.

**chart element** In Excel, any of the items that can be displayed on a chart. Chart elements include the axes, axis titles, chart title, data labels, a data table, error bars, gridlines, a legend, lines, trendlines, and up/down bars.

**chart type** A categorization of charts by the format in which they visually express data. In Excel, chart types include area, bar, column, donut, line, pie, radar, scatter, stock, and surface.

**clip art image** A piece of free, ready-made art that is distributed without copyright. Usually a cartoon, sketch, illustration, or photograph.

**Clipboard** A temporary storage area, shared by Microsoft Office programs or apps, where cut or copied items are stored.

**coauthoring** A collaborative content development process in which documents, workbooks, or presentations are created by multiple people together rather than individually. In Office apps, coauthoring refers to multiple people simultaneously working in a shared file.

**color gradient** A gradual progression from one color to another color, or from one shade to another shade of the same color.

**color scheme** A predefined set of colors that you can apply to text and objects. The colors within a color scheme are assigned to roles, including Background 1 and 2, Text 1 and 2, Accents 1 through 6, Hyperlink, and Followed Hyperlink. Text and objects that are formatted with scheme colors change automatically when you switch or modify the color scheme. See also *theme colors*.

**column** Either the vertical arrangement of text into one or more side-by-side sections, or the vertical arrangement of cells in a table or worksheet.

**column break** A break inserted in the text of a column to force the text below it to move to the next column.

**column chart** A chart that displays data in vertical bars to facilitate data comparison.

**comment** A note or annotation that an author or reviewer adds to a document, worksheet, or slide.

**conditional format** A format, such as cell shading or font color, that Excel automatically applies to cells if a specified condition is true.

**content placeholder** See *placeholder*.

**content template** A file that contains purpose-specific text, images, or other non-design elements that an author can use as a starting point for a similar document, workbook, or presentation.

**continuous section break** A section break that does not affect the flow of text.

**credentials** Information that includes identification and proof of identification that is used to gain access to local and network resources. Examples of credentials are user names and passwords, smart cards, and certificates.

**cursor** A representation on the screen of the input device pointer location.

**custom slide show** A set of slides extracted from a presentation to create a slide show for an audience that doesn't need to view the entire presentation.

**data point** An individual value plotted in a chart.

**data range** Data from a defined internal or external source.

**data series** Related data points that are plotted in a chart. One or more data series in a chart can be plotted. A pie chart has just one data series.

**data source** A file containing variable information, such as names and addresses, that is merged with a main document containing static information.

**demoting** Changing content from a higher level to a lower level; for example, changing a first-level bullet to a second-level bullet or a heading to a subheading. See also *promoting*.

**design template** A file that defines design elements such as the theme (and associated colors, fonts, and effects), character and paragraph styles, background colors, and imagery that an author can apply to a document or use as the basis for a document or presentation.

**dragging**  A way of moving objects by selecting them and then, while the selection device is active (for example, while you are pressing the screen), moving the selection to the new location.

**embedded object**  An object that is wholly inserted into a file. Embedding the object, rather than simply inserting or pasting its contents, ensures that the object retains its original format. If you open the embedded object, you can edit it with the toolbars and menus from the program or app used to create it.

**embedding**  Inserting an independent instance of an object such as a chart, an equation, an image, a video recording, or a font, into a file.

**endnote**  A note that appears at the end of a section or document that explains, comments on, or provides references for text in the main body of a document. See also *footnote, reference mark.*

**Excel table**  A range of cells in a worksheet that has been formatted as a table and that can be managed independently from the data in other rows and columns on the worksheet.

**field**  In Word, a placeholder for information that is supplied from the file properties or a data source. In Excel, a named set of information that is stored in a table column or the area of a user interface into which that data is entered.

**file bar**  The vertical bar on the left side of the Backstage view of an Office for iPad app, from which users can connect to storage locations and open files.

**file format**  The structure or organization of data in a file. The file format is usually indicated by the file name extension.

**File menu**  In an Office for iPad app, the menu that expands when you tap the button labeled with a file icon. It contains commands for managing the file (not its content).

**file name extension**  A set of characters added to the end of a file name that identifies the file type or format.

**fill handle**  In Excel, a cell handle that you can drag to copy data or continue a data series in adjacent cells.

**filter**  A set of criteria that stipulates which data is shown or hidden.

**filtering**  Displaying files or records in a data source that meet specific criteria.

**First Line Indent marker**  The triangle-shaped control, on the top of the horizontal ruler, that indicates the position of the first line of the paragraph.

**font**  A graphic design applied to a collection of numbers, symbols, and characters. A font describes a certain typeface, which can have qualities such as size, spacing, and pitch.

**font effect**  An attribute, such as superscript, small capital letters, or shadow, that can be applied to a font.

**font size**  The height (in points) of a collection of characters, where one point is equal to approximately 1/72 of an inch.

**font style** The emphasis given to a font by using formatting such as bold, italic, underline, or color.

**footer** An area within the bottom margin of a page, worksheet, or slide that can contain information and appears on printouts. A footer typically contains elements such as the copyright holder, page number, file name, or date. See also *header*.

**footnote** A note that appears at the end of a page that explains, comments on, or provides references for text in the main body of a document. See also *endnote*, *reference mark*.

**formatting** See *character formatting*, *paragraph formatting*.

**formula** A sequence of values, cell references, names, functions, or operators in a cell of a table or worksheet that together produce a new value. A formula always begins with an equal sign (=).

**Formula Bar** A horizontal area at the top of the Excel for iPad window in which you display, enter, and edit all cell content.

**function** A prewritten formula that simplifies the process of entering calculations and enables the user to use formulas that might be difficult to build from scratch.

**graphic** Any image, such as a photograph, illustration, or shape, that can be placed as an object on a page or slide or that can be used to illustrate or to add visual interest to a document or presentation.

**gridlines** In a table, nonprinting lines that indicate the cell boundaries. In a chart, lines that visually carry the y-axis values across the plot area.

**handle** A small circle, square, or set of dots that appears at the corner or on the side of a selected object and facilitates moving, sizing, reshaping, or other functions pertaining to the object.

**Hanging Indent marker** The triangle-shaped control, on the bottom of the horizontal ruler, that indicates the left edge of the second and subsequent lines of the paragraph.

**header** An area within the top margin of a page, worksheet, or slide that can contain information and appears on printouts. A header typically contains elements such as the title, page number, or author name. See also *footer*.

**heading font** The first font listed in a set of theme fonts, which is by default applied to all titles and headings in a document, workbook, or presentation.

**hyperlink** A connection from a hyperlink anchor, such as text or a graphic, that you can follow to display a link target such as a file, a location in a file, or a website. Text hyperlinks are usually formatted as colored or underlined text, but sometimes the only indication is that when you point to them, the pointer changes to a hand.

**icon** A small picture or symbol representing a command, file type, function, program, app, or tool.

**indent marker** A marker on the horizontal ruler that controls the indentation of text from the left or right margin.

**justifying** Aligning the left and right edges of each line of text within a paragraph by adjusting the character spacing.

**landscape** The orientation of a screen, page, slide, or image in which the width is greater than the height.

**layout** In Excel, the organization of elements on a chart.

**Left Indent marker** The square-shaped control, on the bottom of the horizontal ruler, that indicates how far text is indented from the left margin.

**legend** A key that identifies the data series plotted in the chart.

**line break** A manual break that forces the text that follows it to the next line. Also called a *text wrapping break*.

**line chart** A type of chart in which data points in a series are connected by a line.

**link** See *hyperlink*, *linked object*.

**linked object** An object that is inserted into a document or slide but that still exists in the source file. When information is linked, the document or slide can be updated automatically if the information in the original document changes.

**local** Stored on the computer or device and not requiring network access. See also *remote*.

**manual page break** A page break inserted to force subsequent information to appear on the next page.

**margin** The blank space outside the printing area on a page.

**master** In PowerPoint, a slide or page on which you define formatting for all slides or pages in a presentation. Each presentation has a set of masters for slides, in addition to masters for speaker notes and audience handouts.

**menu** A list of options, represented as text or graphics, from which a user can choose.

**Microsoft Office Clipboard** See *Clipboard*.

**mixed reference** A cell reference that contains both absolute and relative references.

**Normal view** A view that displays three panes: Thumbnails, Slide, and Notes.

**note container** In OneNote, a flexible bounding box that contains the notes you enter or paste on a page.

**Notes pane** In PowerPoint, the pane in which you enter notes that accompany a slide.

**object** An item, such as a graphic, video clip, sound file, or worksheet, that can be inserted into a document or slide and then selected and modified.

**object anchor** A document element that has been formatted to keep another element (the anchored object, usually an image) in a certain position in a document.

**Office Lens**  An app that captures and digitizes images of text, and then enhances the images to make the text readable and recognizable by Optical Character Recognition technology.

**OneDrive**  The Microsoft online service that lets users access and share documents, photos, and other files from anywhere.

**OneDrive for Business**  A document service that enables organizations to provision and manage online storage for their users.

**orientation**  The direction of a screen, page, slide, image, or other element that can be oriented horizontally or vertically. See also *landscape*, *portrait*.

**padding**  See *cell padding*.

**paragraph**  In word processing, a block of text that ends when you press the Enter key.

**paragraph formatting**  Formatting that controls the structure of a paragraph. Examples include indentation, alignment, line spacing, and pagination.

**paragraph style**  A combination of character formatting and paragraph formatting that is named and stored as a set. Applying the style to a paragraph applies all the formatting characteristics at one time.

**parameter**  The expression of a variable that defines the type of argument required or permitted by a function.

**password**  The string of characters that must be entered to open a password-protected file for editing.

**paste options**  The alternative types of information such as text, formulas, values, absolute values, and formatting that can be pasted from cut or copied content.

**path**  A sequence of folders (directories) that leads to a specific file or folder. A backslash is used to separate each folder in a Windows path, and a forward slash is used to separate each directory in an Internet path.

**PDF (Portable Document Format)**  A fixed-layout file format in which a document appears the same regardless of the computer or device on which it is displayed.

**Photo Stream**  A service supplied with the basic iCloud service that allows users to store their 1,000 most recent photos on the iCloud servers for up to 30 days free of charge.

**pie chart**  A round chart that shows the size of items in a single data series, proportional to the sum of the items.

**pinning**  Adding a file to a group of files that remains at the top of a file list.

**pivoting**  Displaying a different perspective of data in a table by changing or rearranging the available data fields.

**PivotTable**  An interactive technology in Excel or Access that can show dynamic views of the same data from a list or a database.

**placeholder**  A content container on a slide layout that defines the structure and formatting of the content that is entered on the slide.

**plot area** In a two-dimensional chart, the area bounded by the axes, including all data series. In a three-dimensional chart, the area bounded by the axes, including the data series, category names, axis labels, and axis titles.

**Portable Document Format (PDF)** See *PDF*.

**portrait** The orientation of a screen, page, slide, or image in which the height is greater than the width.

**Presenter view** In PowerPoint, a feature that displays slides, notes, thumbnails, and presenter tools on one screen and the Slide Show view of the presentation on another screen.

**promoting** Changing content to a higher level, such as a second-level bullet to a first-level bullet or a subheading to a heading. See also *demoting*.

**property** A setting or attribute of a file, such as the name, size, creation date, author, or read-only status.

**pull quote** Text taken from the body of a document and showcased in a text box to create visual interest.

**range** See *cell range, data range*.

**read-only** A setting that allows a file to be read or copied, but not changed or saved. If you change a read-only file, you can save your changes only if you give the file a new name.

**Recommended Charts** An Excel feature that evaluates data and displays examples of charts that are typically used to present that type of data.

**reference mark** The number or symbol displayed in the body of document when you insert a footnote or endnote.

**relative reference** In a formula, the address of a cell based on the relative position of the cell that contains the formula and the cell referred to. If you copy the formula, the reference automatically adjusts.

**remote** In a storage location that is not directly connected to the computer or device and can be accessed only over a network or Internet connection. See also *local*.

**revision** A change in a document.

**ribbon** A user interface design that organizes commands into logical groups that appear on separate tabs.

**Rotate handle** A handle that you can drag to adjust the angle of rotation of an image.

**row** The horizontal arrangement of cells in a table or spreadsheet.

**section** In a Word document, a portion of the document for which you can configure unique settings such as margins, page orientation, headers and footers, and page numbers.

**section break** The divider between unique sections of a document, represented by a double dotted line.

**selecting** Activating text or an object so that you can manipulate or edit it in some way.

**series axis** The axis (usually the z-axis) used for plotting series information in a chart.

**server** In OneNote, the computer on which the primary copy of a shared notebook is stored. All local notebook copies synchronize with the server version of the notebook.

**shape** In Office apps, a drawing object that can be individually formatted and moved on a page or slide.

**sharing** The act of making a file available in a shared storage location for read/write or read-only access by other computer users.

**sheet tab** A control that is used to select or manage a worksheet within a workbook.

**sidebar** A text box placed adjacent to document content that contains contextually relevant information.

**sizing handle** A small circle, square, or set of dots that appears at the corner or on the side of a selected object. You drag these handles to change the size of the object horizontally, vertically, or proportionally.

**slide layout** A slide that builds on a slide master and defines the static content and content placeholders for slides based on that layout.

**slide master** A common base slide that defines the slide size, master layout, themes, colors, fonts, effects, and background styles for a set of slide layouts.

**Slide pane** In PowerPoint, the area in Normal view in which you edit the currently selected slide.

**Slide Show view** In PowerPoint, the basic view in which you deliver an electronic presentation to an audience. Slide Show view displays only the active slide.

**Smart Guide** A vertical or horizontal dotted line that appears on a slide to help align slide elements.

**SmartArt** An Office feature that allows users to quickly and easily create professional-looking information diagrams.

**sort** To organize information (for example, in paragraphs or in a table or worksheet column) in a specific order.

**source file** A file that contains information that is linked, embedded, or merged into another file.

**status bar** An area at the bottom of an app window or program window that displays indicators and controls.

**style** Formatting that is named and stored as a set. See also *character style*, *paragraph style*, *table style*.

**subtotal** An intermediate partial sum, quantity, or amount.

**tab character** A character used to align lines and columns on screen and in print. The position and alignment of content controlled by tab characters is defined by tab stops. See also *tab stop*.

**tab (ribbon)** An organizational element of the ribbon that displays related groups of buttons.

**tab stop** A location on the horizontal ruler that indicates how far to indent text or where to begin a column of text.

**tabbed list** A list that arranges text in simple columns separated by left, right, centered, or decimal tab stops.

**table** One or more rows of cells commonly used to display numbers and other items for quick reference and analysis. Items in a table are organized in rows and columns.

**table style** A set of formatting options, such as font, border style, and row banding, that are applied to a table. The regions of a table, such as the header row, header column, and data area, can be variously formatted.

**target** A file, location, object, or webpage that is displayed from a link or hyperlink.

**template** A file that serves as the basis for new documents, workbooks, or presentations with a similar design or purpose. See also *content template*, *design template*.

**text box** A container for text content that can be moved and formatted independently of the rest of the document.

**text wrapping** The way text wraps around an object on the page.

**text wrapping break** A manual break that forces the text that follows it to the next line. Also known as a *line break*.

**theme** A set of coordinated design elements including colors, fonts, and effects.

**theme colors** The color scheme associated with a theme. See also *color scheme*.

**theme effects** A set of visual attributes for graphics that is associated with a theme.

**theme fonts** A set of two fonts, one applied to slide titles (heading font) and one applied to all other text on a slide (body font) that is associated with a theme.

**thumbnail** A small representation of an item, such as a slide, an image, or a theme. Thumbnails are typically used to provide visual identifiers for related items.

**Thumbnails pane** In PowerPoint, the pane in Normal view that displays thumbnails of the slides in a presentation and allows you to display a specific slide in the Slide pane by tapping its thumbnail.

**title bar** The horizontal bar at the top of a window that contains the name of the window. Most title bars also contain boxes or buttons for closing and resizing the window.

**title slide** The introductory slide in a presentation.

**tool tab** A tab containing groups of commands that are pertinent only to a specific type of document or slide element such as a picture, table, or text box. Tool tabs appear only when relevant content is selected. See also *tab (ribbon)*.

**toolbar** A row, column, or block of buttons or icons that represent tasks or commands within an app or program.

**transition** An effect that specifies how the display changes as you move from one slide to another.

**user interface** The portion of an app or program with which the user interacts.

**value axis** The axis used for plotting values in a chart. Usually the y-axis.

**web browser** Software that interprets HTML files, formats them into webpages, and displays them. A web browser, such as Internet Explorer, can follow hyperlinks, respond to requests to download files, and play sound or video files that are embedded in webpages.

**webpage** A World Wide Web document. A webpage typically consists of an HTML file, with associated files for graphics and sets of instructions called *scripts*. It is identified by a Uniform Resource Locator (URL).

**word wrap** The process of breaking lines of text automatically to stay within the page margins of a document or within window boundaries.

**WordArt object** A text object you create with ready-made effects and to which you can apply additional formatting options.

**workbook** In Excel, a file containing related worksheets.

**worksheet** In Excel, the primary document used to store and work with data. A worksheet consists of cells that are organized in columns and rows; a worksheet is always stored in a workbook.

**x-axis** The horizontal reference line on a grid, chart, or graph that has horizontal and vertical dimensions.

**y-axis** The vertical reference line on a grid, chart, or graph that has horizontal and vertical dimensions.

**z-axis** The axis that is perpendicular to the x-axis and y-axis in a three-dimensional chart or graph; the z-axis is used to represent depth.

# Index

# About the author

**Joan Lambert** has worked closely with Microsoft technologies since 1986, and in the training and certification industry since 1997. As President and CEO of Online Training Solutions, Inc. (OTSI), Joan guides the translation of technical information and requirements into useful, relevant, and measurable resources for people who are seeking certification of their computer skills or who simply want to get things done efficiently.

Joan is the author or coauthor of more than three dozen books about Windows and Office (for Windows and for Mac) and three generations of Microsoft Office Specialist certification study guides. She enthusiastically shares her love of technology through her participation in the creation of books, learning materials, and certification exams, and greatly enjoys communicating the benefits of new technologies by delivering training and facilitating learning events. Joan is a Microsoft Certified Professional, Microsoft Office Specialist Master (for Office 2013, Office 2010, and Office 2007), Microsoft Certified Technology Specialist (for Windows and Windows Server), Microsoft Certified Technology Associate (for Windows), Microsoft Dynamics Specialist, and Microsoft Certified Trainer.

Joan currently lives in a small town in Texas with her simply divine daughter, Trinity, two slightly naughty dogs, a naturally superior cat, a vast assortment of fish, and the super-automatic espresso machine that runs the house.

Joan's team at OTSI specializes in the design and creation of Office, SharePoint, and Windows training solutions and the production of online and printed training resources.

For more information about OTSI, visit *www.otsi.com* or follow us on Facebook at *www.facebook.com/Online.Training.Solutions.Inc* for advance information about upcoming training resources and informative tidbits about technology and publishing.

# Acknowledgments

I am extremely grateful for the support of the many people without whom this book would not exist, including these talented members of America's finest publishing team at OTSI:

- Barb Levy, for reviewing and laying out content, and for advocating for readers who primarily use Mac computers

- Jaime Odell, for devising creative practice tasks and proofreading the final product

- Jean Trenary, for perfecting the layout template and guiding our production processes

- Jeanne Craver, for processing and pixelating graphics

- Kathy Krause, for thoughtful copyediting and content support, and for shepherding the project through to completion

- Steve Lambert, for providing the automated solutions that helped us to work more efficiently on this book and will simplify processes for future books

- Susie Carr and Krista Wall, for thoroughly indexing this book so readers can find the information they're looking for

I deeply appreciate the time and efforts of my fellow redheaded trainer, Linda Larkan at Skylark Services, who helped to document and review procedures; and of Carol Dillingham, Rosemary Caperton, and the team at Microsoft Press—past and present—who made this and so many other books possible.

Finally, this book would not have come into being without the advice of my resident iDevice expert, Trinity, and the life lessons taught to me by my father, Steve, who got me into this game in the first place by including my depiction of *Robots in Love* in one of his earliest books, *Presentation Graphics on the Apple Macintosh*. I am so fortunate to work with my amazing family members. Thank you both for your unfailing support, and for inspiring and reminding me to enjoy life every day.

# Now that you've read the book...

## Tell us what you think!

Was it useful?
Did it teach you what you wanted to learn?
Was there room for improvement?

**Let us know at http://aka.ms/tellpress**

Your feedback goes directly to the staff at Microsoft Press,
and we read every one of your responses. Thanks in advance!

 Microsoft